Paige!

thanks so!

The

MENTAL

YENTL

For my Michael

&

EJ, Max, and Aaron

The
MENTAL
YENTL

Stories from a Lifelong Student of Crazy

Sally Fingerett

 Green Fingers Music & Press, LLC

Author's Note: This is a work of creative nonfiction. Some of the events described happened as related; other were expanded and changed. A few individuals are composites of more than one person, and a few names have been changed.

Copyright © 2015 by Sally Fingerett

First printing, 2015

ISBN: 978-0-9961494-5-7

Printed in the United States by Green Fingers Music & Press, LLC

Ordering Information:
Quantity sales: Special discounts are available on quantity purchases.
Please contact the publisher at:
GreenFingersMusicAndPress@gmail.com

Cover illustrations by Flash Rosenberg
Author photo by Raymond LaVoie
Cover design by Sarah Allgire
Interior design by Katherine Matthews

Cover illustration copyright © 2015 by Sally Fingerett

Interior typefaces include Garamond, Segoe Script, and Californian FB.

CONTENTS

Chapter Seven   311
It's Time to Celebrate the Crazy

Finale

Introduction

MEET THE MENTAL YENTL

I come from a long line of medicated women.

During my childhood, on any given Sunday, my parents would drag us kids (my older brother, older sister, and me) into the car and drive to the ritual extended family dinner. Mom and Dad were smokers back then, and with the windows rolled up against the nasty Chicago winter, it was an unbearable one-hour commute from our house in South Shore to Division Street, where my grandparents lived above their bakery.

During these Sunday dinners, I found myself mesmerized by my loony Aunt Lill and Aunt Rose. I loved how the company of a few extra animated and histrionic women could diffuse my mother's nutty personality. For some reason "crazy" in a group was entertaining, while one-on-one with "crazy" was just terrifying.

Though I adored these women deeply and cherished their affection, I had no intention of becoming like them. But DNA has its own agenda, and I eventually recognized a great many similarities between us. Due to my own critical thinking and obsessive drive to make sense of things, I have become a MENTAL YENTL—a student of crazy.

I can explain.

"Mental" is a fairly obvious choice—though, I admit, not terribly P.C.

It's the word "Yentl" that I have taken liberty with. In the Barbra Streisand film *Yentl,* based on the Isaac Bashevis Singer's tale of "Yentl the Yeshiva Boy," Babs plays a young girl who defies tradition to become a scholar during a time when Jewish women were not allowed to read sacred texts. In my mind, a Yentl can be any female who wishes to uncover the deeper meaning of whatever it is she yearns to hold close to her soul. Therefore, today, I am a Mental Yentl, someone who lovingly studies and appreciates the fine art of wackadoodle.

I'm thinking there are many of us Mental Yentls out there.

We would be those unknowing students who spent our early lives at the feet of many neurotic masters. These matriarchs, whether they were clinically diagnosed or just quirky, loud, and vivid, guided us through our formative years while believing we would grow up to apply *the mother's* lessons, cook *the mother's* recipes, and marry the man of *the mother's* dreams just like they had been pressured to do. And, in our efforts to do right by our familial tribes, we struggle to balance our independence and guilt as we fall in love with the right guy but marry the wrong guy, and then have babies we have no idea what to do with, only to divorce the guys we have no idea what to do with.

After that, we choose jobs outside the home, learn to cook healthier, stay single or remarry, raise our children, and then launch our children. And sadly, with but a few minutes to catch our breath, we find ourselves enduring great loss as we bury an assortment of family members, and realize the front line is gone, and it's now our turn.

Life itself is wackadoodle.

I now sit at the head of my family's table, and from my chair, I dedicate this collection of stories, essays, song lyrics, and general undefined *mishegas** as a love letter to my families' matriarchs *"of blessed memory."* It is my intention to honor and validate the remarkable women who came to those Sunday dinners clutching their emotional baggage, knowing they would have much preferred a lovely pocketbook.

—*L'dor v'dor** (From generation to generation)

*FYI As a Mental Yentl, my world of words has been infiltrated with Yiddish since I was born. Yiddish is the tongue of my people, and this expressive language has become the endearing slang of our daily vernacular.

But not everyone knows Yiddish, of course, and since it is not in my nature to stir up a dose of crazy-making, I've included a Yiddish glossary at the end of this book. It is my pleasure to do this for those readers who haven't been to New York City or seen a Woody Allen or Billy Crystal movie. We here at Mental Central wouldn't want you to aggravate yourself or get a heartburn, but rather enjoy these stories with a cookie, a lovely glass of milk, and a Glossary.

So *bubeleh,** just flip to the back of this book, and in alphabetical order, you'll find whatever it is that you don't understand. *Gezundheit**

Chapter One

HERE'S TO

THE WOMEN

THE GARFINKEL GIRLS

As a little girl, my mother, Naomi, desperately wanted a brother or sister. Almost as soon as she could talk, Naomi nagged her parents, Sam and Rose, for a baby. Though they took their sweet time, my mother got just what she wanted. In the summer of 1931, seven-year-old Naomi became a big sister to Mindell, a beautiful baby girl. Nothing brought her more joy than diapering, feeding, cooing, and loving her little sister, Minnie.

The Garfinkel family lived in a one-bedroom, third-floor, walk-up apartment on Chicago's South Side. Sam tended to his school supply and candy store, sixteen blocks away. Rose helped her husband at the store and cared for their two little girls. She doted on them, committed to giving her daughters all the wonderful freedoms and opportunities that a mother could want for her children. They weren't rich, but they weren't poor. Happy and settled, Rose and Sam were two Eastern European Jewish immigrants living the American dream.

In the early evening of October 19, Rose was preparing dinner while Naomi sat at the kitchen table, stitching a rag doll for three-month-old Minnie. Suddenly, a thunderous knocking at the front door shattered the quiet of their apartment. Startled, Naomi stuck herself with the sewing needle. She knew her father was expected home at any moment, but he would never bang on the front door that way.

Rose told Naomi to stay back with the baby and flew from the kitchen to investigate the commotion. Naomi peeked around the corner to see two policemen standing at the front door. She had never seen policemen up close before. Disregarding her mother's instructions, she scooped up baby Minnie from her cradle and headed toward the living room.

There, she saw her mother weeping. The police had just informed Rose that her husband had been shot and killed.

Less than two miles away, a bandit had entered Sam's store, pulled out a gun, and demanded all the money in the cash register. But Sam had no intention of yielding to this hoodlum, this lawless thief who would dare to rob such a hardworking man with a wife and two young daughters.

According to the *Chicago Daily Tribune*, when Sam refused to hand over his cash, the robber put his gun to Sam's abdomen and fired. Before the police could arrive, the thief took off on foot, never to be captured. Critically wounded, Sam was transported to a local hospital, where he died hours later.

My grandfather was forty-two years old.

My mother's parents were born in Lodz, Poland, but didn't meet until they settled in Chicago. Sam Garfinkel traveled from Poland to steamy Galveston, Texas, in 1913, at the age of twenty-four. Seven years later, on a cold December day in 1920, twenty-one-year-old Rose Hertzberg landed on the shores of Portland, Maine. From these two entry points, separated by two thousand miles and seven years, Sam and Rose both headed for the Midwest.

How these two young adults from Lodz, Poland, met and married in Chicago remains a mystery, although many immigrants arrived in the United States carrying the name and address of a family friend or relative who had already made the journey to America. In Chicago's early settlement years, Eastern European communities were formed by "old country neighbors," or what were then called *lantzmen*.* These neighborhoods became surrogate *shtetls** of the old-world towns left behind, built by citizens homesick for their people and villages.

My mother knew almost nothing about her parents' early lives, except that my grandfather, Sam, fell in love with my grandmother, "Rose from Lodz," in the 1920s. Ten years older than Rose, Sam was ready to settle down, so he proposed to her. They married and went full tilt into building a life together in Chicago, their new hometown.

Sadly, their American dream was short-lived. Four years after Sam's death, my grandmother, Rose Hertzberg Garfinkel, died of cancer at the age of thirty-six.

When their mother died, Naomi was eleven years old, and my Aunt Minnie was not quite five. No one explained the specifics of Rose's cancer to them. Instead, the girls were told that they would now live at the Chicago Home for Jewish Orphans on 62nd and Drexel in Hyde Park on the South Side. Traumatized and grief-stricken, the Garfinkel girls went quietly.

Due to their seven-year age difference, Naomi and Minnie slept in different wings of the orphanage, and soon after their arrival, Naomi was sent to live with a foster family. Mistreated and miserably lonely for Minnie, she begged to go back to the orphanage and was, indeed, quickly returned. My mother then devoted herself to watching over her younger sister.

About six months after the girls settled in, a lovely family came looking to adopt a little girl. They immediately spotted Minnie and chose the sweet, adorable five-year-old. While preparing the paper work, authorities discovered that Rose's will prohibited the girls from being adopted separately. Whoever took one, took both. Unfortunately, this would not work for the family that wanted Minnie, so my aunt stayed in the orphanage and remained a Garfinkel girl.

In the 1930s and 1940s, the services available for traumatized children were limited. My mother never spoke of receiving any professional counseling, but fondly recalled the amazing friendships and support she found in the close-knit group of kids from the "Home." Many years later, Chicago Jewish Orphan reunions were held once every decade. My mother and Aunt Minnie never missed an opportunity to reconnect with these companions whose childhoods had also been marked by tragedy.

With each other's help, Naomi and Minnie worked hard to overcome their heartbreaking past. They spoke their own sister-language. Their dynamic love for one another rendered them inseparable, and they remained each other's everything for the rest of their lives.

When Naomi was a sophomore at Hyde Park High, her friend Rochelle planned a party and insisted that she attend. Rochelle and her core circle of girls were a privileged group and adored

Naomi. They decided to dress up their orphaned friend, and see if they could find her a beau.

Naomi wore Rochelle's gold pencil skirt, Ruthie's brown blouse, and Esther's low-heeled pumps and tortoiseshell barrettes. The wool skirt itched, the blouse was tight, and the pumps pinched, but Naomi felt the physical torment was worth it. The girls cheered in agreement that she was quite the *looker*.

Bill Fingerett walked in, took one look at Naomi, and that was it. My father fell in love with her magnetic and wacky personality—not to mention her terrific bustline and fabulous legs. They married two years later when she was eighteen. My father was twenty.

Bill Fingerett's mother did not approve of Naomi Garfinkel.

"What? She comes from nothing, she has no people, she's a nothing!" his mother, Anna, cried. "She's had a miserable life and that's something to worry about."

But Bill was in love and would not be swayed.

It was 1943, and Bill's friends were shipping out to fight the war. Bill invited his parents to attend a farewell party for one of his good buddies. To Anna and Jacob Fingerett's surprise, when they arrived at the party, they were greeted by a rabbi, eleven-year-old Minnie, and a crowd of Bill and Naomi's friends standing around a *chuppah*.* Naomi had an orchid pinned to the lapel of her summer suit-dress, while a mother-of-the-groom corsage had been set aside for Anna.

In the only Polaroid snapshot of my parents' wedding, the guests are squished together, laughing and sweating in the late July heat. My mother is smiling the smile of someone loved and adored, my father looks dashing, handsome, and proud . . . and my grandmother looks like she's just eaten a bad piece of herring.

As a newlywed, Naomi did her best to reinvent herself. She took a huge emotional sigh and set about creating a warm home and family life for her husband. But, no matter how hard she tried, Naomi felt like a trespasser in her husband's world. Her disdainful mother-in-law treated the new bride like an unwelcome outsider.

Like all beginnings, beautiful and happy

Thankfully, Naomi's Hyde Park High School chums stood by their motherless friend. Each girl shared her own mother's traditional family recipes and housekeeping tips—from briskets and chicken soup to washing windows and soaking tablecloths. Those devoted friends knew that Naomi's only desire was to be a successful wife and mother with a family of her own. A family that would never leave her.

Naomi and Bill visited Minnie at every opportunity, and as Minnie reached her high school years, Naomi made sure her sister had all the niceties a teenage girl desired. By the time Minnie turned seventeen in 1948, she was staying with Naomi and Bill for entire weekends as the official babysitter for their new baby, Rosalyn. Once again, Minnie and Naomi were part of a family unit.

In 1951, Naomi and Bill planned Minnie's wedding. A lavish kosher affair, the ceremony was held in a beautiful synagogue, where Minnie wore an exquisite off-white gown with a long silk train. Acting as mother and father, Bill and Naomi walked her down the aisle in the traditional processional to the *chuppah** and hired the best professional photographer on the circuit to capture the entire event on film. Naomi was ecstatic. She stood by Minnie's side, proud to have given her sister the wedding she herself had dreamed of.

The Garfinkel girls had only wanted a chance at a happy ending. And, for several years, life was very good.

Over the next few decades, in a small ranch house with three active kids and a husband who had become more human and less superhero, my mother's well-being began to disintegrate. Exhausted from trying to win her mother-in-law's affection and overwhelmed by the physical and constant demands of raising children, my mother fell into a depression.

Once again, her Hyde Park High girlfriends tried to help her: "Forget about the old goose, you don't need her—you have us!" "Come for lunch and play mah-jongg. Harriet always serves Jordan Almonds, and her husband buys the really good cigarettes." "Come on, Na, just try a little!"

Despite their efforts, Naomi's emotional foundation began to crack, and she slowly crumbled into pieces. After many episodes and years of doctors' visits, the professionals finally figured her out. Long before bipolar disorder became a diagnostic term *du jour*, my poor suffering mother was labeled a manic-depressive in the mid-1970s and instructed to take three doses of lithium a day. She willingly and unwillingly continued to do so until her death in 2001.

As grown women, Naomi and Minnie had an intensely devoted relationship. Neither made an important decision without the other sister voicing her strong and lengthy opinions. They spoke to each other every morning on the phone, even though they lived a few short blocks apart. They loved each other fiercely, and they laughed or argued daily. They took turns at mothering each other, desperately trying to fill the void created so long ago in childhood.

Minnie and her husband, Sheldon, divorced in the mid-1980s after twenty-nine years of marriage. With her two children grown, she landed a good-paying job in sales and moved into lovely single-girl apartment on Chicago's North Lake Shore Drive. Minnie enjoyed dating and working and living by her whims. Answering to no one, she had a facelift, spent a fortune on a sexy new wardrobe, and decided to find love by being lovable.

She quickly met Jerry, a wiry pit bull of a man who matched Minnie's passion for working hard and playing hard. Completely smitten after just a few months of dating, she invited Jerry to move into her apartment. They were terrific together, and my mother relaxed, knowing her sister was no longer alone in the big city.

Then, just four years later, without illness and without warning, Jerry dropped dead. A sudden heart attack took him right down. One minute he was lighting a cigar and opening a beer, and the next minute he was gone.

Minnie felt heartbroken and forsaken—and pissed. Everyone she loved, except her big sister, eventually left her. Naomi, understanding the benefits of therapy, helped Minnie find a wonderful support group. Once a week, Minnie attended a Jewish singles grief-and-loss discussion meeting. Hoping to find some comfort, she made a new circle of friends who ultimately changed her life. Bernie, a longtime member of the group, noticed Minnie right away. He begged her to join him for dinner, but Minnie just kept saying no.

"Why bother with men?" she told my mother.

But Bernie kept asking. Six months later, Minnie finally said, "Yes, but just for coffee."

For their first date, Bernie drove her to a Greek diner, where he gallantly held open the door. Minnie walked in and stopped short, her mouth wide open. Three glass cases, filled with desserts, were all lined up by the front door. She saw pies of every flavor, meringue cakes in pastel colors, and coconut and chocolate pastries spinning round and round in the cases.

Bernie knew that she loved sweets, and he was a man with a mission.

He ordered four different kinds of pie and two coffees, hoping to impress her with his generosity. He wanted to give her the world, and if she was only going to allow him to give her coffee and pie, then he'd give her a world of pie.

He then began to tell his story. He'd been happily married for forty-seven years when his wife passed out from an aneurysm and died immediately. A year later, his grief was now manageable, but he was lonely. "I miss married life," Bernie admitted, "and need a woman in my home and by my side."

He also told Minnie that she didn't have to love him, but if she could find it in her heart to date and possibly marry him, she would never have to work again. He would happily support her for the rest of her life. Minnie, a sophisticated woman of the world, knew what he meant by this. She found his straight up directness shocking and strangely attractive.

They dated for an appropriate amount of time, and then my Aunt Minnie took Bernie as her second husband. She was fifty-nine and he was seventy-two.

He boasted of being "the luckiest man on Earth," and called her "*My Mindy.*"

A year after marrying Bernie, Minnie was diagnosed with breast, appendix, and colon cancers. Despite the diagnoses, she promised her adoring husband that she would not go quietly. In turn, he proved to be a stalwart companion. During the nine years that followed, he stayed by her side during every one of her thirteen surgeries.

In that ninth year, her doctors agreed they couldn't do anything more for Minnie.

This news gave Naomi a stomachache. It hurt to eat, though she was hungry. She lost forty pounds in three months. Tests showed nothing, but exploratory surgery revealed everything.

Six months after that operation, Naomi died from stomach cancer—just sixteen days after her dear Minnie died of everything cancer. At seventy-six and sixty-nine, the Garfinkel girls were no longer seven years apart. They would never be apart again.

I'm the baby of my family. Once my siblings went off to school, my mother and I had the world to ourselves for a few years before I entered kindergarten. Several mornings a week, we would hop on the Jeffery Boulevard #5 bus to do "our" grocery shopping.

I loved these outings to the A&P. At the store, my mother picked me up and plunked me onto the Formica counter next to the Eight O'Clock coffee grinder. Then, she left me sitting there, alone, while she roamed the aisles and enjoyed her shopping. I happily chatted with all the "mommy ladies" as they poured their bags of beans into the enormous fire-engine-red industrial coffee grinder. I sat mesmerized, as the shiny red machine magically turned coffee from odd little pellets into a fine brown dust that would fly into my hair if I leaned over and got too close. But even better yet, if I was a good girl and stayed put, the reward would be bites of my mother's Hershey Bar as we stood in line at the cash register.

It seemed so easy to be good, knowing there was candy involved.

On outings like this, my mother would tell me stories of *The Orphanage*. I remember feeling so sad for her because she didn't have a mommy and daddy to love her and give her chocolate. I was too young to contain that kind of grief, but I remember being petrified that, if I wasn't a perfect little girl, G–d would take my parents away and I'd be an orphan, too.

Thus began my career as a G–d-fearing, candy-loving, designated daughter.

MY MEDICATED WOMEN
The Fingerett Family

My father's mother, Grandma Anna, was a tough nut to crack. She took years and years to openly accept my mother as a daughter-in-law. Thankfully, her two daughters—Aunt Lill and Aunt Rose—recognized Naomi's like-minded willingness to be a warm family member and embraced their new sister-in-law from the start.

My mother deeply cherished these women as well. Aunt Rose, the older sister, was a hefty woman who favored her mother and—according to my mother—was Grandma Anna's favorite daughter. Soft and kind, inclusive and easygoing, Aunt Rose was smushy and lovable. She possessed a lovely, lilting voice and constantly sang beautiful old Yiddish songs around the house without inhibition. Everyone spoke of her professional potential, but instead, she married Uncle Alan, had four kids, and ran her home and family from inside her large and flowy muumuu. Prematurely gray, Aunt Rose had little regard for vanity and preferred being a relaxed and comfortable woman who enjoyed making everyone else comfortable.

Aunt Lill seemed like her sister's opposite, although she too loved to sing and knew all the lyrics of the big band hits from her swinging youth. Movie-star gorgeous, Aunt Lill barely needed makeup—but was never without lipstick. Her flaming red hair, pulled back in a bun, framed her face with a dramatic widow's peak. Her twinkly eyes always looked as if they were smiling. At bar mitzvahs and weddings, Aunt Lill always dazzled, dressed in just-the-right, never over-the-top outfits that accentuated her small waist and curvy (read big) bottom. Her vivacious personality matched her earthy and beautiful essence. The men went wild for her, but only lucky Uncle Ralph caught her.

Aunt Lill loved to host the family's Sunday dinner gatherings, and we loved eating at her house. She made the best brisket of all the Aunties. After finishing my second helping, I would leave the kids' table and slowly walk the long stretch toward the bathroom in the back of the house, by the bedrooms. I'd linger in the narrow hallway and stare at the walls where Aunt Lill hung the family's old photos. Most of these black-and-whites in dusty antique frames belonged to my uncle's side of the family. We all gossiped about my uncle's people at dinner because they weren't there and we were.

I loved those old photographs, full of faces I didn't know. I stood in the hallway wondering if they were Holocaust people or family from the olden times in the faraway land of Minsk and Pinsk, wherever that was. I stared at the photographs, thinking, *what did they do for their jobs in Minsk and Pinsk, and did they have a JCC in Minsk and Pinsk, and did the kids in Minsk and Pinsk beg to quit Hebrew School, like me?*

Eventually, I put my thoughts away and continued walking to the bathroom. Once inside, I closed the door firmly behind me. With great aplomb, I'd fake-flush the toilet to muffle the sound as I opened the creaky medicine cabinet. I had no idea what I was looking for, but I just *had* to see how other people lived.

After snooping among the pill bottles and cans of deodorant and hair spray, I'd find my way into my aunt and uncle's bedroom. It looked just like my parents' bedroom, with a big grown-up bed covered in a flowery and puffy bedspread, topped with perfectly placed ruffled pillowcases with fancy stitching, and round foam bolsters you weren't supposed to sleep on. Studio portraits of my cousins as toddlers wearing baby-sized corrective eyeglasses hung on the wall over the headboard. My uncle's nightstand wasn't all that interesting—just an ashtray full of unfiltered Camel cigarette butts.

But my aunt's nightstand, with its organized chaos, was a thing to behold.

A smudgy water glass and numerous pill bottles crowded around a stack of books, with *Dr. Spock* covering the naughty *Peyton Place*. On top of the books, she kept the mandatory roll of toilet paper to blot her bedtime lipstick, catch her husband's messy sneezes, and hold her four-dollar wash-and-set in place with bobby pins while she slept.

I usually returned just as the grown-ups finished dinner. Everybody cleared the table together. However, my boy cousins knew how to screw up so they could get out of doing whatever it was they didn't want to do. They bumped into one another, supposedly trying to help, till somebody yelled, "You kids, just get outta of the way!"

Once the dishes were done and the kitchen cleaned, the adults took their coffee and cigarettes in the living room for a rest. A hyperactive kid, I quickly annoyed my siblings and cousins. As a result, I often chose to hang out in the living room with the grown-ups, where I made myself useful as a jet-fast errand runner for the tired ladies who had spent the evening on their feet. After the men settled in the dining room to smoke and play cards, I sat quietly and waited for the "*Sally, be-a-dear*" assignments to begin:

"*Sally, be-a-dear*, and bring Mommy her purse, I need a gum."

"*Sally, be-a-dear*, and get Auntie Rose a glass of tap from the kitchen, and then go into the dining room where Uncle Alan's gonna hand you a pill for me. Thanks, cookie!"

"*Sally, be-a-dear*, and run to the bathroom medicine cabinet and grab the bottle with the red cap, and while you're back there, grab Uncle Ralph's Camels from his nightstand. Go fast, dolly, I think the Bears are winning, and I don't want him to catch you!"

Growing up, I never once gave much thought to the "pill drill." The women in my family needed me, and I needed to be needed.

At that time, I was too young to comprehend the issues my aunts faced in their own daily lives. I knew that Uncle Ralph and Aunt Lill had adopted my cousins, Gary and Ricky, in the early 1950s. Years later, I learned more. Soon after applying to become adoptive parents in 1948, Aunt Lill and Uncle Ralph were given a beautiful newborn baby girl. Aunt Lill named her Dawn in honor of their new beginning. Baby Dawn had light wispy blond hair and blue eyes that stayed blue. She was cherubic and joyful and the entire family celebrated her arrival and toasted Lill and Ralph's happiness. For six months, they loved and cared for that baby girl. Then the birth mother had a change of heart, and Dawn was taken away from my Aunt Lill.

I cannot, for the life of me, imagine going through this.

In my memory, there was never a day where Aunt Rose wore anything but her gray hair and muumuu. When I was five years old, we kids were all told that Aunt Rose was sick and the doctors were working hard to make her well. No one told us what was wrong exactly, nor did we pry. A few years into her struggle, I somehow became aware that she was heroically fighting ovarian and breast cancer, undergoing every treatment available. She wanted more time, so that she might raise her young children a little while longer. After an eight-year battle, she passed away at the age of forty-eight. Her youngest was eleven.

At Aunt Rose's funeral, I watched my sobbing sixty-eight-year-old grandmother throw herself over her eldest child's casket, bereft and screaming, "Take me, dear G–d, take me, not her, please!" over and over, until the Uncles had to physically hold her up and carry her to a chair by the gravesite. I had never known a human heart could break into pieces. But now I did.

What I do know, looking back, is this—familial love is mysterious, and the depth of love women carry for their children defies all measure and description.

The task of being a good daughter is not always easy. But if I succeed, as my reward, dear G–d, allow me to keep my children till I die.

SONG: *THE RETURN*

Tossed to the stars, and a baby goes sailing
Out on a sea, under quiet night skies
Dark blue and waiting, it's there she does carry
Out and away, it's her heart that will never return

Born of a love where the gift is the giving
Born of two hearts—is just one pair of eyes
Deep blue and wanting, your soul and your reason
Caught unaware, it's your old life that never returns

Promise me—promise me, you will outlive me
That's the natural order, the way it should be
Then break from me and take from me all you can carry
Its nature—it's nurture, and then it's your turn
And as I teach you, I learn

Tossed in the air, and your baby goes flying
Into the sun, under wide open skies
Bright blue and shining, she's earthbound and running
There in her eyes, it's your love that will always return

JEWISH KID BORN ON CHRISTMAS DAY

When I was growing up, music was a language spoken fluently in our home.

In his youth, my father had been a passionate musician and marvelous singer. Strikingly handsome and poised, he performed in Gilbert and Sullivan operettas during high school. An amazing violinist with tremendous potential, he gave up his dreams of joining the Chicago Civic Orchestra and became an accountant to earn a stable income.

My father's love affair with music, however, never ceased. At bedtime, he stood in the hallway between our bedrooms with his violin tucked underneath his chin and took requests. He interspersed "Pop Goes the Weasel" and "London Bridge is Falling Down" with classical passages from the great composers. We three kids fell asleep to the sounds of our dad's magnificent talents, and to this day, my eyes refuse to stay open whenever I hear a violin solo.

In 1958, when I was four years old, my mother joined the Columbia Record Club. Once a month, vinyl albums arrived in the mail, and if Mom liked them, she'd keep them and send in her check. She loved all kinds of music and our record player's

24

turntable spun constantly, especially after *Port Said** arrived. This recording showcased the accomplished Lebanese tenor Mohammed El-Bakkar, singing haunting melodies accompanied by instruments that were completely unfamiliar to my ears— sitars and cymbals, strange drums and voices that whined in minor keys that almost sounded like our rabbi from shul. The photograph on the album's cardboard front cover was equally foreign. A raven-haired, nearly naked belly dancer, draped in blue and pink veils, had been caught mid hip-swing, with her arms raised high above her strategically placed pasties. My mother fell madly in love with these seductive rhythms and melodies and played this LP daily—for years. The racy cardboard sleeve, however, ended up lining the bottom of her girdle drawer, a guaranteed no-man's-land.

I, too, loved that recording. In the summer, after an early dinner, my mother would usher me into the living room and put *Port Said* on the turntable to entertain me while she cleaned up the kitchen. I remember the late day sun shining through the living room's picture window. After changing into a clean white undershirt, petticoat, and party shoes, I pranced around, casting a giant-sized shadow on the floor, as the room filled with a dusky-gold glow from the setting sun.

"Mommy, I'm shadow dancing!" I yelled with delight. "Come see, come see!"

Many times, my mother sprang to life, abandoning a dirty kitchen to join me in the living room. With a dish towel thrown over her shoulder and sudsy rubber gloves still on her hands, she'd attempt to dance like the half-naked lady on the album cover. We laughed hysterically as she clapped her hands and tried to snap her rubbery fingers, flinging soapy water everywhere. Due to her lack of rhythm, the squeaky latex gloves *never* hit the beat of the pulsating bongos and did nothing more than make a mess on the carpet. She was goofy and ridiculous, and I loved watching her love music.

My folks agreed that owning a highly sophisticated hi-fi stereo system was a family priority. Dad built a coffee table specifically designed to house and protect the turntable, tuner components, and pricey speakers. Each day after dinner, he'd stretch out on the living room couch to relax and listen to classical music on Chicago's WFMT. He also tuned in for the radio station's weekly variety show, *The Midnight Special*. Launched and hosted in 1953 by a very young Mike Nichols (the famed Broadway performer and Oscar Award-winning director), this syndicated radio show still features, according to WFMT, "folk music & farce, show tunes & satire, madness & escape."

I was six years old when my father *finally* let me stay up late to listen to *The Midnight Special*. Airing every Saturday night at ten p.m., this program introduced us to the beautiful voices of Joan Baez and Judy Collins, the grinding blues of Huddie Ledbetter and Big Bill Broonzy, and the sophisticated comedy of newcomers like David Steinberg, Bill Cosby, and the duo of Nichols and Elaine May.

My dad and I marveled at Woody Guthrie and Pete Seeger. Their folk songs always had repetitive choruses, making them easy to learn and impossible to forget. He'd grab his violin to jam with the radio. Right there in the living room, I watched my father float away in the moment. Enthralled by his blissful face, I understood that I was hearing and seeing—pure joy.

Right around this time, my Dad bought a used upright piano from a friend of a friend of a friend. The keys worked, and the battered instrument was quite serviceable for kids, but it was in lousy physical condition. Mom decided to spiff up this potentially beautiful piece of furniture by refinishing the faded, scratched wood surface with a thick coat of high-gloss, white enamel paint. Next, she bought three cans of gold and silver lamé spray-paint-sparkles and just let it fly. I have no idea where she got her decorating ideas from, but the piano looked like my *Tante** Faigie's flashy Formica countertop.

I went wild for this bright and shiny look, and couldn't wait for the paint to dry.

Grandma Anna stopped by and gave my mother's handiwork the hairy eyeball. "This piece of *drek** does not belong in a living room. It belongs in a whorehouse!"

The next day my father and some neighbors moved the piano to the basement rec room.

My heart soared at the prospect of the piano being banished to the basement. This meant I wouldn't bother anyone if I wanted to monkey around on it, especially on a Sunday morning. I would wake up early with those Saturday evening *Midnight Special* songs still stuck in my head, and I'd sneak down to the basement. While everyone else slept, I quietly plunked on the keys, trying to recreate the melodies I had heard the night before. During my search for the right notes, I hit a few wrong ones, but figuring out how to play these songs felt like a wonderful game. Frankly, I just assumed everyone could sit down with an instrument and play a tune they had just heard. My father did it with his violin; I did with a sparkly piano.

I didn't know about sheet music back then. Somehow, I had a memory that held onto every melody I heard. I called it my *rememory*. Musical sentences sat between my ears and took over my thoughts, and then they jingle-jangled in my heart and soul before finding their way down to my fingers and out onto the piano keys. For me, having music float from the inside of my head to the outside of my head gave me a sense of calm and physical comfort. The seams in my socks stopped bothering me, the wool sweater I was forced to wear when playing in the basement stopped itching, and for those hours at the piano, my mother's odd behavior didn't matter. One might say I copped a bit of a buzz.

I now spoke my father's language, and I wanted to speak it all the time. More often than not, I chose to stay downstairs in the basement with my best friend, the piano. I spent hours sounding out pop songs from the radio, and soon made a life-altering discovery: *I could dink around and create new melodies all by myself.*

I soon lost interest in the radio songs, and devoted all my time to making up my own goofy lyrics and simple melodies. When I sat down at the piano, the world as I knew it fell away completely. I climbed inside my little songs and stayed there until someone came down to the basement to retrieve me.

My first compositions were inane childhood ditties about being born on Christmas Day. I hated my birthday because sharing the date with the Baby Jesus had turned out to be a pretty crappy deal. I never once got to bring cupcakes to class for my special day, or have the teacher ask me to erase the board in honor of turning a year older. And being Jewish didn't make it any less dreadful, because my birthday occasionally fell on Chanukah. This meant I got *ditzed** on gifts, receiving only one present for the two events. Faced with these injustices, I found great comfort in making up songs about how lousy I had it in December.

The piano remained my constant companion during the lonely and boring Christmas break. I played endlessly since there was no reason to stop; I had no school to wake up for and no shopping to do, as we Jews refused to venture out during the Christmas pre-holiday shopping madness. The TV offered little comfort with its live broadcasts of various church masses from all over the Chicagoland area, and the Christmas movies just made me sad that we didn't share the day with the ENTIRE WORLD!

Though my long-term *rememory* has diminished, I do recall that these childish and offensive Christmas-bashing tunes stunned my mother, who threatened to wash my mouth out with soap: *"You may not degrade that lovely piano with your potty songs about Christmas, Sally. Shame on you!"*

As an adult, I am finally free to chronicle the personal trials and pitiable miseries inflicted by my Christmas Birthday. And now, here is my non-potty version of my *white-girl blues*.

SONG: JEWISH KID BORN ON CHRISTMAS DAY TALKING BLUES

Back in 1954, down in Chicago by the South Shore
Baby girl is born that Christmas morn
Ooh, here comes drama
Of those Christmas babies that arrive
She's one of the lucky—in the first five
She wins free diapers—whole year's supply
Ooh, got a happy mama
The hospital nurses were more than delighted
To help with the names, they get all excited
"Name her Mary Carol? Or how 'bout Christine?
There's always Judy or Josephine. You know, use the letter J
In honor of . . . shhh, the Baby Jesus"

But the parents were having none of that
So they gently replied to avoid a spat
"Oh, thank you for those names
We're not Christmas people, so if it's all the same
We thought we'd go with something Jewish
Something Hebraic
We're gonna call her Esther Shaindel!"
That's quite a handle for a brand-new baby
And a trend was starting in the 1950s
Names were getting Americanized, downsized, de-ethnicized
A futile attempt to depolarize, so the family decides to be
Translatin'—truncatin'—ultimately—assimilatin'
So the beautiful and biblical name of Esther Shaindel gets
Homogenized on down
They call her Sally—that would be me

Now being born on Christmas really sucks
I got a lot to say and you can trust
My litany will be very long
For years I've tried to write this song
I'm a cranky old broad with no decorum
I'm stealing licks from a talking blues forum
It's my turn to have my say
'Cuz I'm a Jewish kid, born on Christmas Day
(*Sung*) I'm a Jewish kid, Jewish kid born on Christmas Day

I remember back, when I turned five
No birthday party would ever jive
No little friends could come around
'Cuz the Jewish ones had all left town
They went to Florida, Christmas break at *Bubbe's** house
And the Gentile ones? Well, come on, it's Christmas!
Back then, gas stations and movie theatres were closed
There was nothing open, goodness knows
Just one rickety Chinese restaurant

"Happy birthday, Sally, have whatever you want . . ."
What do I know?—I'm five!
They give me rice and a fortune cookie!

On our way back home from eating Chinese
We'd drive up and down the icy streets
Peeking into windows—see Christmas trees
We'd have us a contest
Which side of the street had the best Christmas lights
Sparkly houses, lit up bright
But I'm a little girl, I start to cry, I don't understand why
The Baby Jesus is out in the cold
In the front yard manger, covered in snow
Why didn't they bring him in where it was nice and warm
Near the fireplace, where the stockings were hung?
Let him open presents with the girls and the boys
Give him Christmas cookies—let him play with toys
I'd give him my fortune cookie, my fortune said
"Learn many languages—go far"
I wanted to learn to speak Catholic, and go to Christmas
(*Sung*) I'm a Jewish kid, Jewish kid born on Christmas Day

I turned ten in 1964, and I was miserable down to my core
Radio and TV were a horrid bore, remember—before cable?
Radio blasting choirs from the Vatican
TV humming with off-the-air patterns
Christmas people rushing everywhere, for us
Alienation and despair
There was nothing to do but sit and wait, and wait and wait
As the world came to a screeching halt
Midday on December 24th
Folks said "Don't worry, kids, it's over soon"
Felt like we were lost, marooned
Thankful our cousins from Skokie would visit
Aunt Lill was planning on bringing a brisket

She called to say they were out of gas
Stations were closed, they'd have to pass
"Ohhh, Happy Birthday, Sally . . ."
My mom starts to bake a cake—we're out of eggs. OY!

Well, really, I could go on and on
No doubt this is one depressing song
Truth is no one forgets my birthday
'Cuz they know it's a drag, and they all call to say
"Hey, what a drag," and I say, "Yeah, thanks"
And then I ask them what they got for Chanukah
'Cuz now, this year, it's also Chanukah—Damn!
I get birthday calls on Christmas Eve
So now I call it Birthday Eve
Just a chosen few get Birthday Eve, who? I'll tell ya!
Humphrey Bogart, Jimmy Buffet
Annie Lennox, and Sissy Spacek
I wonder if they all get birthday presents
Wrapped in Christmas paper
"Look, it's Charlie Brown with Lucy and Linus dressed as the
    three wise men standing over Snoopy as the Baby Jesus"

In spite of myself, I've grown up
Trying not to be a bitter adult
But the biggest *mishegas** of all
Is when I'm out shopping at the mall
I've had a lovely time perusing
And my credit card is perched for using
The cashier asks for my ID, I hand it over
He takes a peek, and then I hold my breath
As I wait to see if he notices . . . Yep, he notices
Stand back—here it comes, every time
"Oh, you're a Christmas Baby!"

Right then and there I have to make a choice
To just say thanks, or raise my voice
And let loose with my talking blues
But hopefully, I'm smart enough to choose
To just let it go—turn the other ear
Because that's what the . . . shhh, Baby Jesus would do
He too was a Jewish kid, Jewish kid born on Christmas Day!

*You must Google *Port Said.*

THE BALLAD OF
HARRY AND ESTHER

For the Jewish holiday meals of my childhood, my mother, aunts, and grandmother took turns hosting. This meant surrendering one's kitchen to the other women in the family and allowing them to make a complete mess of things as everyone shared in the chaotic preparations for the meal's religious rituals. Hosting also meant opening your home to family and friends, as well as strangers in need of comfort and community.

When I was five years old, my mother tried to explain just who these people were, and how we were related. As she gave me the rundown, I glazed over the first time she said "second cousin *once removed*." I mentally *once removed* my own self from the conversation and decided to simplify matters. Any lady who carried a pocket book was an Aunt and any man in a collared shirt was an Uncle.

The old Auntie Ladies would grab me and hug me and pinch me while spitting out Yiddish phrases that meant nice things, but sounded like sneezes. The old Uncle Men wore their pants up to their armpits and did stupid magic tricks with quarters.

The guest list always included the same roster of usual suspects. We only saw these people at the more sacred Jewish holiday dinners, the bigger weddings and bar mitzvahs, and for sure, every funeral.

Rosh Hashanah and Passover served as the seminal checkpoints for the older folks. They pinched the cheeks of the newest baby, heard the latest developments in everyone's personal life, and of course, passed judgments that *hopefully* sounded like words of encouragement, love, and concern. Year after year, the greetings were always the same, just progressively louder than the year before.

- **"You look fabulous!** Have you lost a little weight? Ohhh, I see you had that thing taken off your forehead—very nice!"

- **"I told you to call Herman**—he could have gotten you a deal! Why would you waste money? What's wrong with you?"

- **"How's your mother and that eye?** Was the doctor able to fix it? *Kinahora, poo-poo-poo,** she should live and be well! She should see only wonderful things, and never have to wear an eye patch like my brother-in-law Lenny, poor man. He can't drive, he can't go bowling, and when he walks—he drifts a little to the left, like he's drunk, but he's not. I told him to take that BB gun away from his son, but no! No one listens to me! Now, he's had to drop out of the JCC's bowling league, and he was quite the star of the team, a wonderful bowler, but now he's a misery to be around."

- **"It's been too long! Don't be such a stranger.** Our phone rings—you should call it sometime!"

Once in a while, an elderly relative cornered me with a question. As a child, I had yet to learn how to make two-way conversation. But I knew how to be polite—sort of.

OLD PERSON: Tell me, sweetheart, what grade are you in? Do you get good marks?

SALLY: I'm in first grade. What's a mark?

OLD PERSON: *Kutchkie*,* come here and tell me about your school!

SALLY: It's red brick, and the bathrooms are stinky.

OLD PERSON: So, are you as smart as your big sister? I hear she always gets straight As.

SALLY: How do you know my sister?

Before these large family dinner parties, the hostess's dining room, which sat undisturbed for the other 362 non-holiday days a year, underwent an extraordinary transition. The sacred, six-foot dining room table, normally treated like a museum piece and covered with a table runner and a vase of silk flowers, would be pulled apart to house all four leaves, bringing this elegant little six-top to its maximum banquet length.

But why stop there, when you had to feed eighteen adults in one place?

Card tables were added at both ends. To create the illusion of one long surface, the hostess overlapped antique lace cloths over the three tables. Then some poor *yutz*,* sat in that one spot where the table heights were ever so slightly uneven, and his dinner plate wobbled from *the crack*. Too bad, fooled you, you're stuck now!

As children, we never got to sit at this long and lovely table. Banished to some other room, we were hidden away at the *Kids' Table*, where anyone could pick their nose in peace and put icky food in a napkin to flush down a toilet rather than die eating it. Dining unsupervised with my cousins had its merits.

But still, I wanted to sit at the big, lovely table where the salt-and-pepper shakers matched the plates and bowls, where water was served in long-stemmed goblets like the ones in picture books about kings and queens, and where there were so many forks that if you dropped one you'd still have another fork—right where you found the first one.

I wanted to sit with my mother and hear all the stories and gossip, shared across the table and told in the astonishing mixture of our family's three different languages: English, Yiddish, and Yelling. But no—little girls weren't allowed at the grown-ups' table. Instead, I managed to weasel my way *under* the table, and scrunch-sit quietly for hours. I easily dodged the restless feet of the old men. An accidental kick from a worn-out wingtip didn't scare me. But when the old Aunties took off their low-heeled pumps to give their bunions a rest, well, it was all I could to do to stifle my gag. Encased in thick support socks the color of skin, their ankles were the size of arms, and the things on their toes filled my nightmares for years.

But hiding amongst those weird ickies were worth it. I got to hear, firsthand, all the name-calling and swear words and so many other wonderful, *terrible* things.

I remember one elderly couple who always sat next to my grandparents at our dinners. The lady had big shoulders and muscular arms like a man, but her pretty face was beautifully done up with rouge and lipstick and false eyelashes. She waved her enormous hands in the air when she spoke, and I couldn't take my eyes off her jingling charm bracelets and her fingers loaded with diamond rings, and her long, pointy fingernails, painted fire-engine red.

At the table, she sat a head taller than her husband. However, when the two of them stood up, they were nose-to-nose in height. I decided that her husband had devised a *very* special magic trick, allowing him to grow when he stood, and shrink when he sat. This gimmick was so much better than the stupid quarter tricks the other uncles performed. I instantly liked this large fancy Auntie Lady and this stretchy Uncle Man, and I suspected that, if I crouched beneath their end of the table, I would hear tremendous amounts of *terrible* things.

One Rosh Hashanah, when I was six years old, my mother let me sit on her lap after my boy cousins ditzed* me. I was *kvetchy** and upset. She hoisted me up, put her arms around me, and gave me a pile of pistachio nuts to comfort me. Oh, this was heaven. All the pastries and nuts were within arm's reach, and I had the best seat in the house—with a panoramic view of all the relatives.

And there, sitting across from me, was the super-cheerful and lively fancy Auntie Lady! She talked and gestured nonstop, her hands raised well above her bosom area. Everyone sitting nearby had already moved their water glasses and *Kiddush** cups to avoid disaster. The loudest among a table of *shrayers,** she was the center of the after-dinner conversations.

In a voice that made every sentence sound like an important secret, the Auntie Lady launched into a story about a shoe repairman who lived in their building. Everyone at the table quickly hushed to hear her . . . except for stretchy Uncle Man, who started fiddling with his wineglass. Already half a head shorter than Auntie Lady, he sank lower in his seat.

Then, he spoke.

"Really, Esther, there's no reason to spend so much time with that guy. You stand so close to him," he chided.

"Harry, please, you're being ridiculous," she said. "He's a tenant, and I was just being friendly."

Now I knew! The Uncle Man was named Harry, and the Auntie Lady was Esther.

She rolled her eyes and whispered to her audience at the table, "Really, it's just that I love the odor of shoe polish, and I can't help myself. How can he be jealous of a smell, I ask you?" She searched each face at the table for agreement.

I leaned forward, wondering if I could someday stick my nose in shoe polish, too.

HARRY: Well, you might like the smell, but I don't like the smell, and if I don't like the smell, I don't think you should go out of your way to smell the smell.

ESTHER: Why can't I like a smell, even if you don't like the smell? It's my nose and it's on my face. What's the difference to you if I wanna smell a smell?

HARRY: Because it lingers on you, and I can tell you've been smelling the smell. You're my wife, and I don't want you smelling like a shoe!

ESTHER: But if I smell like a shoe, at least I smell like a well-cared-for shoe. I can't believe you're upset by this!

HARRY: I'm not upset by this. I just don't understand your need to stick your nose up into the shoe repairman's business or his smells.

ESTHER: Sorry, Harry, it's my nose, and it will smell whatever it wants to smell, and I don't want to hear another word, the end!

My mouth dropped open. I couldn't believe that Auntie Esther had, just now, been so mean to the fun, stretchy Uncle Harry. In front of the entire family, she had spoken to him like he was a kid and she was a mad mom. Uncle Harry looked away, took a big gulp of his wine, and grabbed his cigar. With a loud skootch of his chair, he stood up, stepped away from the table, and headed outside for a smoke.

Everyone at the table yelled after him, "Harry, no need to leave the table! Awww, come on back, it was funny! No?"

By then, he was out the door. The family's silence didn't last but a second, and then people moved on to the next tidbit of gossip and news.

Lying in bed that night, I couldn't stop thinking about the incident at the grown-ups' table. Stretchy Uncle Harry had been hurt and angry, and beautiful Auntie Esther didn't seem to care. I climbed out of bed and found my mother in her room.

"Mommy, why did Auntie Esther and Uncle Harry argue?" I asked. "She was so mean to him, and then he ditzed her and walked out. It's like they don't even like each other. Why did they ever get married?"

As she took off her earrings, my mother looked into the big mirror hanging above her dresser. She didn't turn around and face me. Instead, our eyes met in the mirror.

"Don't worry about them, cookie-noodle, they're perfectly happy. I promise you, Sally Girl, what they have is a thing of beauty and it's not for us to question. Now go back to bed."

SONG: *THE BALLAD OF HARRY AND ESTHER*

He met her in college, there in the ballroom
He met her while learning to dance
He was inwardly awkward, and she was outgoing
She seemed to be spinning so fast
Always up-tempo, always one step ahead
Again and again, she'd say no
He wanted her for his partner
But she moved on with another
But still he loved her so

There in the frat house, now they were seniors
He met her while drinking a beer
He was painfully quiet—she was drunk, loud, and boisterous
Crazy, but they married that year
She was a noisy girl, she railed in high decibels
And he always went with the flow
Then came the babies, she got fat, she went crazy
But still he loved her so

True love, true love
It's strong like a diamond, strong like her tears
True love, true love, it's a mystery—a mystery

There in her bedroom, he opens her window
She's caught in that season of change
She feels so hopeless, so ugly and fruitless
To him her beauty remains
He sometimes wonders how he ever caught her
He knows that he'll never let go
But she tries to test him—she will nag and upset him
But still he loves her so

True love, true love
It's strong like her diamonds, strong like her fears
True love, true love, it's a mystery—a mystery

There on the front porch, all alone after supper
He met her just closing his eyes
She passed on before him, the one girl who adored him
She ordered him home one last time
They were always together—she was always demanding
He wasn't one to say no
He wanted her for his partner and
In that ballroom, he joined her
Because he loved her so

THE RED MAN
Dedicated to Red Skelton

As the youngest of three kids, each born three years apart, I mastered the art of staying out of everyone's way at an early age.

Our parents were typical hard-working people, as parents go. Consistently weary and outrageously loud, our folks did the best they could while raising us with very little money, in a tiny six-room house. The five of us shared just under eleven-hundred square feet of space.

Since we kids were always bumping into one another, we would occasionally retreat into our own special areas. My teenage sister monopolized our only bathroom for hours on end. My brother commandeered the family TV to watch his scary science fiction and boring cowboy shows. And me? Well . . . I took the kitchen sink.

When I needed to hide from the chaos of family life, I'd climb onto my mother's step stool, start the water running, and grab a wiry S.O.S soap pad. With some little school tune playing in my head, I scrubbed and detailed my mother's entire collection of soup pots and broiling pans and cookie sheets. I cleaned anything that would keep me looking occupied and important. Somehow, dishwashing rendered me invisible. It was magic.

As often as we fought, we still loved and adored each other, deep down. But, growing up in a crowded, postwar tract house in the 1950s, we couldn't help being a bunch of roughhousing, smart-mouthing, and demanding mischief-makers.

However, on Tuesdays, we were perfect children, pretending no injustice offended us, therefore causing no retaliation. On Tuesdays, no Fingerett child misbehaved, lest we be banished for the evening. On Tuesdays, there was too much at stake, so we imposed an unspoken truce and suspended all hostilities.

We were angels—in anticipation of *The Red Skelton Hour*.

We lived for Tuesday nights, losing ourselves in the antics of Red Skelton's comedic alter egos—the adorable hobo Freddie the Freeloader, country-bumpkin Clem Kadiddlehopper, and Junior the Mean Widdle Kid, who was my favorite character.

As Junior, Red became a naughty little boy who always admitted that he had, indeed, done something wrong by announcing, "I dood it."

I, however, kept insisting Junior had said, "I doodied."

My mother, who had to stifle her own amusement, would threaten to wash my mouth out with soap at the very kitchen sink where I took care of her cookware.

In front of that small TV in the living room, with our folks on the couch and us kids on the floor, our whole family laughed out loud to see someone else stumble through awkward social exchanges and endure embarrassingly goofy misunderstandings. I marveled at how things could go so wrong for Red's characters and then somehow end well. During those precious sixty minutes, my world felt warm and loving. When that hour was over, I remember how Red looked me square in the eye, and with a wave farewell, bid me, "Good night and may G–d bless."

I floated to bed with a blessing from my favorite friend.

Throughout my life, Red Skelton has remained my childhood champion. With my little girl eyes, I witnessed a grown man, unafraid to be a misfit or a *widdle kid*, all the while remaining adorable and loveable. I marveled at how he made us laugh together, united in the shared experience of being in on the same joke. I watched my parents relax and my siblings soften, and I knew right then and there, that I wanted to be that person who people wanted to watch, and be with, and laugh with, and love.

In 1982, during the early stages of cable television, I rediscovered many great old TV shows from my youth. But I could not find *The Red Skelton Hour*. I later learned that Red had refused to participate in the new cable medium, due to the violence and lack of decency in prime-time programming. I was heartbroken to realize that generations to come would never witness his brilliant craft and talent.

I missed this warm and loving TV star from my childhood and wondered—what would have happened, if Red Skelton hadn't happened to me?

SONG: THE RED MAN

Come Tuesday, I would dream away
Right through a school day, it was a fool's day for me
Come Tuesday, we'd have dinner at half past six
Wrap the foil, get the TV fixed
To watch the Red Man, we'd watch the Red Man
Oh Mama, please let me stay up late
Kadiddlehopper just found the bar
Mama, I want to be a star, I wanna make 'em laugh
I wanna make the people laugh, just like the Red Man

Come Tuesday, I'd ignore the ringing of the phone
I'm never home when I'm with the Red Man
Come Tuesday, I'd remember all I'd hear
I'd practice in the mirror
To be the Red Man, just like the Red Man
Oh Mama, please let me stay up late
Kadiddlehopper just drank the bar
Mama, I want to be a star, I wanna make 'em laugh
I wanna make the people laugh, just like the Red Man

Last Tuesday, I had a fitful dream
There was no Red Man
There was no laughter anymore
And all the babies lately being born
Would never know the clown
Or the love that went down
Come Tuesday

Oh Mama, please let me stay up late
Kadiddlehopper just left the bar
Mama, I want to be a star, I wanna make 'em laugh
I wanna make the people laugh, just like the Red Man
Goodnight, goodnight, goodnight
And may G–d Bless, Red Man

I wrote the song "The Red Man" in 1982, and recorded it in 1983. My friend Fran Kovac passed along the cassette to a friend, a bellman at the hotel where Red stayed at during his Columbus show. This kind bellman gave the tape to Red, who quickly grabbed a bottle of white wine, autographed it, and had the bellman send it to me. I have never opened this bottle.

A few months later, in February 1984, I received an envelope from Red's musical director, Jerry Kaye. Red must have listened to my song, and then written the letter that I've transcribed on the following page.

January 1984

Dear Sally,

Thank you, "Dear Heart." Your songs are beautiful. As for "Red Man"—I have received many awards in my lifetime, but I cannot remember anything that has ever touched my emotions with such a heartfelt warmth.

I am sure we met in Columbus—we tried to get into a studio so that I could hear your music—but the studio was closed or something like that happened.

When I go home, I will play your record for my folks. I am sure they too will be as proud of your "talent" as all who hear you. Take good care of your dear self—that way you will be taking (care) of my dear friend. You're a lovely human.

May all good things in your life be to your liking.

Thank you, Dear.

Love,
Red Skelton

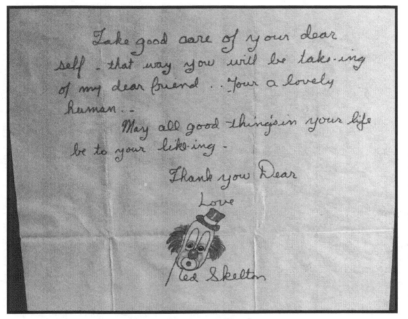

Red's signature, with hand-colored clown drawing.
The complete letter, beautifully framed, hangs on my office wall.

RIPPED FROM THE CITY

My Very Own

American Diaspora*

*DIASPORA   *noun:* the dispersion or spreading of something that was originally localized (as a people or language or culture). The body of Jews (or Jewish communities) outside Palestine or modern Israel.

I was eighteen months old when my family moved into our brand-new house in a Jewish neighborhood in Chicago called South Shore. Built in 1956, our tiny, three-bedroom, one-bathroom, orange brick ranch sat in a row of identical houses. With young families in minds, each house featured a large picture window in the living room where mothers could sit with coffee and a newspaper and watch their children play in the front yard. With elderly relatives in mind, every front porch came equipped with a wrought iron railing to assist aging grandparents as they hauled their weary immigrant souls up the steps into their offspring's new American dream home.

Our house, located three doors from the corner of Jeffery Boulevard and South 91st Street, sat just a few feet away from the city bus stop. The Jeffery Boulevard bus was our lifeline to everywhere—the grocery store, the doctor's office, and of course, downtown to State Street.

All the neighborhood kids took great advantage of the freedoms the bus offered. As long as we had correct change, we had wings.

A pack of us seventh-grade girls, after weeks of whining and promising to stick together, finally received permission to ride the bus downtown for an unchaperoned shopping trip. Armed with our mothers' charge cards and warnings to guard our purses, we raced around the Loop, making sure to hit our three favorite department stores—Marshall Field's, Carson Pirie Scott, and Goldblatt's. Stopping first to overspray ourselves with Chantilly and Ambush perfume samples, we then began our hunt for wool skirts and alpaca cardigan sweaters that came with dyed-to-match knee socks.

Some of us had older sisters who took the bus to Hyde Park under the guise of visiting the Museum of Science and Industry. Truth be told, these young ladies would apply forbidden lipstick and flirt with premed students at the University of Chicago library, a few streets away from the museum. When Janice Patempkin's Uncle Sheldon caught her making out with a boy named Troy over by the reference stacks, all hell broke loose for that group of girls, and almost ruined it for the rest of us.

But the boys got away with murder. Our older brothers took the bus up to 79th street and transferred east to Rainbow Beach, where it was rumored to be thick with *fast girls* tanning in the sun. More often than not, these unsuccessful Frankie-Avalon-wannabes struck out. But when the bus brought them back home, they stepped out onto the sidewalk with their cool slouchy posture, flicked their unfinished cigarettes, and made sure they had minty-fresh breath—and not a hint of sand in their pants pockets.

That bus was everything to us. All of us.

Growing up in my *shtetl** world, it seemed natural to assume that every family in our neighborhood was a Jewish family. Each day after school, hundreds of kids gathered at the Henry N. Hart Jewish Community Center (JCC), just down the block from our house. The JCC offered music, art, and dance classes, in addition to hosting sports teams for all ages. From toddlers to teenagers, everyone hung out at the JCC.

Since no self-respecting Jewish neighborhood dared to call itself a Jewish neighborhood without a serious delicatessen, we had Marcon's—located right next door to the JCC. On Sunday mornings at Marcon's, everyone caught up on the news and gossip as they waited in line to order bagels, lox, whitefish salad, and corned beef with just the right amount of fat. I myself never returned home from this deli without purchasing a bar of *halvah.**

With our JCC and deli sharing the same block of Jeffery Boulevard, it was convenient that our conservative synagogue—Rodfei Sholom-Oir Chodosh—looked on from across the street.

Founded in 1957 by South Shore Jews of my parents' generation, this shul spiritually housed roughly eight hundred families. Built with plenty of classrooms for Sunday school, a magnificent modern sanctuary, and a large social hall, this synagogue was the epicenter for Hebrew education and religious life-cycle events. My sister Roz, my brother Steve, and I attended countless bar and bat mitzvahs of friends we'd known since our preschool days at the JCC.

Rodfei Sholom-Oir Chodosh flourished for ten years (1957–1967). As the congregation entered its second decade, our South Side neighborhood began to grow more diverse and underwent socioeconomic changes. By the end of the 1960s, the upwardly mobile Jewish families had fled to the suburbs. Like dominoes, family after family moved to Skokie, Highland Park, Deerfield, Homewood, and Flossmoor.

Having not quite finished raising their children in this culturally vibrant and *hamishe** middle-class urban area, many parents were heartbroken to leave their warm and wonderful self-made American *shtetl.** In 1970, with just a handful of Jewish households remaining, our congregation disbanded after thirteen years, and the synagogue closed its doors for good.

Most of my friends moved away immediately after our eighth-grade graduation in 1968. My folks didn't quite know what to do—stay or go? We had a perfectly lovely home, they figured, so why leave?

We remained in the little orange brick ranch for two more years, until I was nearly molested by a gang while walking to high school. By spring 1970, my frightened parents had decided to leave South Shore, just like hundreds of families before us.

With Roz and Steve away at college, my folks chose to downsize to a small co-op apartment southeast of Chicago. How they found Calumet City, Illinois, remains a mystery. Just a sneeze away from the Indiana border, this blue-collar town once dreamed of becoming a suburb of Chicago, but had remained a small, forgotten, working-class neighborhood.

Instead of living in a freestanding home, we now shared walls with other co-op tenants, in a row of townhouse apartments. Our eight-unit building, one of the six buildings in the complex, sat surrounded on all sides by endless fields of untilled prairie. Barren, with only a promise of landscaping, our desolate cul-du-sac's driveway emptied out onto a newly paved two-lane road that stretched on for miles and led straight to nowhere anyone would want to go.

That fall, I enrolled as a junior at Thornridge High School and commuted on a yellow school bus, just like a farmer's kid.

In Calumet City, I was without options or public transportation. I no longer lived on a busy street with access to the Jeffery Boulevard #5 bus to everywhere. I lost contact with my old friends, since I couldn't call them without incurring long-distance charges.

Gone were the after-school gatherings at the JCC, and snack sessions at Marcon's Deli where we shared fries and Cokes and debriefed each other on who had kissed who, and who had purchased the latest 45-rpm single at Mr. T's record shop on 87th Street. Gone were the companions I had played with since kindergarten—the friends who shared a common childhood, knew my personal history, and kept my secrets.

I was gone, and they were gone.

I desperately missed my cultural Jewish identity. In my new school's cafeteria, everyone was blond and blue-eyed, and drank milk with their ham sandwiches. I readily assumed they were all

Catholic, Lutheran, Presbyterian, and whatever else there might be that wasn't Jewish.

There were no Jews in Calumet City. Not a one.

Oh, wait, there were three—my mother, my father, and me.

This move affected us all, and though I had long been accustomed to my mother's occasional rants and her bouts of depression, I now noticed her behavior becoming strange and histrionic. One day, she would shriek with contagious laughter as we watched *The Mary Tyler Moore Show*. The next morning, I might discover that my funny, up-tempo mom had been awake all night, seething over an imagined personal slight. Then, without warning, an unspecified mental shift would land her in bed for days, tearful and apologetic.

My father and I did everything in our power to be patient and compassionate. We rode out her swiftly changing moods, watching her bounce from depression to agitated mania in the course of a few days. We did what we could, but we were clueless.

Every day, my father left the house at seven in the morning to drive forty-five miles to his office on the northwest side of Chicago. Most nights, he returned home at half past seven, overworked and exhausted. During the school week, it was just my mother and me.

For six months, I came home from school each day unsure which version of my mother would be waiting for me. Sometimes, funny, loud and competent mom met me at the door. Other times, angry, bitter, and agitated mom slammed the front door behind me after she let me in. I quickly got to the point where I hoped to find quiet, sleepy, and neglectful mom. What frightened me most were the unpredictable possibilities.

With life at home so uncertain, I avoided making new friends at Thornridge High School—and I didn't dare go out on dates. We didn't belong to a synagogue, and there wasn't a JCC to be found. Instead, I took a weekend job working the ticket booth at the local movie theater. I willingly spent every Friday and Saturday night happily sequestered inside the box office. Between show times, I ate popcorn and managed to do a little homework—with "little" being the operative word.

Academically, I dropped the ball with a resounding thud. I had to keep an eye on my mother, and my miserable grades were the least of my worries. For the life of me, I couldn't think straight and no one seemed to care that my insomnia was eased by staying up all night teaching myself to play the guitar I had purchased with my earnings from my part-time job.

Eventually, my mother agreed to see a psychiatrist, who medicated her into some sort of holding pattern. My father and I were grateful that she had found a place to start—but we all had much to learn about what made her tick.

Unfortunately, my weary father's own depression became the collateral damage of this upheaval. He dragged himself through long days at work, only to return at night to find a chaotic home run by a frightened teenage girl and an unhinged wife. Now, it took all his strength just to join us for supper, help out a little in the kitchen, and then take himself to bed.

His violin sat neglected in its case. It broke my heart that he no longer "spoke music" here in Calumet City. Now all three of us felt like a foreigners in our new home.

In the middle of my senior year of high school, my parents and I had only one significant conversation about college—they informed me that they couldn't afford to send me. I already knew this. My grades had fallen to the left of lousy, and I hadn't gotten any takers when I brought up college visits and entrance exams, so the whole issue was a non-issue anyway.

I told them not to worry, and that I'd be more than fine. After graduation, I would move back to Chicago, get an apartment, find a day job, and save money for college. Privately, I dreamed of being a singer and breaking into the music business, and I would start with the vibrant club scene on Chicago's north side.

A few months later, my folks admitted that this two-year exile in Calumet City had been rough on us all, and they wanted me to have a wonderful summer. As a graduation gift, they offered me an open-ended airline ticket to Israel to stay with my sister, Roz, who was there teaching English.

I studied my mother's face.

"You need to go, Sally Girl. It's your turn now," she told me.

I graduated from high school at seventeen, and by the time I left for Israel in June 1972, I was *so-outta-there* the front door of our Calumet City apartment couldn't have hit me on the ass— unless it met me at the airport in Tel Aviv.

Once in Israel, I felt reborn. Roz lived in Haifa and had arranged for a solid chunk of time off from teaching to be my Hebrew-speaking tour guide. Our six-year age gap effortlessly fell away as we spent four weeks flitting about the country, touring Israel's many significant and historical sites. Roz loved watching me discover the exotic foods, biblical desert vistas, and the native Israelis—known as *Sabras**—she had come to know and love during her year there.

For both my sister and me, the highlight of this trip was spending time with our relatives. In Israel, as a seventeen-year-old American, I met my mother's *mother's* side of the family for the first time.

Though my mother had been orphaned at the age of eleven, her mother (the late Rose Hertzberg Garfinkel) had surviving family overseas.

After the war years, my mother had discovered that Rose had three siblings. Her two brothers, Avraham and Jacob Hertzberg, had left Russia on foot and immigrated to Israel in the 1930s, while a sister (first name unknown at this writing) remained in Europe, married a man with the last name of Glazer, and had two children.

The Glazer family was sent to Auschwitz during the war. The story goes that when the family first entered the concentration camp, the mother (my mother's aunt) stood in one line clutching the hands of her son and daughter, while the father stood across the field in the men's work line. Mietik, the thirteen-year-old son, left his mother's side and ran across the vast compound to join his father. Guards lifted their rifles and took aim at the young boy, but before they could shoot, the main officer halted them. Mietik cried out that he was strong and could work with the men. The guards gathered around the boy, pinching him up and down, and in the randomness of a fated moment, they scowled and sent him to stand in the men's line. Somehow, Mietik survived his years in the camp, while his mother, father, and sister perished. When the war was over, Mietik Glazer, now a young man, made his way through a displaced persons camp to join his uncles and their families in Israel.

At first, I found it odd that my orphaned mother had aunts and uncles and first cousins alive and well, just halfway around the globe. I was told, however, that the Hertzberg brothers *had* tried to bring their widowed sister Rose and her two daughters, Naomi and Minnie, to Israel after my grandfather Sam was shot and killed. But, in 1931, no one had the financial resources to assist, and Rose died before Avraham and Jacob could afford the arrangements. (*See "The Garfinkel Girls."*)

To honor both their long-lost sister, Rose, and her American granddaughters, Sally and Roz, the remaining Hertzbergs and Glazers joyously opened their homes and hearts, wanting to know and love us.

One day, while waiting for the bus to take me to visit my family, I noticed a group of elderly women sharing the bench in front of my sister's apartment building. These *zaftig** *bubbe** types, with their ample bosoms spilling out of their sleeveless dresses, sat and fanned themselves under the hot desert sun, *kibbitzing** in Yiddish.

Yiddish! My heart skipped a beat! It seemed that my newly discovered family—along with everyone in Israel—made it a point to speak Hebrew (the new official language of Israel), but these women were yakking away in the same Yiddish dialect I remembered from my childhood in South Shore.

Maybe their people were from the same Russian or Polish village as my people? I stepped in closer to ask.

Then I saw, on the inside of each woman's wrist, the tattoo of her concentration camp number.

"Oh no!" I gasped, before I could stop myself. My hand covered my mouth and I turned away. I had seen videos and documentaries about the Holocaust in Sunday school, but I had never seen a real tattoo before. Immediate thoughts of war, along with the vision of the dark greenish-bluish markings on their forearms, stunned me. Tears welled up in my eyes.

"Sveethaaht," one woman called out to me.

I was busted. I turned back to acknowledge her.

She pointed a gnarly finger at me. "Don't feel bad for us!" She sounded exactly like my grandmother.

"Vee survived," the *bubbe* continued in her heavy Eastern European accent. "Vee lived! And now . . . vee live good . . . in this land, vee are home!"

She saw the tears in my eyes and motioned for me to step closer.

"Sveethaaht," she said, her voice softer, "Come to me, take mine hand."

I stepped closer and stretched out my hand. She wrapped her rough, arthritic, spotted hands around mine.

"Better you should feel bad for those who don't live. Never forget them, *kutchkeleh.**"

Kutchkeleh. No one had called me by this term of endearment for years. I studied the old woman's face and I could no longer hold back—tears spilled down my cheeks. She squeezed my hand, and I felt the stunning strength she must have used to survive the war some thirty years earlier.

"Don't you vurry about us, Sveethaaht, vee vill be fine and so vill you. But now, ve have a job. Ve must make it our responsibility to never forget them. Never."

I nodded yes, took a deep breath, and saw my bus approaching. She gave my hand a peck of a kiss and then let go, with a smile and a final "*Kutchkeleh.*"

I boarded my bus and sank into a seat. I cried and cried, and then cried some more.

I will never forget that moment. That was the moment I learned to never forget.

Many years after those first exchanges with Holocaust survivors, I had good friends in Columbus who took their entire family to Israel to celebrate their daughter Jamie as she became a bat mitzvah in the Holy Land. They commissioned me to write a song for the film they were producing of this trip. After looking at the photographs of Jamie, a petite American girl carrying the Torah scrolls on her tiny shoulders, I went straight to my diaries from the 1972 trip to Israel and revisited my own teenage experience.

There in my journals, I discovered that Israel's very essence had changed me profoundly. I had been spiritually moved by the overpowering sense of belonging. I made a vow at seventeen that I would be more than just a child of Jewish parents. I knew in my soul that, should I ever become a parent, I would be a Jewish one.

SONG: *I'LL BE THE ONE*

Here in this land I am home—I'm not alone, not alone
I'm just one of many who belong
I'm not alone, I'm not alone
For so many years, I have dreamed of this day

When I'm put to the test
I am asked to stand and take my place
I'm asked to be strong like a soldier
To always remember, and carry the truth on my shoulder
And be a faithful protector of this light that's shining
I'll be the one, to carry on, to carry on
Mighty and faithful and strong
I'll be the one, to carry on, to carry on
Here in this desert I will stand—I'm not alone—not alone
My soul now belongs to this land
My future is here, in every grain of sand
History tells us that there'd be a day
When we're put to the test
We are asked to stand and take our place
We're asked to be strong like a soldier
To always remember, and carry the truth on our shoulder
And be the faithful protector of this light that's shining
I'll be the one, to carry on, to carry on
For thousands of years, I've been strong
I'll be the one, to carry on, to carry on
I see these mountains and oceans
I hear of past generations
I have my own destination
It is I who've been chosen
I'll be the one, to carry on, to carry on
I dedicate a promise to go on—I'll be the one
In this world, in this life, I will be—this eternal light

***Kutchkeleh** I've been called "kutchkie" by relatives in Chicago,
  and here I was, a world away from home, and this stranger said,
  "kutchkeleh." It was an out-of-body experience. This woman
  must have been a *lantzman** of my family from Europe.
  Seriously amazing.

Chapter Two

A NICE JEWISH GIRL WALKS INTO A BAR...

DIPPED BACK
IN THE CITY

When I returned from Israel in September 1972, I went home to my family's tiny condo on the cul-de-sac in Calumet City. I was back where I started—isolated from friends and living with my parents. Without a job or car, I felt trapped.

All my childhood friends from South Shore were on their way to college. Many of them had chosen the University of Illinois in Champaign and had paired up as roommates in the same dormitory. I knew that I'd eventually experience college—once I saved up enough money. But I was also determined to be a musician when I grew up. Now I had to figure out, for myself, how to pull this off.

First, I had to find a way to make a living and get the hell out of Dodge—but I was only seventeen.

Apparently, I had angels watching over me. A neighbor who commuted every day to downtown Chicago told me that her office had a secretarial position open. She knew I had taken typing in high school and had wicked fabulous clerical skills. I gladly and gratefully accepted the job, and said yes to her offer of free transportation in her car. The full-time salary felt like gobs of money and her kindness made the forty-five-minute ride into the city a pleasure. This gig was a serious blessing.

At night and on weekends, I hid in my bedroom. I rarely ventured out with friends or spent my earnings, preferring to save every penny. I kept my focus on the freedoms that a big bank account would afford me. When I turned eighteen that December, I'd be prepared to bolt.

During those few months in Calumet City, I listened to WFMT's *The Midnight Special* every Saturday night, and became obsessed with Steve Goodman and John Prine, Chicago's local songwriters. I had also fallen in love with Crosby, Stills & Nash, James Taylor, Judy Collins, Judee Sill, and of course, Joni Mitchell. When I allowed myself to spend a few dollars, I would purchase their recordings. I obsessively studied each song, memorized the melodies and lyrics, and played along on my guitar or piano. I practiced maniacally, and then I practiced some more.

My eighteenth birthday finally arrived. Legally, I could do as I pleased, but I still needed my folks to be okay with my going. My father looked uncertain, but my mother convinced me she would be fine. And so I went.

Cynthia Flicker, the daughter of one of my mother's Hyde Park High pals, had returned to Chicago after her college graduation from the University of Illinois at Champaign. Four years older than me, she had become a tad rudderless after receiving a BA in English Lit rather than the expected MRS degree her parents thought they were paying for.

Our mothers were thrilled that we'd be together in the big scary city, while Cynthia and I were even more thrilled to move out of our parents' homes.

Together, we signed a lease for a one-bedroom, third-floor walk-up apartment in the East Rogers Park area near Loyola University. Cynthia and I loved our dilapidated apartment with its ancient plumbing and worn-out carpeting. Fifty years of stark white paint prohibited the doors from closing and the windows from opening. We set up twin mattresses in our shared bedroom and plundered our grandmothers' basements for tables, chairs, and cast-off frying pans. Cynthia's aunt gave us a sofa made of itchy-scratchy fabric that we covered with a king-size Martex sheet we bought on sale. The coat closet off the living room had been converted into a kitchen where the half-size refrigerator's door cleared the oven by a fraction of an inch. Our tiny flat offered only two windows—and each looked out onto the brick wall of the building next door. The lobby and hallways smelled of foods we couldn't identify, and in winter, the steam heat from the overactive radiators turned our apartment into a sauna, leaving us with brilliant complexions.

I couldn't have been happier. I enjoyed my secretarial job and started dating. I came to understand that I was quite likable. Cynthia, a large-boned brunette with a million-watt smile, thrived at her receptionist job (she never learned to type!) and got down to the serious business of husband-shopping.

Back in the early 1970s, young girls like us were bursting at the seams with independence. We loved taking responsibility for our own rent, and even with our cockroaches, we flourished in our little apartment. We were out to reinvent ourselves.

For a few months, I felt wonderful, free, and optimistic. I loved the way I looked and how people responded to me. Each day felt like an exciting new adventure.

Then, my mother had her big-time, Technicolor, grand-finale nervous breakdown.

She had dealt with depression for years and had recently suffered from severe hormonal imbalances due to menopause. As if that wasn't enough, the poor gal had neglected her dental care when we were kids and now required oral surgery to remove all her teeth. She would need to be fitted for a complete set of upper and lower dentures. No woman, let alone a fragile one like my mother, should ever have to endure such dramatic physical and emotional changes—all at once.

She didn't stand a chance. At the age of forty-nine, my poor mother went over the unknowable edge. I was nineteen.

Under outrageous duress, my father had no option but to have her admitted to Michael Reese Hospital. I immediately went to see her. Agitated and vehement, she told me not to come anymore—she didn't want me to see her this way.

"Sally Girl, unless you're willing to become a five year old and be my baby, there's nothing you can do for me. You grew up, and I'm not a mother anymore. It's my tough luck, not yours." She said this with a bitterness that ripped my heart in two.

My father, along with her caseworker, suggested that I steer clear. Smacked with the stunning realization that her mental illness merited a lengthy hospital stay, I took a step back and waited for instructions. I prayed that her doctors could dig down deep inside my mother's psyche and get to the bottom of the exhausting misery that had been her life.

Her six-week stay at Michael Reese allowed the doctors to finally diagnose her correctly and prescribe the latest in pharmaceutical regimens. After years and years of misdiagnoses and faulty medications, my mother discovered that her illness now had a name—manic-depression. (Nowadays, we call it bipolar disorder.)

Her traumatic childhood—losing her father to gun violence at seven years old and her mother to cancer four years later—had clearly taken a psychological toll. Naomi Garfinkel Fingerett had desperately wanted to be a good wife and mother, and these two jobs became her entire existence. Over the years, she had repeatedly faced off against anxiety and depression. As her children grew up and left the house, her sense of identity crumbled. I was the baby of the family, and as the door in Calumet City closed behind me, her last safety net had been attached to my shoe.

She plummeted and crashed.

It would be years and years before I learned to accept that I couldn't save her, and I couldn't blame her—I could only love her. That being said, I spent my life begging for forgiveness.

Upon her release from the hospital, my mother regained her balance and became humbly apologetic and determined. She quickly purchased a wristwatch with an alarm she could set to remind her to take her three daily doses of lithium. My father had threatened that if she didn't take her meds as prescribed, he'd send her to the moon. Upon hearing this, she stored extra watches in the kitchen junk drawer, next to the surplus batteries and egg timers.

I researched my mother's diagnosis of manic-depression and learned that her DNA might someday bite me in the ass. Right then, I decided that I needed to get busy and make my life happen—before all that caught up with me.

Back uptown in our little apartment, Cynthia and I had different ideas about this new feminist revolution we kept hearing about.

Many women were finally realizing that no one *gives* you control—you have to *take* control. Ideals, fashions, work opportunities, and gender politics were changing so fast we could barely grab it all. Cynthia had been raised to marry, have children, keep a lovely home . . . and that was about it. After learning that I was genetically predisposed to wonk out and lose my mind at some point, I feared that eventually turning into my mother was a fait accompli. I assumed I was unmarriageable.

Late at night, over tea and chocolate-covered graham crackers, Cynthia and I often had deep and mystifying "what if" conversations. What does a girl do if she's not interested in marriage after college? Or babies after marriage? Or mah-jongg and bridge games after the kids were grown and gone?

In my office, many young gals were actively seeking a career, rather than a job, while a few of the middle-aged women in my department insisted they preferred clerical work over kitchen detail. On television, Mary Richards and Rhoda Morgenstern were women of a certain age without men, not to mention Betty White's Sue Ann Nevins, an independent man-chaser with a haughty demeanor and a wicked tongue.

Possible role models flowed everywhere around us, and we were stymied by the options. Suddenly, life for our gender had become a virtual *free swim*. Young women like us needed to be watchful when considering these new life choices, lest we drown in our indecision.

While Cynthia continued her search for true love and marriage, the constant threat of the dreaded "Naomi Disease" colored my decision making, so I went with what I felt had been chosen for me since I was a young girl.

Music.

I now lived in the best city ever for aspiring musicians. Chicago offered an astounding array of clubs and coffeehouses that featured folk music and blues, seven nights a week. Every bar boasted a four a.m. liquor license (five a.m. on Saturday nights), and each establishment had to fill their stages with hours and hours of live music.

On Mondays and Tuesdays, all the hip and happening "joints" on Lincoln Avenue held open mic nights that offered beginners a place to try out their skills and gain some practical experience in front of live human beings. Anyone with a guitar and some guts could show up to a club at eight o'clock and put their name on the open mic list. Hopefully, by midnight, they'd get the chance to stand on the stage in front of a room full of strangers and perform their three best songs.

Because the audiences primarily consisted of other hopeful singer-songwriters, these open stages served as both classroom and laboratory for amateurs. Often, we heard rumors that the manager occasionally stuck his head out from behind the bar and had a listen. He'd choose some lucky scruffy Bob Dylan wannabe or a voluptuous blonde Joni Mitchell sound-alike and offer them an opening slot during a prime-time weekend show. That big-break gig of twenty minutes in the spotlight paid $25, which most performers ended up handing back to the bar to pay for the liquid courage they needed to perform.

I scored my first real gig in February 1974 at the No Exit Cafe, a Chicago institution that opened in 1958 and enjoyed a mythical underground reputation as the nation's oldest coffeehouse in continuous operation. Located on the corner of Lunt and Glenwood in Rogers Park, this bohemian hangout had a gigantic espresso machine with a steam wand for frothing milk. The vibrating stainless steel and copper contraption made so much noise that it drowned out the 'L' train that rattled the building's front door. Cozy, friendly, and laid-back, the Cafe was lined with dark mahogany bookshelves overflowing with plants and books. Dusty, old, gouged tables and unmatched rickety chairs were available for the science nerds and geeks who spent hours playing chess, checkers, and the Chinese stone game of Go.

Warm and inviting in winter, the coffeehouse was famous for its Russian tea—hot Earl Grey tea blended with strawberry preserves. Served in tall water glasses set into fancy brass bases with handles, this sugary and highly caffeinated specialty kept the chess players buzzed. Unfortunately for the guitar players onstage, the vibrating whirr of the steamer wand as it frothed the preserves into the tea often upstaged their vocal talents and delicate fingerpicking. The folk music audiences complained about the espresso machine's noise, and yet no one stopped ordering Russian tea.

It was worth every decibel.

Soon, I had no trouble finding places to play for pay. I reworked many of the dud songs I had written in high school and wrote new ones that voiced my sensibility. I grew my hair down to my tush and worked my way up the ranks and onto the stages of the Lincoln Avenue club scene. To me, I had *arrived* when I snagged a gig opening for John Prine at the Earl of Old Town, the hippest folk venue in the city.

Eventually, I left my day job at the insurance office and became a receptionist (and later a bookkeeper) at Chicago Recording Company, a trendy and happening recording studio in the North Michigan Avenue area. I met studio musicians and occasionally landed gigs singing radio and TV commercial jingles myself.

Everything fell into place. I spent my weekdays steeped in the business of music, and on weekends, I belonged to the Lincoln Avenue community of hippie musicians. We were a family of scruffy artists who shared contacts and showed tremendous support for each other's talents and goals.

Late at night, after finishing our own gigs, we'd traipse over to another musician's show and silently witness a great after-hours performance or the midnight debut of a new song. As the night came to a close, we'd harmonize from our seats at the bar, only to be called up on stage to share the microphone with our cohorts. When this happened to me, I positioned myself to sing straight into the microphone while throwing a hairy eyeball toward the guitar player's hands to learn (and steal) his instrumental licks.

I thrived onstage with these musical masters. I admired them, respected them, and did my best not to sleep with them, because the world was changing in 1974, and the feminist revolution had me believing that I should aspire to be the star—not the groupie.

One Saturday, Cynthia needed to pick up a wedding gift for a sorority sister from college, so I accompanied her downtown to Marshall Field's. Stopping at the bridal registry department, we were handed a clipboard with eight pages of *things* the bride could chose for her home. On each page, many *things* were listed, and check marks showed which *things* had already been purchased by other guests. This prevented people from buying the same *thing* twice. The bride had picked out every*thing* she desired, and these pages listed her preferred china pattern, crystal goblets, and sterling silver bread baskets, not to mention her selected models of blender, toaster, and Dutch oven, whatever that is. Also listed were her color choices for towels, bed linens, tablecloths, and dinner napkins. These were the *things* every home would need.

Incredulous, I flipped through the pages and thought, well, here's one way to get a bunch of stuff—just get married! It's a regular do me, show me, buy me, love me, give me, affair.

I was one-part grossed out—and three-parts jealous.

"Cynthia," I asked, "is this something you want to do when you get married?"

"Register, you mean?" she said. "Yeah, my mother already told me in no uncertain terms how all she's been doing is buying wedding gifts for her friends' kids, and she expects them to do the same for me when I get married. Can you imagine my mother, Phyllis Flicker, allowing me to elope or get a PhD instead of letting her plan a big wedding? Could' ja bust?"

I shook my head. I was sure my mother felt the same way.

Cynthia chose a cutting board and had it sent to the bride's house. After buying ourselves some Frango mints at Field's, we made our way back home on the 'L' train, sitting quietly with our own thoughts. We were intelligent girls who had been raised by Jewish mothers, and our destinies were dictated by strong-willed families. My parents were holding out for me to bring home a nice Jewish boy to marry, but there on the 'L' I could only think about how to circumvent my preordained future— stuff or no stuff.

Exhausted from the overstimulation of a hectic Saturday downtown, I found the rhythm of the moving train hypnotic. I closed my eyes for a quick rest, while a mantra kept repeating in my head. The syntax matched the chugga-chugga of the rails.

Do me, show me, buy me, love me . . .

Do me, show me, buy me, love me . . .

Half asleep, I came to when Cynthia elbowed me in the ribs. "Come on, we're here," she said.

We exited the train and walked the two blocks back to our apartment. Cynthia called dibs on the bathroom to primp for her evening's date, while I picked up my guitar and noodled a melody to fit the mantra from the train.

I grabbed a pen and jotted the mantra down. More words followed so quickly, I almost missed them.

Do me, show me, buy me, love me, give me,
Don't forget to tell me that you need me.
Do me, show me, buy me, love me, give me,
All the world, 'cuz I'm your girl,
Do me, show me, buy me, love me, give me,
Right now. When? Right now.

This song flew out of me—first the chorus and then a verse, and then another verse. I spent days and days writing, trimming, carving, and polishing the song, preparing it for the stage.

Still, I was hesitant to perform it. As a novelty song, I worried that it could be taken the wrong way. Would people experience the lyric as an anthem for spoiled brats, or would they understand that I had written this piece with my tongue firmly planted in my cheek?

Live performance is the true laboratory and I wouldn't know a thing until I played this song in front of an audience. So I nervously took my new tune for a test on a Monday night open mic stage. I couldn't have been more surprised when, thank goodness, audiences sang along, and laughed in all the right places. Score!

Forty years (and two husbands) later, I'm not sure how this song will be received. Some people may take it as a satirical song, or a snide song, or just a plain goofy and silly song. I was young and snarky when I wrote it, and *I'm older than that now.*

However, in light of our modern day concerns with kindness and political correctness, I can't believe I have the *chutzpah** to put this song out there again.

Ooh, snap (*insert bitchy cat meow here*)—I do!

SONG: *DO ME, SHOW ME, BUY ME, LOVE ME, GIVE ME*

When I was just a baby, I was a dandy
Mama said I was as sweet as sugar candy
Growing up a nice girl comes in handy
When you're in the market for a man . . . to

CHORUS
Do me, show me, buy me, love me, give me
Don't forget to tell me that you need me
Do me, show me, buy me, love me, give me
All the world, 'cuz I'm your girl
Do me, show me, buy me, love me, give me
Right now! When? Right now!!

When showing off with hopscotch was my hobby
I vowed that I would give my heart to Tommy
But Tommy vowed to give his heart to Bobby
Do you think it's something that I said? . . . like
CHORUS

Do me, show me, buy me, love me, give me
They say everybody has their price
I want a love to care for me forever
I guarantee that I will treat you right
Just not every night

I went to college just to catch a husband
Mama said, "You can't come home without a husband!"
I stayed in school, I couldn't get a husband
All I got's a PhD. Hmmm! In Women's Studies
And how could I forget about the 60s?
I burned my bra and bought a van to be a hippie
Like for sure it was a total out-of-body experience
But now I take my trips with MASTERCARD!
Do me, show me, buy me, love me
Do me, show me, buy me, love me
Do me, show me, buy me, love me, give me
Right now. When? RIGHT NOW!

GRACEFUL MAN 1976

In 1976, after I turned twenty-one, I signed with a booking agent who specialized in sending performers out on the folk music/coffeehouse circuit. She belonged to the National Association for Campus Activities (NACA). This organization coordinated and promoted a myriad of events on college campuses, where a built-in audience of young adults needed social programming to keep them safe from the evils of off-campus adventures. *Wink-wink.* Booze.

During the 1970s, lucky college students could hear a young Bruce Springsteen or Dan Fogelberg for a mere three-dollar ticket charge. The NACA also presented up-and-coming comedians like Jay Leno and Sinbad—long before they landed on national television.

We all honed our skills by performing for a varied assortment of student audiences. I remember plenty of guys in ripped jeans, Frye boots, and flannel shirts, who showed up drunk and stoned, accompanied by braless, blond hippie chicks wafting of patchouli oil. Twenty minutes into a show, these kids usually passed out in a haze on the student union couches. Scholarship and work-study students, with their short hair, V-neck sweaters, and ever-present book bags, always stayed attentive for the entire concert. Grateful to have escaped their stifling small towns, they sought out anything that might inspire and expand their world views. But no matter the audience, our job was to entertain and bring the contemporary performing arts to campuses across the United States.

As a teenager, I had dreamed of being Joni Mitchell, and I couldn't wait to experience that gypsy lifestyle. I spent two years touring across the Midwest and up and down the Eastern Seaboard in a blue 1967 Chevy Bel Air that my grandfather had left me. That gas guzzler became my second home. The roomy powder-blue interior had bench seats big enough for me to sleep on, even with my legs fully extended. I napped, changed my clothes, wrote letters home, ate meals, and even played my guitar in that Chevy Bel Air.

I spent day after day behind the wheel. Many of the NACA schools were small and hard to find, located in towns that weren't always listed on Rand McNally's maps. Years ago, road trips took some serious premeditated planning. No matter how skilled I became at travel arrangements, I still got lost at some point—*every* day. Back then, I depended on gas stations with pay phones to save me. Armed with prepaid long-distance calling cards, several ballpoint pens, and a notebook, I would dial some poor college administrator and force him/her to dictate directions over the phone. Nervous and distrustful of my poor penmanship, I followed my barely legible scribbles through the rural and unmarked back roads to my destination.

Despite my best efforts, I usually arrived late and ended up driving all over the campus, winding past dormitories, lecture halls, and sports fields, desperate to find the student union. When I finally located the right building, a crew of freshman student volunteers would greet me, doing their best to look professional and make me comfortable. My performance space could be anything from the big stage in the drama department's main theater to the basement of the chapel's refectory.

Even with the hassles, I loved the travel and I loved making money and my agent loved that I was so willing. No doubt, though, being an itinerant chick-singer-songwriter was a ridiculous way to make a living.

One time, my agent arranged a grueling tour that required performing at four different schools, in four different towns, in a three-day period. In addition to the evening shows, she scheduled me for a "nooner," a midday concert held in the student cafeteria. I stood atop a Formica table and sang my guts out without any amplification, projecting out over a sea of students eating, talking . . . and ignoring me.

The evening gig that followed that dreaded nooner show took place in a cavernous rathskeller on a different campus, ninety-six miles away. My gig was part of the parents' weekend celebration. The dimly lit rathskeller had no stage, so they dumped me next to the popcorn machine at the end of the bar, where I stood eye level with the crowd. The volunteer sound guy, a freshman most likely, pinned a single lavalier microphone on my guitar strap to amplify both my voice and guitar. He plugged this lavalier, designed for spoken lectures and not for music, into a consumer stereo system snatched from some poor *schmo's** dorm room.

I looked down at the puny microphone and the ridiculous sound system and the sticky floor that served as my stage. As I began imagining the expletives I would hurl at my agent over this fiasco, the doors to the room suddenly opened and the students and their parents flowed into the rathskeller in droves, rushing to find tables and claim seats. Shrieks and shouts flew across the room as everyone motioned for friends and family to come and meet one another. Mothers and fathers ordered soft drinks from the bar, while their sons and daughters poured hard liquor from flasks into their sodas.

Trapped in the middle of the standing-room-only crowd, I began my show.

I sang as loud as I could, but the overwhelming crowd noise drowned out my voice. Next to me, the popcorn popper sounded like a machine gun as it endlessly fired out kernels. I kept at it, song after song, two feet from the line of kids pushing and shoving to scoop up bags of popcorn. They stared at me as if I were an embarrassing inconvenience their folks would have to suffer through.

Throughout both of my sixty-minute sets, the people never hushed to listen or acknowledge me with applause. Not once. The frustration and anger made me strum harder and sing louder. But, no matter what I did, I was as insignificant as a penny waiting for change. I was invisible and inaudible, and ultimately, inconsolable.

When my performance time was over, I packed up my stuff, thanked the sound-nerds for their time, accepted my paycheck from the student organizer, and made for the door faster than a flicked piece of popcorn. When I reached my car, I threw my guitar into the trunk, sprawled across the backseat, and cried my eyes out. My hair smelled like scorched oil, my throat was sore from singing above the enormous din, and my heart was broken. This had been a pointless and soul-crushing gig. I sobbed into the dusty upholstery and seriously considered my mother's suggestion that I become a court reporter. I fell asleep in my clothes and woke up the following morning with lead in my veins, not wanting to continue on to the next campus.

At that moment, I came up with a phrase that helped me accept the variables of my work. Sometimes the work is great, but sometimes you're just *"driving for checks."*

I threw on my sunglasses, started the car, and began my struggle to put a dent in the three hundred miles I needed to drive before I could clean myself up and hop onto another stage. For the first time, I dreaded the unknown possibilities waiting for me that night. *Would there be a decent microphone? Would there be speakers mounted high enough above the crowd to be heard? Would there be chairs for the audience, and if so, would they even sit in them?*

And, most importantly, would I have to compete with the rhythm of a friggin' popcorn popper?

A few hundred miles later, I succumbed to exhaustion and hunger. I wanted a big-ass burger, and an even bigger cup of coffee. As a treat, I decided to have my lunch in a chair that wasn't moving at sixty miles per hour.

I pulled into a McDonald's and immediately spotted a huge tour bus in the parking lot with the words "Gallaudet University" on the side. I didn't recognize the school's name, but I knew that I'd be surrounded by college students. Yet again.

"Crap," I muttered.

I prayed for a fast-moving line. I allotted only thirty minutes to relax and eat before continuing on my journey. I grabbed a magazine from the backseat and headed across the parking lot, hoping to take my mind off my mind.

Through the glass window, I saw the entire McDonald's packed with students.

Crap, crap, double crap. I lowered my head and pushed open the door, dreading the din.

But the restaurant was silent. Perplexed, I looked up.

Students sat at nearly every table, gesturing wildly while simultaneously eating their burgers and fries. Hands flailed and fingers fluttered. I had never heard so many people be so quiet.

I had walked into a restaurant full of hearing-impaired students.

I froze.

As I stared at the crowd, a wave of shoulder tapping and finger pointing ran through the room. A sea of curious eyes turned to stare. I can only imagine the nutty look on my face. After a significantly awkward amount of time, I spun around and headed straight for the bathroom.

I stood at the sink and looked straight in the mirror to study my own confusion. My glazed eyes look stunned. A deep furrow ran between my brows.

What the hell was going on out there?

I splashed my face with cold water and realized that, like the night before, I was the avocado swinging from an apple tree. I was the stranger who didn't get the cosmic memo to stay away. I was the intruder, unwelcome and incoherently participating in someone else's communal moment.

Oh, for Pete's sake, it's only a lousy burger! After last night, you really think this is hard? You'll be fine. Go get yourself some fries and a milk shake, overeat, and freak out about the calories instead of this! Take a deep breath and fuh-gedda-boudit!

I left the restroom and purchased my lunch. The crowd had thinned out since some kids had gone outside to smoke. I nabbed an empty table and set my tray and magazine down. Sliding into the hard plastic chair, I reached for my hamburger and stopped. All around me, the students communicated with each other, their hands moving fluidly through the air. I did my best not to stare, but their intensely animated faces fascinated me.

My eyes darted back and forth between watching the students and pretending not to be watching.

I poured the creamer into my coffee while I looked up and then looked back down. I unfolded my hamburger wrapper while I looked up and then looked back down. I used my teeth to open the ketchup packet, and while my teeth argued with the packaging, I looked up and then looked back down.

I had just squirted ketchup over my fries and started eating when a very attractive young man came over and started talking to me—with his hands.

I stared blankly at him. My thoughts went straight back to irrational panic. Why didn't I go to the Denny's on the other side of the highway? Why didn't I pack the car with food while I had the chance? Note to self—buy Tupperware.

I suddenly realized that he wanted to join me. I quickly moved my tray and motioned for him to sit down. He pulled out the chair and flashed me a gazillion-watt grin.

I smiled politely. I couldn't understand why this handsome, dark-haired stranger wanted to communicate with me.

Then he spoke.

"Don't . . . freak . . . out, . . . I . . . read . . . lips." He sounded like he had a few marbles in his mouth, but I had no trouble understanding him.

"I'm . . . not . . . freaked . . . out," I mouthed slowly.

"We . . . don't . . . want . . . you . . . to . . . feel . . . a-lee-en-ated," he said carefully, with great intention.

This time, I smiled a genuine smile, complete with teeth.

"Thank . . . you. You . . . are . . . very . . . kind," I said loudly.

Slowly and deliberately, he explained how his group had traveled from Gallaudet University in Washington, DC, to a conference at Penn State and was now returning home. I was fascinated by his openness, his fearlessness, and his struggle that seemed to be no struggle at all.

I considered telling him that I was a musician, when another student tapped him on the shoulder and gestured toward the bus. It was time to go. *Oh, too soon!*

His eyes twinkled at me as he articulated perfectly, "It . . . was . . . very . . . nice . . . to . . . make . . . your . . . a-quaintance. . . . Good . . . bye . . .and . . . travel . . . safe."

He offered his hand and I took it.

"Thank you for sitting with me. It was lovely to meet you too," I said.

He nodded and continued to hold my hand. Our eyes locked, sending an electrical surge right through me. My face felt flushed, but I brazenly kept my eyes on his. I wanted to ask if he had ever dated a hearing person before. But then he let go of my hand, and he was gone.

After he left, I barely cared that I was eating a cold hamburger and wilted fries. Of all the mysterious and cosmic moments in my life, this one shook me to my core. Yesterday, I'd been completely ignored while singing at screaming decibels, and then today, I had been silent and withdrawn, but completely understood.

That random and magical encounter left an impression on me that, to this day, I recall—loud and clear.

SONG: *GRACEFUL MAN*

Is he a dancer, or is he crazy
The way his hands move all around?
His lips are moving, I hear nothing
He's asking questions without a sound
Asking, would I like to walk through his silent world?
Show me how the silent talk
Graceful Man, graceful hands, how I long to understand

Does he notice people staring
Spelling out his name to me?
My lips are moving, he hears nothing
He dances my name back at me
Asking, would I like to dance through his silent world?
Show me how the silent dance
Graceful Man, graceful hands, how I long to understand

Oh, I long to tell him I'd be his
And to tell him of my loneliness
Oh, but now I see that it's my turn
Now I'm the one who cannot speak—to that
Graceful Man, graceful hands, how I long to understand

He is spinning, moving pictures
He is singing in the wind
Next to him, now I stand silent
With my eyes, I'm listening
Love can be a silent message, tossed out in the wind
With his heart, I know he hears me loving him
Graceful man, graceful hands, how I long to understand

PLAY FOR THEM 1977

San Francisco

I n the spring of 1977, I was invited to perform at an outdoor folk festival in San Francisco. I had never been to the Bay Area, and I couldn't wait to get out there and connect with a dear old friend from summer camp who had settled in Berkeley for college.

Rosa and I met as eleven-year-old bunkmates at Habonim Dror Camp Tavor, a Jewish overnight camp in Three Rivers, Michigan. We immediately clicked and were inseparable that whole summer, and when camp ended, we became devoted lifelong pen pals. Between her home in Detroit and mine in Chicago, we exchanged handwritten letters full of emotional adventures in heartbreak and our shared adolescent-dramatic angst. On our birthdays, we were allowed to place outrageously expensive long-distance phone calls, as our parents held egg timers to watch over the cost.

As an adult now, in my own apartment with my own phone, I freely dialed Rosa's California number. She picked up the phone, and suddenly, I felt the pressure of a self-imposed egg timer.

"Hello, Rosa, it's Sally—calling long-distance from Chicago!" I took a quick breath and kept going. "Listen up! I scored a great gig out in San Francisco in a few weeks. I'd love to see you. If I come a few days early, can I crash with you?"

"Yes, yes, and yes! I'm totally *plotzing**! We can have a slumber party!" Rosa's warmth flew through the phone line.

"I'll bring my camp T-shirt!" I said.

"And I've got the Ouija board here. We play it all the time in Berkeley."

"Can we binge on Gummi Worms like we use to?"

"If we can braid each other's hair like we used to."

"Will do, Mildew!" I would do anything for her.

I gave her my flight info and travel plans. Then we said goodbye with smoochie noises, and hung up quickly. I yipped and yapped around my apartment, overjoyed at the thought that I'd soon be on my way to hang out with the very gal who taught me how to tweeze my eyebrows and use a tampon.

When I packed my bag two weeks later, I made sure to include my camp T-shirt and the one photograph that always sent us into hysterics. It's a black-and-white shot of two best friends being naughty. We're standing on a cabin porch dressed in only sunglasses, camp sailor hats, flowered underpants, and stark-white training bras.

If you looked close enough, you could see the hair on our legs.

The flight to San Francisco went off without a hitch, but I landed at eleven p.m. local time, which felt like one a.m. to my Chicago-timed body. I had insisted Rosa let me worry about ground transportation. I was a musician with a paying gig, and she was in the middle of college finals.

Walking through the empty airport, I saw the skeletal staff closing up newsstands and food counters. My eyes felt dry and tired, and I longed to shut them. I hauled my weary self down the escalator to the baggage carousel, sat down, and waited for my guitar case and luggage.

In all fairness, I couldn't call my stuff *luggage*. Unlike my mother, with her matching set of American Tourister, I traveled with a huge, wilderness-camping/hitchhiking backpack, fastened to a four-foot-tall, aerodynamic aluminum frame. I could *thumb* my way to the moon and back with my possessions evenly distributed up and down the length of my spine, from my neck down to my butt. My tattered sleeping bag, strapped to the frame's bottom rung, slapped my ass as I walked. This contraption allowed me to carry my guitar case in one hand and flip my long bangs out of my eyes with the other.

I slumped in the hard airport chair and closed my tired eyes. Just then, the bags arrived, crashing onto the conveyor belt with shocking thuds. I jolted up and out of my chair and saw my backpack and guitar case inching towards me. I grabbed the frame and yanked the backpack off the carrier and swung it onto my back, but I wasn't fast enough to catch the guitar case. I thought of chasing it down the beltway, but the lead in my veins forced me to wait for it to come around again.

Calculating its approach, I bent over to retrieve the guitar at precisely the right moment—but forgot that I had a four-foot aluminum backpack strapped to my five-foot-three body. With a surprised yelp, I tipped forward and almost somersaulted onto the conveyor belt. Through sheer force of will, I found my footing and grabbed my guitar case. I glanced around to make sure no one had seen this horribly awkward maneuver, and then slithered away.

Outside at the taxi stand, I stepped up to the curb and nodded to the next cab in the queue. With great relief, I dumped my cargo on the ground for the cabbie to worry about.

The taxi driver, an obvious remnant from the Haight-Ashbury days, was tall and skinny in a malnourished kind of way. His jeans, colorless T-shirt, and high tops gave him a youthful appearance, but his long, thin, graying ponytail and leathery, wrinkled skin said *aging hippie.*

We exchanged smiles as he picked up my guitar and frame-pack and walked around to the taxi's trunk.

"Musician, huh?" he asked.

"Yeah," I said, too tired for small talk.

He opened his trunk and studied the interior.

In addition to an enormous spare tire, the trunk contained a large tool box, a book bag, a television-sized cardboard box of vinyl LPs, and two brown grocery bags, bursting with produce.

Out came his stuff, in went my stuff, then in went his stuff, but he couldn't make it work, so out came his stuff; then out came my stuff. This went on and on. By now, it was nearly midnight.

I couldn't figure out whether he had spatial relation issues—or was just high.

Finally, I politely asked if I could help.

"No, it's good." He gritted his teeth. "I've almost got it."

Skeptical, I stood back to let him work.

"We're good," he said.

I don't think so.

"We're fine."

I don't think so.

"Give me a minute"

You've had twenty already.

"I can smash it down more." He lowered the trunk lid and got ready to push down with his full body weight.

NOOO! My guitar case was in that trunk! I threw myself in front of the cabbie.

"Let me take that!" I slipped my hand through the guitar case's handle. I slowly pulled the guitar from the overstuffed trunk and gently placed it on the ground near the curb.

He brushed the sweat from his face with his T-shirt. "Okay, hey, like, let me try this, like, one last time." He was begging now. He lifted my backpack out of the trunk and leaned it against the rear bumper.

"I just need to meditate on the square footage." He stepped back and stared blankly into the trunk.

Seriously, he's going to meditate?

Finally, my brain burst. I was done with his *mishegas*, his visualizing, and his pondering of space and square footage. I snapped—s*crew this!*

I went reeling into my unattractive default mode, "Miserable Bitch of Death," or as I prefer to call it—Plan B. I lifted my backpack, banged it against my leg, swore a little louder than I would have otherwise preferred, and swung the whole frame into the backseat of the car. I hugged my guitar case to my chest like a baby, and flung myself into the backseat, nearly landing on top of my backpack.

Done and done, and PS, I was done.

"All right, then. This is fine." I motioned to him. "Let's go!"

He wordlessly got in the front seat and started the car. Then, as if nothing stressful had happened, he said, "Where to ma'am?"

He had to be totally stoned.

I handed off the address, planted my eyes out the window, and kept them there. Once we were in motion, my own lousy mood lifted a little, and I began to enjoy the magnificent city lights. The hilly streets with row houses built into the tilted earth amazed me. I marveled at how all the parked cars appeared to be linked together, lined up, bumper-to-bumper-to-bumper, with not an inch to spare. I quietly opened my window to alleviate the BO emanating from the front seat. The balmy air wafted in, scented with flowers, marijuana, and dead fish—all at the same time.

Finally, the cabbie turned onto Rosa's street. The car slowed down and pulled over to Rosa's curb, and without the incoming breeze, his BO got the best of me.

"Hey, we made it! We're here and we're fine." He sounded surprised

That's what you think.

I took out my wallet. "Thanks, this was great," I lied. "Can I bother you for a receipt?"

"Huh . . . what? A receipt? Hmmm, oh, you mean to show you paid?" He looked like I'd just asked him for some lint from his belly button

Yep, he was high—and probably tripping too. I was lucky to be alive.

"Never mind," I said, passing him some bills. I tipped him more than I should have, but that's what Grace Slick would have done.

Note to self: *Stay clear of any drugs you might be offered here in California. Stick with the devil you know—wine and candy.*

The taxi pulled away, and I gathered my things.

Rosa had mentioned her neighborhood might appear questionable, but that I shouldn't be frightened—"My area is thick with grad students like me, and nobody bothers us 'cuz we all have the same amount of nothing. All the landlords are slummy jerks and they take advantage of our desperation and lack of funds."

Indeed, her block featured a miserable array of dilapidated old houses, and my heart began to beat faster than normal.

Mysterious, overgrown foliage hid the windows of her bungalow. If there was a porch light, it wasn't on. I searched for a sidewalk to her front steps. Instead, I discovered a treacherous maze of broken concrete with exposed tree roots bursting out from between the jagged chunks. Tall weeds sprouted from every crack beneath my feet. Lugging my crap along this crippled walkway presented a huge challenge. I carefully watched my feet and slowly made it to the front porch.

The smell of pot and patchouli wafted through the doorjamb and hit me full on. I went to ring the doorbell, but couldn't locate it in the darkness.

Is everything difficult in California—cabdrivers, sidewalks, and *doorbells?*

I stood still in the moonlight and squinted all around the doorframe. Finally, I found the doorbell mounted high on the right side of the wood molding. I reached up and pushed with my right index finger, but heard no ring. *That's odd.* I pushed again, but still no ring.

Then, my senses slowly connected, one synapse at a time.

Wait, that's not a doorbell. Did my finger just go completely through something squishy, wet, and slimy? Did I just ring a slug? What the ... !

My screams and curses brought Rosa to the door. I didn't know whether to laugh or cry, but for sure, I wanted to hurl.

"Sally, you're here!" Rosa threw open the door and gave me a hug.

"Shit, oh shit, oh shit, I rang the doorbell, but it wasn't a doorbell, it was a slug, why is the doorbell made out of slug and not out of doorbell?" I gave her a left-armed hug, while keeping my disgusting and slimy right index finger pointed toward the ceiling.

"You're okay sweetie! But that's so ewww—let me get you a joint." She said this like she was offering me a Band-Aid. "Come in, let me take your things, and we'll get you fixed up."

I set my backpack and guitar case down in the foyer. Rosa led me to the kitchen sink and she flicked on the light. Her kinky-curly, hennaed hair cascaded down her back and gave off a beautiful red glow under the sink's fluorescent bulb. Barefoot and dressed in a long gauzy nightgown, Rosa wore her tortoise-shell eyeglasses in their predictable headband position. She'd been in bed studying, of course, because she was the smartest girl I knew. Awarded a full scholarship to UC Berkeley, Rosa planned to get her law degree and then, of course, change the world.

We leaned over the sink and I shoved my icky finger right up in her face. She smiled and made sarcastic *there-there* noises while she sprinkled Ajax powder cleanser over my whole hand. She reminded me to breathe, and that if I needed to puke, it was perfectly natural and not to feel bad. She'd always been a calming influence, and now she'd grown into an earth-mother-extraordinaire who thought nothing of humans and nature colliding in unfortunate situations such as this.

With my hand scrubbed clean and smelling like bleach, we settled down at her kitchen table for girl-time. She offered me pot or wine, but I asked for a saltine and herbal tea to calm my uneasy stomach. She lit herself a *doobie.**

"Wait here, I've got our Gummi Worms in my bedroom." Rosa got up from her chair.

"NO, NO! I just did a mind meld with a worm-snail. My Gummi Worm-eating days are over," I said. "What else ya got?"

Rosa, like me, loved penny candy.

"Not to worry." she said. "I've got Smarties, candy necklaces, and some natural, homemade Bit-O-Honey from the farmers' market."

Yep, that's my Rosa.

We spent the next day walking through her favorite parts of Berkeley, checking out little bohemian shops and cheap cafés. We ate as we walked—sharing crispy tart apples, wedges of hard cheese, and French baguettes dipped into our creamy, sugary coffees. We discussed her academic potential and professional goals and my fear of not having anything to fall back on— should I not become the next Aretha Franklin, Joni Mitchell, Carole King, Judee Sill, or Carly Simon. We spent the entire day outdoors, on foot, just being together. That evening, I conked out early from delayed jet lag and fresh air, while Rosa studied long into the night.

On my second day there, Rosa had class commitments, so I equipped myself with street maps of San Francisco and brochures of trolley routes and touristy highlights. Then I took Bay Area Rapid Transit (BART) across the Bay Bridge for a day of sightseeing. After her day of classes, Rosa would join me for dinner to celebrate our glorious visit.

Once I arrived at Fisherman's Wharf, I turned around to see that I had entered busker heaven. Everywhere I looked, street musicians, magicians, jugglers, and mimes populated the sidewalks in front of shops and galleries. Out-of-towners were encouraged to stop and watch performances, and then show their appreciation with spare change—or better yet, dollar bills, tossed into instrument cases left open on the sidewalk.

I walked along Jefferson Street, reading the hand-painted signs propped in front of the buskers. I read sign after sign:

"How do I get to Carnegie Hall? Practice, practice, practice—and your dollar bills."

"Vietnam Vet. This guitar saved my life . . . help save this guitar, needs repairs."

"Help with rent money—or take me home?"

There was no shortage of homeless-looking vagabond-beat-poet-angst-ridden-guitar-playing-brilliant-songwriters with hair that hadn't been washed since the Kennedy administration. However, I also witnessed many esoteric and charming oddities.

First, I stumbled upon a slender blonde ballerina dressed in a bright turquoise leotard and magenta toe shoes. With her hips swirling, she kept three yellow Hula-Hoops twirling around her waist while simultaneously playing the harmonica and standing *en pointe*. Next, I walked past a solo classical violinist, dressed in a T-shirt printed to look like a tuxedo. A block later, I discovered a seven-foot-tall pantomime artist, stuck inside (of course) an invisible box, standing next to a guy singing Appalachian folk songs while scrubbing a galvanized washboard with sewing thimbles on his fingers.

Then I heard Him.

I slowly turned around, scanning the streets for the body that belonged to this golden voice. I followed the sound like a child searching for the Pied Piper.

Then I found Him.

Tan, athletic, and sexy, he wore *nice* jeans and pristine brown leather sandals on clean feet. The sleeves of his crisp white cotton shirt were rolled up to his elbows, exposing magnificent, muscular forearms. His wavy golden hair was short for a street musician, and he was freshly shaven. By far, he was the best-dressed and most put-together busker on the street.

I stood there, drawn in by some unexplainable magnetic force field. This golden-musician-boy was so breathtakingly virile that I lost all interest in walking any further to see other performers.

I wondered how I might introduce myself to Him.

Hello, my name is Sally. I'm a musician too! Hey, I have a gig here in town at a blues festival. Wanna come to my gig and sit in? Wanna marry me? We can be Sonny and Cher, or Simon and Garfunkel, you pick . . . I'll be anyone or anything you want me to be!

But, dumb struck by his charisma, I remained speechless. *How could I get Him to notice me?*

Just then, a hefty woman walked by holding a shopping bag from Ghirardelli, the famous chocolatiers. A brilliant inspiration hit me.

I practically sprinted to the store in Ghirardelli Square, a few blocks away. I quickly loaded up on gift-box samplers for Rosa and her roommates and grabbed a few assortments for my mother. Then I roamed the aisles until I found the perfect bar of dark chocolate for my soon-to-be husband, the golden-musician-boy. I paid for my treasures and left the cocoa mecca to head back to his street corner.

During my absence, my future spouse had positioned a cardboard sign inside his open guitar case: "Help send me to med school so I can quit this crazy business."

Oh, how perfect—a guitar-playing doctor! Now I'd be bringing my mother chocolates AND a doctor for a son-in-law.

I inched towards Him and seductively turned my chestal area in his direction. I opened the Ghirardelli shopping bag, slowly pulled out the chocolate bar, and gently placed it on the green faux-fur lining of his guitar case. Then I stepped back and pushed my long hair away from my face so I could flash Him a big smile.

I sincerely believed my little plan would work. *This* would be the fairy-tale beginning to our life together. After we met on the street, we would discover that we had so many wonderful things in common—I was a musician (with a paid gig for heaven's sake) and he was the struggling pre-med guitar player. He would become the singing doctor and I would be his beautiful singing wife, and we'd live happily ever after, hopefully just two blocks from a chocolate factory. Amen.

But his eyes were closed. His head bobbed up and down as he sang a riveting rock tune. Damn, I couldn't tell if he'd actually seen me put the candy bar inside his case.

The sun came out bright and hot. Suddenly, three busloads of tourists disembarked and stopped in the beautiful sunshine to listen to my golden-musician-boy. Each passing group dug into their pockets and fanny packs to throw money at the movie-star-handsome performer. It rained quarters, dimes, and nickels.

Dollars floated down in slow motion, as the tourists raved about his amazing talents.

"Isn't he wonderful! He's so handsome! He should be on TV! Why isn't he on TV? He should at least be on the radio. I don't see why he's not on the radio! Have you ever heard of him before? What's his name? Why don't we know his name? None of these musicians seem to want anyone to know their names, why can't we know their names?"

The loose change inside his case became a mountain of silver.

Finally, the crowd began a collective move towards the knife swallower standing in front of a bodega selling iced coffees and snow cones.

As I stepped aside to let the throngs pass, I glanced into the guitar case and froze in horror. The weighty pile of coins had warmed under the sun's pummeling heat, causing the chocolate bar to melt and ooze out of its wrapper. The green plush faux-fur lining now revealed a mound of coins covered in sticky brown goo. At any second, my beloved might turn his head and see the candy-coated carnage.

I immediately spun on my heels and took off, walking for blocks and blocks, looking for a place to hide. I slipped into an air-conditioned diner, tucked myself in a booth, ordered a coffee, took out a pen, and wrote this song.

If you're out there, oh golden-musician-boy, this song's for you.

SONG: *PLAY FOR THEM*

Tourist attractions attract him
The tourists are ready to spend
So he plays for them, right on the street, he sings to them
You know he'd like to talk to them, oh no
He's only there to play for them
For change or a bill, the crowd gathers at will
While he plays for them

Pretty women passing by, flowers in skirts
He laughs, he's high
While he plays for them, right on the street, he sings to them
You know he'd like to talk to them, oh no
He's only there to play for them
For a smile or a wink, he knows what they think
While he plays for them

His pals come by to sympathize
Request his best with hopeful eyes
While he plays for them, right on the street, he sings to them
You know he'd like to talk to them, oh no
He's only there to play for them
But at dinner tonight, they're gonna turn up the lights
And he'll play for them

His girl back home in Kansas City cries but never tells
Where he plays for them
Right on the street, he sings to them
You know he'd like to talk to them, oh no
He's only there to play for them
She knows he'll return, a little wounded and burned
'Cause he played for them

I'd like to ask if we could meet
When he gets his act off this heartless street
Where he plays for them
Right on the street, he sings to them
You know I'd like to talk to him, oh no
He's only there to play for them
We don't know his name, but I guess that's the game
When you play for them

*Doobie Seriously if you don't know what this is, I cannot take
responsibility for telling you. Ask your children.

ASK ANY MERMAID 1978

I n 1978, my agent, Gypsy Schwartz, heard that the Buffalo Gals, a groundbreaking all-female bluegrass band, needed to replace two musicians who were leaving the group. Martha Trachtenberg, their guitar player, had chosen to pursue a graduate degree, while Nancy Josephson, the bass player, had chosen to tour with the legendary David Bromberg. (She married him two years later.)

An astute agent with an eye for trends, my pal Gypsy had noticed the rising sophistication of contemporary bluegrass groups, and suggested that this could be a tremendous opportunity for me to work with top-notch musicians. Women musicians at that!

My audition fell effortlessly into place. After sending my demo and press kit to the Buffalo Gals, Gypsy arranged for an audition. I was already scheduled to drive from Chicago to Savannah for a gig, so pulling over in Tennessee to meet with the Gals would be easy enough.

The exciting possibilities of living and working in a new part of the country had me ten feet in the air with my nose pointed south.

I met the band at the Nashville apartment of the group's founder and innovative banjo player, Susie Monick. There in her living room, the Buffalo Gals welcomed me with open arms, coffee, and pastries—like it was a bridge party. Sprawled out on tattered old couches and easy chairs, the four ladies were makeup-free, with hair flowing everywhere. They all wore hoop earrings, jean shorts, sandals, T-shirts, and their instruments. We instantly fell into an easy sorority-sister-banter, discussing our favorite songwriters, the latest trends in guitar making, and the hip new music festivals being staged around the country.

After an hour of chitchat, we agreed that we had much in common, and it was time to get down to the business of music. I pulled out my beat-up Gibson J-45 Sunburst acoustic guitar. Suddenly, I had no idea what to play and I felt a little shy. Taking a deep breath, I chose to share an original song with them. Hoping to wow the girls, I pulled out my flat pick and threw in the only bluegrass guitar riff I knew and sang my heart out with all the twang I could muster.

All of a sudden, Nancy Garwood, the bass player, stood up from her rickety Goodwill rocking chair. I thought she was going to leave the room and my heart fell a little. Instead, she hoisted her huge stand-up bass into position and began thumping out big bottom notes in perfect time with me. Next, Nell Levin placed her violin under her chin and tucked her head down to hold the fiddle in place, so she could adjust her bow with both hands. Eyes closed, she listened intensely and plucked the strings *pizzicato* with her finger until she found the perfect entry point. Offering the loveliest musical sentence, Nell lifted the song into a magnificent sphere where all the rough edges became smooth and elegant. Elaine Eliah stood up, tossed her mandolin strap over her shoulder, and began chunk-a-chunking a solid backbone rhythm accented with fast-moving musical phrases, placed perfectly between the lyric sentences. Susie, who wore her banjo like a second skin, began frailing, adding a bouncy counterpoint rhythm.

My arms were covered in goose bumps and I could hardly sing through my ecstatic smile. I burst out laughing when Susie broke out some jazz-style horn parts on her banjo and Elaine echoed her back on the mandolin. These brilliantly talented women had never heard my song before this moment, yet played along with me like they'd been rehearsing for days. Our musical chemistry was ethereal, and no one could deny the electricity that flowed through the room.

I finished the song and lowered my guitar. Gypsy-the-Agent had been right. The Buffalo Gals' contemporary musical vision and creative use of bluegrass instruments had placed them on the front lines of a genre revolution. I wanted to be a part of this amazing group. We had just shared a moment where notes and rhythms did all the talking, and everything that needed to be said had been spoken.

I waited for someone to say something.

The ladies made eye contact with one another. Just like high school, I was on the outside—wanting in. I had no idea how bands made these decisions and wondered if the Buffalo Gals had some kind of girl code. I just stood there awkwardly, holding my guitar.

Susie broke the silence. "Okay, then."

Looking serious, she walked over to me with her hand extended. By the time she crossed the room, she was smiling.

We shook hands as the Gals all cheered, "Welcome to Nashville!"

I was hired!

I couldn't wait to hop onboard as the band's singer/guitar-player and immerse myself in this eclectic new world of roots and country music. I made it to Savannah, finished my gig, and drove back to Chicago, where I quickly subleased my apartment. My mother wasn't too happy about my moving away, but I promised her I wouldn't fall in love with a Baptist or eat a hot dog that wasn't kosher.

Then I headed to Nashville!

On the west side of the city, I rented a small room in a house full of musicians. I threw a mattress on the floor and spent the next twelve months on the road with the Gals. After traveling as a solo performer for the previous two years, working with these soul-sister-musicians was a hoot. We toured continually, playing everywhere from roadside bars in rural Mississippi, Alabama, and Louisiana to high-profile folk festivals in West Virginia and upstate New York. We shared stages with the likes of Ralph Stanley, Bill Monroe, Doc Watson, and the late John Hartford.

I saw parts of America that I would never have seen otherwise. I found the landscapes and people in these rural communities fascinating. The Buffalo Gals were gypsy vagabonds tearing up the highway with five suitcases, five purses, and five instruments, all squished inside two Volkswagen Beetles.

Elaine and I usually paired up in my orange Beetle (four on the floor, no clutch) while Susie and Nell joined Nancy in her navy-blue Bug. We caravanned around the country, honking and making funny faces out open windows as we passed one another on roadways. We made regular pit stops, as women are known to do, and the two vehicles got separated now and then. In those days, before cell phones, we sometimes lost track of each other for hours, until we were reunited at the next gig for sound check.

One such separation took place during an all-night road trip from Gary, Indiana, to Ronceverte, West Virginia. I can't recall how, but by midnight, it was every Bug for itself. Well equipped to manage the long journey through the night, Elaine and I were wired on chocolate bars and black coffee. Bored with the darkness and absence of scenery, Elaine pulled out her mandolin and played while I drove. We sang for hours and hours, keeping ourselves awake and cognizant through the winding roads of southern Ohio and western West Virginia.

Around three o'clock in the morning, I suddenly realized that, while we were singing and harmonizing, we were also running out of gas.

"Start looking for a filling station," I told Elaine

"What? Are you kidding?" she said. "What's going to be open at this hour?"

A wave of panic hit me. She was right. We were in mountainous terrain, cautiously motoring through the creepiest little towns we'd ever seen. Even if we found a gas station, chances are it would be closed.

We were screwed.

Finally, after driving around bend after bend on a tight and winding two-lane road, I spotted a bright yellow circle shining through the trees.

"Elaine!" I shrieked. "Look, it's a Shell sign!"

Surely if it was lit, it was open.

We both took a deep sigh of relief, and I drove up and over the crest of the mountain. Suddenly, the Shell sign expanded before us—and we realized that it had been a mirage. We had come face-to-face with a bright yellow full moon.

Exhausted, and still not completely convinced that this *wasn't* a Shell sign, I opened my window and reached out. But my fingers grabbed nothing but cool night air.

Damn! This fantastic golden disc was indeed, the moon.

We were totally hosed.

To distract ourselves from the fear of being stranded in *Deliverance* country, Elaine and I played the great road game *Bargain with G–d*. This was a contest to see who was the most willing to quit their evil ways in exchange for a gas station. I vowed to give up peanut M&M's for a whole week, while Elaine vowed to give up driving with *me*. Soon, we were howling with laughter. In fact, we were laughing so hard that we didn't notice when the long stretch of tedious back roads ended. Suddenly, just ahead of us, we saw the entrance of Interstate 77—with all signs pointing towards Charleston, West Virginia.

And there, by the on-ramp, lit up in its fluorescent glory, was the most *beautiful* twenty-four-hour truck stop we'd ever seen. I told Elaine that I would gladly add plain M&M's to my bargain with G–d to cover her debt, lest she never drive with me again.

We traveled well as a team, and if Elaine and I ever disagreed, we laughed our way through our pretend-fighting. We were wonderful together.

After that show in West Virginia, the Buffalo Gals headed south to a festival in Sarasota, Florida. Under an early morning summer sun, I did my best to follow behind Nell, Susie, and

Nancy in their blue VW Bug. Of course, a few hours into the journey, Elaine wanted to stop.

"Hey, Sally," she said from her designated passenger seat. "Get off at the next exit. I need to make a phone call."

"Oh, come on!" I whined. "Once we pull over, we'll fall back and lose the girls, and then we'll have to pay attention to where we're going." I wanted to bean her.

"Nah, I'll be good and watch out for signs, I promise." She patted the map in her lap. "I'll keep my eye on this the whole way down."

"Oh, man, I was digging the mindlessness of this drive." I sighed. "This better be important, 'cuz you're gonna have to do all the concentrating . . . and you'll have to treat me to coffee and doughnuts."

Elaine agreed, and I got off at the next exit and pulled into a crowded parking lot. Elaine grabbed her wallet and dug out her phone calling card. She got out of the car, stopping to bend over and make the customary adjustments to her pants.

After sitting for hours and hours in a car with no air conditioning, there was always a wedgie to take care of. And if you were wearing shorts, it was imperative to pull the leg part down to keep your thighs from rubbing before you started walking in the heat. This one deft move could save a girl from the meanest of rashes. With everything in place, Elaine headed for the pay phone.

I closed my eyes to rest, and a few minutes later, Elaine kicked the side of the car to wake me from my meditation.

"Hey! Ohhhppinnadoor!" *Kick-kick.* "Ohhhpppinnadoor!"

She had a large coffee in each hand, and a giant bag of Krispy Kreme doughnuts dangled from her teeth. This stop was *so* totally worth it now. I leaned over and pulled the handle from inside the car and pushed open the door for her.

She handed me a coffee and I took the bag of doughnuts from her teeth.

"Success!" she said.

"I can see! Krispy Kreme—nice touch!" I was pleased that she fully understood the need to indulge me and get the really good doughnuts.

"No, I mean I got a hold of my old college boyfriend on the phone to let him know we're playing in Sarasota. He wants to take the whole band out sailing. He'll get a bunch of friends together and we can make a day of it!"

I felt a little sick. "Oh, gee, hmmm, that's nice, but I'll have to let you know."

"What do you mean, 'you'll have to let me know'?" she cried. "What's the matter with you? It'll be outrageous! He's a great guy with a yacht and I'm sure his buddies are terrific, and we'll have a whole day of partying out on the water!"

I shook my head. "Elaine, I just saw that movie *Jaws*, and I don't think I could handle it. Plus, I've never ever been out on a boat before, EVER."

"Sally, you'll be with us Gals, and it'll be fun, and you'll wear a life jacket and a cute hat, and we'll catch some rays." Elaine was pleading with me now. "Do it for me, because I know you'll love it. Remember—I didn't give up driving with you for my *Bargain-with-G–d* debt. If I have to play that Shell-station-mirage card, I will. You have *got* to come out sailing with us."

"I'll think about it." I started the car, took the bag of doughnuts, took a bite out of each one, took a big hit of coffee, and got us back on the highway.

Elaine's passion for adventure was contagious and I knew that her friends were always wacky delights. Plus, the guilt of disappointing her would be way worse than being eaten by a shark. Forty-five miles and three Original Glazed doughnuts later, I agreed to go.

The morning after our Florida gig, all five of us gals rushed through Kmart for the essentials: flip-flops, sunglasses, wide-brimmed hats, sunscreen, and junk food. I told the girls I'd meet them in the checkout lane so I could run and nab our beloved Good & Plenty, along with a few last-minute items.

This sailing escapade had me by the short hairs, and I wanted to make sure all my hairs were taken care of. I also needed to organize my personal affects, since I was putting my life at risk. First, I hunted down a waterproof purse to hold my driver's license and a self-penned note that read, *"If found, please contact Naomi Fingerett at 312–555–5555, and since you'll need to soften the blow, do yourself a favor and tell her that her daughter drowned while trying to meet a future husband."*

I estimated that we had a fifty-fifty chance of capsizing, so I was probably gonna die, and the authorities would need to notify my loved ones quickly. They couldn't waste time goofing around looking for my next-of-kin-people, because my next-of-kin-people were Jewish and they would have to bury me fast, within the time frame of Jewish law.

I also picked up a razor and some waterproof makeup, not caring that the girls would tease me and call me a princess. If the U.S. Coast Guard had to dredge me up from the deep dark bottom and force my mother to pay retail for a last-minute flight to Florida, JUST to identify my body, I believed it was imperative that my corpse wore lipstick and looked nice. This, of course, only mattered if the *Jaws* shark hadn't eaten my face first.

In the end, despite my world-class sunburn, dreadful hangover, and the too-late realization that one should never shave her legs two hours prior to swimming in the salty ocean, I lived to tell the tale. We had abundant and delicious food, impeccable weather, and ice-cold beers. We made our own music and sang till we were hoarse. We laughed so hard, that we had to instantaneously fling ourselves back into the ocean, rather than have little girl *accidents* right there on the deck. We stayed out on the water till sunset, when the evening's chill put an end to the day.

In the company of great girlfriends and handsome sailors, my maiden ocean voyage was a total success. I left my neurotic fears behind and put my faith in the good friends who ultimately had my back. Obviously, I was not eaten by sharks, and to my surprise, I didn't barf once (while on the boat).

Thirty-eight years later, I still cherish these wonderful memories, that waterproof purse, and *MY FRIEND ELAINE*.

SONG: *ASK ANY MERMAID*

Out on the ocean, up on the high deck, under a clear sky
Sunburn, and wanting more
I'm sorry I've never done this before
Isn't it crazy I'm not even seasick—it's up with the sails
And out with your laughter, it's the freedom you're after

I think I'll go and find me some men
Talk like a sailor, act like a sailor
Brag and boast and tie on a big one
And like the waves, we'll all go
Dancing, rolling, crashing, down to the shore
Oh look at me—I'm out on the sea
It's such a wonder—I've fallen under a mermaid's spell

The smell of the ocean, everyone's hungry
Cast out your lines and down with your fishing pole
What could you possibly catch in a net with those holes?
Pardon me captain, you must be mistaken
You chop their heads off, I'll do the pots and pans
Good lord—we'll fry them up as soon as we can
The sun's taken off, music's the ransom
I've got the squeeze-box—who's got the mandolin?
I think the time is right to find me some men
Sing like a sailor, act like a sailor
Brag and boast and tie on a big one
And like the waves, we'll all go
Dancing, rolling, crashing, down to the shore
Oh look at me—I'm out on the sea
It's such a wonder—I've fallen under a mermaid's spell

Out on the ocean, up on the high deck, under a clear sky
Sunburn and wanting more and more and more
Sorry I've never done this before!

POEM: THE RUNNING 1979

He was running from his mother's table when I met him
He was racing at breakneck speed, not looking back
This renegade son from a good family
Looked fast—just standing still
He had no idea he was running
When he found me flying overhead, breaking rules in midair
Soaring over boundaries set by parents
Who bargained and threatened to not forgive
But they would
And so we met
The running Jewish boy and the flying Jewish girl
In motion and removed from our families' tables
We were introduced in June and married that October
As radical hippies with identical passions
We believed we were unique and destined
On our wedding night, my mother pulled me aside
"Sally Girl, you found a good boy from a good family
Now, I can forgive you for all that flying around"
Somehow, I had unknowingly fixed
What I had unknowingly broken
As newlyweds, we bought a table of our own
Embracing customs, traditions, and community
Still and grounded, moving slowly forward
We began a history of our own making
There would be no more running

Chapter Three

THE ONLY
CONSISTENT THING
IS INCONSISTENCY

WILD BERRIES

Dan Green and I were introduced by mutual friends in Chicago on June 1, 1979. I had just hopped down off the stage after doing a set at the Barbarossa on Rush Street, and saw a group of folks I knew sitting at the bar. I went over to say hello.

I immediately fell into a conversation with Dan. Like me, he was a performer. He also owned and operated a recording studio/production company, Amerisound, in Columbus, Ohio. He had traveled to Chicago to purchase some new gear.

Between my work at Chicago Recording Company and my own career as a singer-songwriter, I had a lot in common with Dan, and we got along famously. By some cosmic force, everything fell into place, and it was love at first sight.

By July, Dan and I were engaged. We set a wedding date for that October.

My parents were overjoyed. They couldn't have been happier that I would be settling down with a like-minded Nice Jewish Boy. Dan's parents adored me, and I adored them. I had always known that you don't just marry a guy—you marry his family. And I wanted each and every one of them to be my family.

As hapless hippie musicians, Dan and I didn't quite comprehend the bride-and-groom-wedding-business, so we told my mother that she had complete control. We had only one request. "Ma, we want an outrageous sweet table," I told her at our one and only sit-down meeting. "I want halvah, Dan wants Jordan almonds, and we both think a chocolate wedding cake would be cool. Other than that, this party is your gig. Tell us how many people we can each invite, where and what time you plan to hold this shebang, and we'll be there."

We all agreed that we would be married in Chicago, allowing my mother to run the show. In Naomi's world, giving her free rein to enjoy the planning, preparations, and decision making was a dream come true.

I purchased my wedding dress at a small Calumet City bridal shop. I found a simple and elegant "very-shiny-bride-girl" gown. Full-length with an empire waist, the dress didn't have one of those storybook trains that drags and follows behind you, but I thought the beautiful white-on-white lace over the boobal area and the scooped neckline made for a lovely bodice. It fit, it flattered, it needed absolutely no alterations or hemming, it came with a matching veil, and (*drum roll, please*) I found it on the sample rack during a sale for just $100. Dan didn't want to wear a ring, so I bought myself a stock gold wedding band that he could give me at the ceremony. On the afternoon of the wedding, I did my own hair and makeup in the bathroom of the rental hall facility. I didn't know any better or different.

Our parents walked us down the aisle to songs we had written for the wedding. A very dear pianist friend played the processional music on a borrowed electronic keyboard. My brother-in-law, Norman the Rabbi, officiated the vows, and our *chuppah** was hoisted on poles and supported by our siblings and friends. It was simple, it was small, we took photos, our mothers wept, our grandmothers didn't like each other—but, of course, the sweet table rocked. Amen.

We spent our wedding night in a downtown Chicago hotel, opening up cards and checks, laughing about how we wanted to use the money to buy candy. Instead of a honeymoon, we headed back to Columbus, Ohio. Eager to start our new life, we couldn't wait to get back to Amerisound and start the process of growing the company.

I was twenty-four and Dan was twenty-eight.

As a newly married couple, we settled into a routine of sorts. We hunkered down and began recording rock bands and other musicians at the studio. Creative agencies hired us to write *jingles* for radio and TV commercials. On weekend nights, Dan and I continued to perform at local bars and clubs as solo artists. I had stopped traveling and preferred to stay close to home, enjoying our social circle of musicians and advertising pals.

But, after two years of married life, I missed Chicago and I missed touring. I hadn't stayed put for such a long time since I was a teenager. I felt a little wanderlust coming on, and decided to take a brief road trip.

Some old Chicago musician-friends were performing in Cleveland, and invited me to visit. For me, the one-hundred-and-fifty-mile drive from Columbus to Cleveland wouldn't even merit packing a lunch. Also, I'd heard that Cleveland's downtown had some fabulous department stores on par with my hometown Marshall Field's. This would be a lovely little getaway.

With my plans in place, I left Columbus early one day in December. At nine a.m., the air felt frigid, but the skies were bright and sunny. About an hour into my drive, clouds rolled in and a light snow began to fall. Cars slowed down in the slush, and I worried that I'd be spending the day *getting to* Cleveland, instead of spending the day *shopping* in Cleveland.

Damn.

About thirty miles into my trip, I noticed a bundled up figure hitchhiking on the right shoulder of northbound Interstate 71.

Had it not been for her childlike mittens, hot pink magenta scarf, and long, flowing blond hair, I would have never considered that this loner could be a girl hitchhiker.

What the hell? Does this tiny little thing have a mother, and does this mother know her daughter is hitchhiking on a major interstate in the winter?

I slowly pulled over onto the shoulder and let the cars continue on their way. I honked my horn, looked into my rearview mirror, and watched as the standing human-bundle became a running human-bundle. As she approached, I kept thinking—*Oy, walk, don't run! Oy, walk, don't run!*

And then, there she was, at the front passenger door window, with her smiling eyes and her runny nose. She couldn't have been more than sixteen.

I leaned over the seat, opened the door, and barked, "Throw your shit in the back, and get in!" A blast of cold air smacked me in the face and filled the entire car with wind.

She was swift and mighty, and with a grunt and a toss, her green army-style duffle bag flew right into place on the backseat. The next thing I knew, she was in the front seat next to me, wiping her nose on her sleeve.

"Wow, like thanks. Really, like, I'm totally grateful," she said.

I reached into the glove compartment and grabbed a miniature-size packet of Kleenex, the kind that my mother always kept in her purse. I handed her the packet. "Here, dolly, take these."

"Thanks so much. I'm really gross, aren't I?" She laughed.

"Nah, it's icy cold out there," I said. "All right then, what's your name and where are you off to? And please tell me you're over eighteen."

"Cicely, Boston, and I'm twenty. And you?"

"Sally, Cleveland, older than you." I grinned. "Nice to meet you, Cicely Boston."

"Well, Sally Cleveland, if you could, like, drop me around I-80 and I can hitch through Pennsylvania, or if you're going into downtown Cleveland, I could, like, ride with you all the way to I-90, then head across upstate New York on the throughway. Either way, I'm cool."

"Well, Cicely Boston, you sure do know your geography!" I said.

I started the car and slowly steered back onto the highway, relieved that my passenger was sunshiny and most likely wouldn't pull a gun on me.

"Hey," I said, "How about we make it to I-90, and we can grab lunch there—my treat?"

"Wow, how kind. Thanks!"

Her nostrils were dry and her eyes were smiling. It was then I noticed that her nose was pierced.

We immediately bonded as we discussed the merits of Joni Mitchell's songwriting, and how sad it was that Joni couldn't get to Woodstock due to the traffic. We had just started debating Joan Baez's current politics when we reached the interchange where I-71 bumped into I-90, just a little south of downtown Cleveland. I exited the highway and pulled into a Friendly's parking lot. We laughed about loving grilled cheese sandwiches with tomato soup, and agreed that, no matter how cold it was outside, if you're dining at Friendly's, ice cream sundaes were always required.

We found a booth and proceeded to unzip and unwind ourselves from our jackets and scarves. We settled into our seats, studied our menus, and placed our orders. Now that I wasn't driving, I could pin her down with the questions that had been rattling around my brain.

"Cicely, you have to tell me about your family and all this traveling. How can your mother take it?"

"Oh, yeah, she's like totally cool with this. She and my stepdad are up in Alaska working on pipelines or something. I visited them last summer. Man, it's like really pretty there, but like, really far away. But maybe she'll come and see me in India sometime."

What?

"India?" I'm sure I sounded horrified and incredulous. "When you said you were going to Boston, I assumed you were on your way to college."

"Well, I got into Antioch here in Ohio, and I tried it for a while, but it's not for me. Maybe I'll do college again later, but first I have the craziest desire to go to India."

"My goodness, that's some desire you got there. India, that's big."

"Yeah, well, first I'm heading to Boston to hang with my yogi. There's a whole group up there, and like, we might all just go to India together. For sure, I really want to travel as a cook in different ashrams and see the world." Now her sunshiny way and calm demeanor made sense.

"Well," I said, "now's the time to do it, girl."

I told her about my earlier days as a traveling singer-songwriter, driving from gig to gig, sometimes living in my car. I filled her in on the great friends I had made performing all over the country, working solo shows and playing bluegrass with the Buffalo Gals. "But after a while, Cicely, traveling gets old," I continued. "Before you know it, you fall in love and get married, and all of a sudden, there's a cast of characters who worry about you when all you've done is sneeze."

She looked at me and laughed. Then her eyes turned sad, and I swear I saw her make a mental note to never become someone like me.

I looked down at my coffee cup and realized what I had just said. I *did* love being a part of a new family, and I especially loved having a comfortable home base. But suddenly, I wondered if my autonomous, impetuous, freewheeling days were over.

My heart sank.

The waitress came and laid the bill on the table. I snatched it up, grabbed my wallet, and paid the check. I reached for my coat. "Well, Cicely Boston, you have the best life ever. Be careful out there, and I'm wishing you the safest journey and most wonderful adventures. I'll be thinking of you, dolly."

She put her hand on my arm. "Hey, do you have a pen and some paper? Why don't I give you my ashram address in India? If you ever get there, come and find me!"

I knew I'd never make it to India, but I took the address she scribbled on the back of an old grocery list I found in my purse. "I'll write to you," I said. "And you can let me know you got there safely."

I was not her mother, but at that moment, I would have driven her all the way to India.

We hugged and said our good-byes. I got in my car and watched her walk toward the highway ramp heading in the other direction. I started this song lyric in my car as I waited for her to find a ride. Not wanting to lose the words, I pulled out my journal and started writing. When I looked up again, she was gone.

SONG: *WILD BERRIES*

A young girl on the highway, stranded in the snow
December, south of Cleveland, Ohio
I'm stopping out of pity for a stranger I don't know
Just a young girl on the highway—like me so long ago
I check my rearview mirror and I'm taken by surprise
By silver-studded strands of hair
In the bangs around my eyes— oh, my eyes
She's frail, but she is handsome, just nineteen or so
Dropping out of Antioch and drifting like the snow
On her way to Boston to make dinner for some friends
"Guess to where I'm off to next?" she said
"India—like the wind I'm off and running
I'm alone, there is no race"
I saw a silver-studded diamond pin and
A smile upon her face—oh, her face—it said
CHORUS
Come with me, go with me

We will be free birds again
You'll see, just like me
We will be free birds and when
You fly there's no time, only
Your wings and you're free

She speaks of her adventures—Alaska and the ice
Wild berries on a doorstep in springtime paradise
I'm off to the city to window-shop downtown
I make a little money—like a slave, it ties you down
But this spirit right beside me, she's off to see the world
And my silver-studded memory longs to be
Just like this girl—oh, this girl—she says
CHORUS

My free bird generation has come and gone
What's left behind—but a young girl on the highway
The last berry on the vine
Our lost, forgotten causes lie deep within her eyes
Where berries grow on doorsteps, there in paradise
And I look into her garden, I see myself upon that vine
I see silver-studded dew that falls on berries
Lost in time—lost in time—she says
CHORUS

MAN PLANS, G—D LAUGHS

*O*ver the course of my life, whenever things didn't go my way and disappointment ensued, the same cliché would rear its unsympathetic head.

"Man plans, G—d laughs."

As an advocate of solid planning, I'm convinced that when it came to my life, G—d laughed so hard that he got a gripping side stitch, came down with the hiccups, and had to lie down.

Married life was going well, and our businesses—Amerisound Studios and Jingle Production Company—had wonderful clients. Dan and I wrote the music and lyrics together. Then, while Dan sat at the helm and turned all the buttons and knobs, I stood at the microphone and sang. Everyone and everything was moving in a great direction.

By 1982, I had written a slew of my own artistic, noncommercial songs, and Dan suggested that we produce an album of my solo work. Studio sessions were scheduled and everything fell into place. Amerisound would become a record label and its inaugural release would be *Enclosed*, my first LP (on vinyl!). I signed with a wonderful booking agent, Andy Espo, in Boston, and the gigs poured in. Dan got busy recording bands in the studio, while I got back to the business of touring and performing and (hopefully) selling records. Money was beginning to roll our way, and we decided it was time to start house hunting.

(G–D enters stage right and laughs.)

G–D: Ha-Ha-Ha-Ha-Ha-Ha-Ha!

(G–D laughs so hard he can't stand up straight. Still bent over, he stirs the pot that is our life, and begins gasping for air between fits of hysterical guffawing. Then, because he's elderly, his laughter turns to horrible wheezing that appears to be dangerous and out of control. Thankfully, he exits stage left and is taken to a hospital, but he doesn't have to wait in line 'cuz he knows people.)

Just as we completed the production of my album, Dan's father had a fatal heart attack at the age of sixty-four. Six months after that, I was heading north on Route 23 through northwestern Ohio on my way to a gig. I got caught in a whiteout blizzard that dropped eighteen inches of snow in four hours. As I struggled to see through the thick white mess blowing and swirling everywhere, I drove at attention—sitting straight up and leaning forward, to get as close to my windshield as possible.

I literally never saw the rear end of the creamy white Buick—even as I drove right into it.

With a jolt, my car crashed into the Buick. My seat belt held me tight, but my head snapped forward. My mouth smashed into the steering wheel. Once my Civic stopped, I instinctively took off my seat belt and prepared to exit the car. At that moment, a Peterbilt semi rammed me broadside on the driver's side. The impact catapulted me out of my seat. My face and body slammed into the dashboard and, with the Civic in continuous motion, the dashboard slammed into me. The

Peterbilt and car finally came to a standstill. I grabbed the passenger door handle and tumbled out onto the ground.

The next day, I would discover a black-and-blue mark in the shape of a steering wheel on my ass.

Many hours later, I sat waiting my turn in the emergency room of the Blanchard Valley hospital in Findlay, Ohio. I heard the nurse telephone my poor husband back in Columbus to inform him that his wife had been in a twenty-car pileup on the highway. I fell apart, thinking of Dan. He had just lost his father six months ago, and now he had to deal with this.

The hospital stitched up my face and lip. The doctor told me that my teeth would need to be wired back together with braces, once I returned home to Columbus. Then, without so much as an aspirin, they released me.

Due to all the confusion at the accident scene, my glasses, purse, and guitar had been left behind in my demolished car. By the time I left the hospital, the Civic had been towed away from the crash site. I was completely without resources. Thankfully, my agent, Andy, located some friends in Findlay who offered to take me in that night, and the Red Cross was dispatched to deliver me there.

The next day, after the blizzard passed and the roads were cleared, Dan drove the ninety-five miles to collect me.

When I saw the look on Dan's face, I felt responsible for his pain.

He put me in his car and drove to the impound lot. He looked inside the Civic, saw all the blood, and cried. We retrieved my things, signed the paperwork, said good-bye to the totaled car forever.

Once we returned to Columbus, I decided that I never wanted to leave home again. I was over the whole touring thing. I wanted us to have a home, and I wanted us to be in it every night, safe and together.

WHATEVER WE DID

Dan and I finally found the perfect house. Built in 1939, the red brick, one-and-half-story Tudor had aged to perfection. Just north of The Ohio State University's campus, this fixer-upper had natural hardwood floors and a funky turquoise semi-updated kitchen from the late 1950s. Quaint and petite at fifteen hundred square feet, the Tudor wasn't too big to heat or clean. This made us both very happy.

After our first year in the house, I became pregnant. The hormonal changes left me with all-day morning sickness and screwed-up sleep patterns. I kept having the same nightmare in which I arrived home from high school to discover that I had left the baby in my locker.

When I told this to my mother, she said, "Sally Girl, G–d doesn't give you a ten-year-old, he gives you a baby, and you grow and learn together. Don't be ridiculous and go take a nap."

Dan couldn't wait to become a father, and I hoped to find assistance once I entered the world's largest and oldest sorority—motherhood.

For me, choosing to have a baby represented a relatively recent decision. As a little girl, I had never been a babysitter, and as an adult, I had never seen myself as a mother. Based on the oddness of my mother's parenting skills, I didn't think I wanted to do something I hadn't enjoyed watching someone else do.

But I loved Dan, we both loved family, and I just held my nose and jumped in.

I hoped for a boy because this business of being a girly girl was not my thing. I didn't know the fashion rules—like when it was safe to wear white or not to wear white. Applying makeup gave me heart palpitations, nail polish was wasted on a musician's fingers, and I never really mastered the art of blow-drying my hair. It would be a shame if I had a little girl.

Many of my South Side childhood pals had already had girl babies. Sheila had Lauren, Karen had Jessica, Alysa had Elana and Janna, Donna B. had Susan, Nancy had Alexa, Donna H. had Lauren and Alexis. But these women lived faraway in cities like San Francisco, St. Louis, Portland, Los Angeles, San Diego, Minneapolis-St. Paul, and though we might share our mothering issues on the phone, we wouldn't be experiencing our children's childhoods together.

I missed them all desperately. If not for my South Side Girls, I don't know how I would have gotten through my younger years. Karen's mother fed me lunch and Sheila's mother let me play their beautiful living room piano and gave me wonderful compliments. I spent countless hours in Alysa's finished basement, where our pretend play alleviated much of my anxiety. Nancy, who remains slender and beautiful, had a kitchen drawer full of candy that we kids were allowed to raid without penalty. Donna H. had four siblings, and her mother owned and operated a mimeographing and clerical services company in their basement, while upstairs, their free-range house burst with chaos and laughter.

Adolescent life with my South Side friends included the occasional scapegoating and triangulation of gossipy girls, but I admired and depended on them. And, although I envied their perfect hair and skinny thighs, I coveted their homes and ever-present mothers even more.

I used to say that I was raised by wolves, but the truth is—I was raised by friends.

SONG: *WHATEVER WE DID*

I lie here homesick, though I lie at home
Awake with thoughts of sweet friends
Now we're grown and gone
Back when we were younger, we clung in a clique
And ran like schools of minnows

Whatever we did, whatever we did
Pretty girls dancing in the gym
Whatever we did, whatever we did
We were spinning on the South Side
Whatever we did, whatever we did
Braced against Chicago's dirty wind
Whatever we did, whatever we did
We were visions from the South Side
That's my neighborhood

We could be cruel, we could be kind
We'd be judgmental to pass the time
Nobody's mama had an only child
We'd lay the law through a lipstick smile
Loyal and faithful, two-faced and then
We vowed to remember, I try to forgive

Whatever we did, whatever we did
I'm looking back, I'm looking in
Whatever we did, whatever we did
We had secrets on the South Side
Whatever we did, whatever we did
Might cut you off, might let you live
Whatever we did, whatever we did
I landed on the outside
That's my neighborhood

Hometown visits are gonna drive you wild
Streets are frosted shiny blue
I tend to think we turned out all right
But I wonder what they've been through

I heard some would do away with men
Some would leave home again and again
Some would chase a dream or two
Find a lover and that's all they do
But you keep a line along the way
It all comes back to you again someday
Who stayed married, who's got kids
There we go again
I wonder how they've truly been

Some would spend their nights at war
Some get hurt and go back for more
Some would find a cross to bear
Carry that burden everywhere
Me I struggle for peace of mind
Live by example, I try to be kind
I will raise a compassionate child
Lessons from the South Side
That's my neighborhood

SAVE ME A SEAT

After arriving home from the hospital with my newborn daughter, Elizabeth Julian (EJ), I eagerly waited for that Earth-Mother-Glow thing to hit. At the childbirth classes, I learned to breathe through the pain, demand the really good drugs early in the game, and of course, be on the lookout for that Earth-Mother-Glow thing.

But, instead of flowing around the house all warm and fuzzy and mushy, I became a miserable new mother with an equally miserable baby.

Poor EJ cried all the time. For weeks, I barely slept, and when I did manage to pass out for a few hours, I woke up feeling worse than I did before. Tending to Elizabeth's cries in the middle of the night, I dragged my addled self to her crib and peered in. *Whose baby is this? I don't mind feeding it, 'cuz it's cute and all, but* somebody *must be missing a baby!*

I felt deficient in the whole area of nurturing. I was undone by how much I didn't know, and petrified by the physical and emotional harm I could easily inflict. Somehow, all the standard-issue blueprints and class notes for parenting had been circulated to everyone but me.

In a paranoid moment, I recalled the awful curse my mother threw at me when I was a teenager—*"You should someday have a daughter of your own who gives you such a heartache!"*

I didn't want to believe in curses, so I decided that *I* was to blame for my baby's unhappiness. My mother's curse must have flown around the planet a time or two and turned inside out—I was the *mother* who gave the daughter the heartache.

That Earth-Mother-Glow thing was a total *no show,* and I felt doomed.

What's wrong with you? I thought.

I knew full well that not everyone struggled like this. One of my girlfriends had given birth to three kids—quickly, expeditiously, and exactly two years apart. Each child was more wonderful than the previous one. These babies came with tiny little angel wings, elegant sleeping patterns, and well-timed nursing habits. After listening to my girlfriend gloat, I just wanted to push her down in the mud.

My baby did *not* come with angel wings. Instead she came with colic. Her inconsolable and heartbreaking cries, coupled with her insomnia, turned me into a raving lunatic.

One morning in the kitchen, unable to put a sentence together, I pulled the yellow pages down from the top of the fridge. I had no idea where to look, but I had to find some help. I flipped the pages, searching through the P's for the Sylvia Plath Hotline, hoping to find an emergency number for new mothers like me. No such luck.

Instead, I called my ob-gyn's office. Thankfully, they put me through to the postpartum nurse on call.

"Here's the deal . . ." I started to cry. " . . . I'm the world's worst mother and I don't know what I was thinking when I had this baby, and oh my goodness, I'm horrified that I'm doing everything wrong and I'm gonna ruin her for life." I choked back a sob. "And my hair is falling out like you wouldn't believe."

"Oh, sweetheart, you'll be fine!" the nurse said. "Let's get you in and have a look at your hormone levels."

"Okay, thanks," I said sheepishly.

This lovely nurse asked about my eating, sleeping, and anxiety issues. She was calm and comforting. We made an appointment for me to come in and have blood work done.

I hung up, relieved. This nurse's reassuring tone gave me hope that I'd be okay and would not end up in a rubber room, wearing my mother's bathrobe.

For those fleeting moments when Baby EJ wasn't screaming, she was really easy on the eyes. She was born with a full head of *long* black hair, and I actually had to take a scissors to her bangs when she was two weeks old. Her dark, soulful eyes sat above chubby cheeks and the fullest pink lips.

About four weeks into her life, she *finally* smiled and coo'ed. Taken aback, I finally smiled and coo'ed. Was it possible that my instability and tension had caused my little girl to have a nervous stomach—a grown-up medical term for tummy ache?

During one of her brief quiet spells, I seized the opportunity for us to have a face-to-face.

"Listen, EJ, this is your mother speaking. Unfortunately, I have no idea what I'm doing here. So if you can hold on until you're fifteen, I promise you'll have plenty of girlfriends with mothers you'll like more than me, and you can hang out at their houses all day if you like. But until that time, you're stuck with who I am, so please have some *rachmones** and go easy on me. For right now, I'm the only mother around, so how about we make a pact to stay in this together, and see how we do?"

I could have sworn I saw a gleam of understanding in her dark eyes. She looked right through me and then she farted. Score!

A few weeks later, EJ and I woke up to a bright and sunny March morning. Winter was winding down, and the icy sidewalks had turned slushy. I thought this would be the perfect day to take Elizabeth outside and introduce her to the neighborhood.

I cautiously placed my tiny six-week-old baby inside a twenty-four-months-sized snowsuit, knowing that it would take two years for her to grow real arms and legs that actually filled out the sleeves and pant legs. For now, I pretended she was wearing a beautiful pink sleeping bag—from Nordstrom no less.

EJ squirmed and wiggled deep in the throes of way too much fabric, sliding around inside the sleeping-bag-snowsuit. I tied the empty pant legs in a knot to keep her afloat. With only a tiny sliver of her face showing, there was, at least, a hint of baby in all that pink.

I placed EJ in her beautiful top-of-the-line Aprica stroller, complete with mud flaps, and out the door we went. My muscles strained as I directed the stroller down our driveway to the street. *Not bad, look at this! I'm pushing a stroller in the snow!! So what if I haven't changed my clothes since last Wednesday—I'm wearing a*

winter coat and a scarf and gloves, and I'm outside pushing the baby, and
I'm going to live!

I made it to the sidewalk in front of our house, and then looked up and down the block. I saw nothing but quiet houses, bare trees, and slush. Then I noticed someone sitting on a front porch swing across the street, three houses down.

I sloshed my way toward the house. A young woman, dressed in sweat pants, slippers, and a lightweight hoodie, sat rocking and talking. At first, I worried she was talking to herself. Then I spotted a wiggling and whimpering bundle of baby blankets next to her on the porch swing. At ten thirty in the morning, I assumed she was rocking to get the baby down for a nap.

She glanced at me and continued ferociously unwrapping a Hershey's kiss. She popped one in her mouth, grabbed the bowl on her lap, and held it out to me.

"Hey, want some? I've got plenty!" She smiled, and the silver wrappers glittered in the sun.

G–d had just thrown me a bone.

Lisa and I became immediate friends, and we spoke or saw each other almost every day. Her daughter, Jessica, was a few months older than EJ, and we both planned to stay home with our kids for as long as possible. Both of us loved to sew and quilt. Sometimes, we shared the cost of a babysitter and indulged in a weekday outing to a fabric store or a matinee, where we hid out in the quiet movie theater, bingeing on our beloved red licorice and Hershey's kisses.

During our second summer together, boredom got the best of us. One day, hungry for lunch, we pushed the strollers to Wendy's on our way home from the neighborhood park. On foot, without a car, we walked the strollers into the drive-thru lane. We simply placed our order at the first window, paid at the second window, and then took our bags and walked away. This became our favorite weekly outing. We loved how people watched us, gobsmacked by our audacity. We eventually trained the babies to wave at the cars of customers in line behind us.

It was our favorite party trick.

We shared a deep affection for pulling off stunts like this and considered ourselves quite the duo—a contemporary version of Lucy and Ethel. The only time we ever disagreed was when I refused to be Ethel. I made it very clear that if she got to be Lucy and I had to be Ethel, then I got to be Wilma and she had to be Betty. She accepted this, but insisted that if she had to be Betty, then at some point, she would get to be Veronica and I had to be Betty. There was never a problem when I pushed to be Laverne because she had no problem being the perky and adorable Shirley. But when the kids misbehaved or got into trouble, conversation wasn't necessary. Lisa was the warm and rational Cagney all the way, and I was loudmouthed Lacey to my core. We were the perfect team.

When the girls were past the toddler stage, they often wanted us to join them in their little-girl games.

"Mommy, will you play fairy-princess-pretend?" Jessica begged, tugging at Lisa's pant leg.

"Sorry, Jess," Lisa said kindly. "I don't want to play fairy-princess-pretend. Choose something else."

"Oh, okay." Jessica turned and left the room.

My mouth dropped open.

"Hey," Lisa said, "I've got rights and she's got choices."

"Wait, we have rights?" I laughed. "But you didn't even make up an excuse. You were *honest*. And she was completely okay with it!"

Lisa shrugged. "Yeah, when I bullshit her, she senses the weasel in me and nags on end. So I cut the crap and go for a concrete absolute. Seems to work, go figure."

My friend's magical life kept unfolding before me.

Lisa and her mother shared the most admirable and magnificent relationship. They adored each other and made *dates* to spend time together. They were spiritually close and emotionally respectful.

Witnessing this made me so jealous that I ached. But seeing my mommy-playdate-partner with her mother confirmed that I had found the perfect parenting mentor. With Lisa in my corner, I had already won the best-friend lottery, and now this sturdy, well-balanced, and loving Midwestern girl was sharing her seamless child-rearing techniques with me. I had no idea at the time that, with her quiet guidance, I would nurture and heal myself while raising my little girl.

When Jessica was three and a half, Lisa had a second daughter. Round and pink, happy and adorable, baby Olivia slowed us down a little with her nap schedules and feedings. But this was okay by me. I stood by, fascinated by Lisa's even-tempered poise and magnificent organizational skills with two daughters at her feet. I'm convinced that her Earth-Mother-Glow thing had multiplied, and had now morphed into superpowers.

Ten months after Olivia's birth, Lisa complained that her tummy wasn't going down in size. She made some calls, checked in with a few doctors, had some lab work, no big deal. And then, BOOM, an operation revealed a significant malignant uterine tumor. The surgeons found the cancer to be aggressive, and they removed her entire reproductive system. Lisa hadn't turned thirty-one yet and had no family history of disease. This horrific turn of events caught everyone completely by surprise.

Her husband, Jeff, jumped into action. After work, he spent long nights researching various options and drug trials. He studied up on complex medical terms in order to explain Lisa's condition and treatments to family and friends. I signed on as a worker bee, assisting with anything asked of me, while Lisa's parents came for an open-ended visit, offering babysitting, meal preparation, and unwavering strength.

Lisa fought with determination and faith. "Somebody gets to be in the surviving fifteen percent—why not me?" she told us. For two years, she endured countless surgeries, prolonged chemotherapies, and relentless radiations. Struggling with continual side effects and illnesses, frightening ultrasounds and disappointing test results, she finally accepted that she wouldn't be getting any better—nothing would change.

She phoned me from her hospital room, her voice defiant.

"Sal, this has to stop. I've had enough. I wanna go home."

"I'll be right there." I hung up the phone and drove straight to the James Cancer Hospital at The Ohio State University.

The elevator stopped on Lisa's floor. The doors opened and I rushed into the corridor. As I entered her room, I found several nurses embracing her. They had cared for Lisa tirelessly and understood her situation. They offered prayers and kind words of unconditional love and acceptance, each nurse supporting her unimaginable, yet very personal decision, to *go home*.

"Your blessings mean the world to me," she told the nurses.

I studied Jeff's face as he gathered Lisa's things together. Tall and normally energetic, he now moved slowly, his shoulders hunched under the weight of knapsacks and worry. Jeff's constant strength and grace had been replaced by unthinkable defeat. I knew he couldn't bear the thought of raising the girls without her, but he could no longer watch the love of his life suffer so.

A social worker handed a few hospice information brochures to Jeff. He turned and held them out for me to see.

"Can you believe this is happening?" he whispered, just to me.

"I'm so sorry, Jeff." I took the brochures from him.

With Lisa packed and ready to leave the hospital for what would be the last time, I wheeled her down to the street, while Jeff went to pull the car around.

At home, Lisa settled into her big easy chair. Wearing her favorite seafoam-green scarf, she looked like a movie star. Frail and elegant, my best friend and spirit guide sat with a battery-operated fanny pack of pain meds strapped to her waist. With the push of a button, this pack dispensed as-needed pain medication via a shunt in her chest.

I finished vacuuming, put the Hoover away, and grabbed two glasses of iced tea to join her for a chat.

"Thanks so much, Betty," Lisa said weakly. "I don't know why a vacuumed carpet gives me such a buzz."

"Hey Wilma, we all know it's the little things," I said. *'Cuz the big things are just too damn big.*

'You know what, Ethel?" Lisa asked quietly.

"Yes, Lucy?"

"There's something to be said for getting hit by a bus. It would be so much simpler than this," she whispered.

"Well, I agree that getting hit by a bus does offer an element of surprise and freedom and spontaneity," I began. "But think about how shitty the driver would feel, and then all the people in the street, they'd be freakin' out, and the traffic tie-ups and the paper work and, oh my G–d, police reports. Oh, and then your kids don't get a chance to say good-bye."

"Yeah." She laughed. "You're right."

I finished getting both her and the house ready for the next shift of helpers. I left and wept my way home.

I spent the rest of that day and night writing her song. The next afternoon, I played it for her as my gift, and she asked if I would sing it at her funeral. Two months later, I did.

This is for my Lucy.

SONG: *SAVE ME A SEAT*
for Lisa Anderson Webb 1958–1992

She's standing in a hard rain, waiting for the bus
Homeward bound
There with her umbrella, she's had enough
Homeward bound
She's ready for the journey in her heart of hearts
Homeward bound
Once those doors swing open, they let the healing start
Homeward bound

CHORUS
Get you a place by the window, grab the aisle for me
Someday, when it's my turn
Look around you and there I'll be
You better save me a seat, oh, save me a seat

You don't need to transfer on the freedom bus
Because it's one-way bound
You don't need a token if in G–d you trust
Homeward bound
Lay down your weary burden, travel as you please
Homeward bound
The tired and the weary find comfort in release
Homeward bound
CHORUS

They don't laugh at white girls who love their R&B
Homeward bound
You'll be dancing by the river, let your soul run free
Homeward bound
She's ready to get ready—she's got everything in a line
Homeward bound
You gave the gift of courage, go on, girl, it's time
Homeward bound
CHORUS

She's standing in a hard rain, waiting for the bus
Homeward bound
Closing her umbrella, she hands it back to us
Homeward bound
Wave good-bye at your window, put up your big old feet
You'll always live inside my heart
Hold a spot for me
You better save me a seat, oh, save me a seat

BUBBE CHICKEN

Just like my grandma
wished she could make

In 1913, my father's mother, Anna Skroden, traveled alone from Vilna (in Russia or Poland or Lithuania, depending on the day) to Chicago. Sixteen-year-old Anna arrived and joined her older sister Mayim (Mollie) as a seamstress at Hart Schaffner & Marx Men's Clothiers. Anna quickly excelled and became the first woman promoted to the rank of joiner. This highly regarded group of experienced tailors fastened (joined) the difficult shoulder and sleeve seams that the average sewer couldn't handle. Anna loved her job and took great pride in her accomplishments. She did her best to ignore the antagonizing catcalls her male co-workers sent her way. She felt she had just as much right to make a living as these *yutzes.**

A few years later, she met my grandfather, Jacob Fingerett. Anna found him pleasant enough, and after the man she truly loved ran off with someone else, she agreed to marry Jacob. This is information she surely could have kept to herself, but my grandmother lived her life as an honest—and very loud—open book.

My Grandfather Jake was a gentle, sweet, and handsome man who had planned to be an actor. As a teenager, he went to various portrait studios and posed in borrowed cowboy costumes, hoping to become a moving picture star in California. But, after meeting Anna, he realized what a blunder it would be to leave town and possibly lose this girl. My grandpa might have been a good-looking dreamer, but he was no dummy. He chose a brilliant woman to be his wife and the mother of their four children, while he quietly and graciously accepted the fact that she was going to be the boss of everyone.

After marrying Jake, my grandmother left Hart Schaffner & Marx and became one of the original mover-and-shaker multitaskers who could do it all. Fast and furious when it came to raising the children, Anna also managed the sales counter and cash register of the bakery she and Jake opened on Division Street. Jake drove the delivery truck, while Anna's customers adored her. She knew enough to speak Russian to the Russians, Polish to the Poles, and Yiddish and English to the rest. Fingerett's Bakery did quite well in its day.

Anna thought life in America was wonderful. They had a two-bedroom apartment above the bakery, with three beds for the six of them and a real kitchen. She often proclaimed indoor plumbing "a *mechayeh**" and thought nothing of storing her gefilte fish ingredients (a live carp!) in the bathtub. (That poor carp was an unintended participant in one of my greatest childhood traumas. To this day, I jump at the sight of a live fish.)

In keeping with Jewish family traditions, Anna always demanded the family come together for Friday night's Shabbat meal. She stepped away from the cash register, lit the Sabbath candles, said the blessings, ate dinner with her family, and—for one night—she didn't yell at anyone.

In 1976, when I was in my early twenties, I made a Sunday afternoon pilgrimage to visit my grandparents. Now in their late seventies and retired, they still lived in the same apartment, above their closed bakery. Decrepit buildings lined the block and gang members sat on milk crates by the curb waiting for "deliveries." I parked my beat-up Volkswagen Beetle on Division Street and nervously walked to their side entrance door, next to the bakery. After I hit the buzzer, they let me in. I was astounded that, after decades of buzzing, the buzzer still buzzed. Go figure.

My grandmother greeted me with a huge hug, looked me up and down, and let out a tired sigh. I had long hair with bangs way down into my eyes, and wore faded blue jeans, Frye boots, and of course, no bra. She's disappointed in me, I thought. She's probably upset that I would come and visit without my brassiere, having risked my life just walking past the hoodlums loitering on the street, *kinahora.**

Looking back, I realize that my grandmother wasn't unhappy with me, but rather, she was saddened that the times were changing and she had run out of steam to change with them.

For decades, she had ruled her family with a tight and inflexible grip, wearing her uniform of flesh-colored support hose, sensible brown leather lace-up shoes, and a colorless dress that somehow allowed for the longest and biggest bosom(s) ever. I think she would have loved to have been able to shed her emotional limitations and modesty, along with her size 42DDD bra.

My grandmother died in 1992 at the age of ninety-six and refused to believe that she had been an early version of a modern feminist. Yet, she often spoke of how she admired those of us dedicated to the women's movement. It's funny, now that I think of it, that she never once wore a pair of pants . . . except verbally.

My grandmother often admitted that when it came to cooking, her heart wasn't in it. When she had to be in the kitchen, she recreated the meals she had watched her own mother prepare, back in the old country. Food was served hot, mushy, and tasteless. Everybody eat, everybody get back to work.

I cannot, in good conscience, include any of my grandma's recipes because, frankly, we're not gonna have any feather plucking and head chopping in this book. I loved her to pieces, but as a child, I found her cooking to be the stuff nightmares are made of.

Instead, I'd like to offer a wonderful way to make the "Bubbe Chicken" we Jewish people are so wild about. In this recipe, there are three seasonings that, if laid on heavily enough, will create the Russian/Polish wonderfulness that makes old hallways in Jewish ghettos smell so much better than they might have otherwise. *Ess, mine kinder.**

RECIPE:
Division Street Bubbe Chicken

INGREDIENTS:

4 ounces Manischewitz wine
1 to 2 shots vodka
Whole roasting chicken *I buy small 4- to 5-pounders.*
8 carrots (peeled and cut into 2-inch logs)
1 large onion, quartered and then separated
Onion powder (not onion salt*). Just go with the flow of the text
   below.*
Garlic powder (not garlic salt) *Just go with the flow of the text below.*
Paprika *I have no idea what to tell you other than to just go with the flow
   of the text below.*
Italian salad dressing *Check in your fridge 'cuz everyone keeps Italian
   dressing around. If not, a little olive oil then.*
Salt and pepper too, to your taste. *For some reason, I salt only after
   cooking. I've been told to step up the salt, but I'm just quirky that way.
   Plus, I feel taste buds are really personal.*

DIRECTIONS:

Preheat the oven to 350 degrees.

Pour the vodka shots into the Manischewitz and then throw in an ice cube, if desired. Set the glass on the countertop near your workspace. You might sip this nectar of the czars, or you might knock this puppy right on down. Either way, it will make having to be in the kitchen that much more enjoyable. No need for me to tell you how to drink this. Just go for it.

Under cold water, wash the chicken and see if you can pull some of the fat out from under the skin, scraping what you can. Though we're replicating an old family recipe, no one wants to look like they came from the old world of Vilna, so we're going to cut the calorie count if at all possible.

Lay the chicken, breast side down, in a roasting pan that's not too much bigger than the circumference of the chicken. Smother/cover with garlic, onion, and paprika powders. Really "go there." Don't be afraid. Overdo it. Trust me. Flip over the chicken and repeat the seasoning event. Then pour/rub a little Italian salad dressing or olive oil. You will be cooking this chicken with the breast side up.

Stuff a few peeled and cut carrots into the breast cavity of the chicken and then distribute the remaining carrots and onion pieces all around the pan. (Parsnips can be added as well. Any root vegetable works great, but it's a question of taste.) Add 2 cups of water—or more if need be—so when you stick your finger in the pan, the water reaches your first knuckle.

Cover the chicken for the first 20 minutes, then uncover. Total cook time should be about 25 minutes per pound. Maybe 30 minutes, depending on your oven and your chicken. If you have a 4-pound chicken, we're talking an hour at least, with basting at the end to make the skin golden brown. You'll taste, you'll *plotz*,* you'll thank me, and—all of a sudden—you'll feel Eastern European.

If I've left anything out, don't worry, just punt, go with your gut, channel your own version of a young woman whose family lives in another part of the world, and you have to forage your own way around a kitchen. No one will starve.

Serve the chicken and cooked carrots with, maybe, a nice noodle kugel, but if not, a baked potato would also be lovely. Don't forget to make a salad—you should eat your greens—and if you've got, open a can of cranberry sauce, it goes good. Try to sit and eat your dinner at the table like a *mensch** and maybe do your dishes before the vodka/Manischewitz buzz wears off.

You're welcome.

HOME IS WHERE THE HEART IS

I wrote this song in 1990, just as EJ was getting ready to turn four years old. Our quiet sleepy neighborhood near The Ohio State University's campus was home to domestic diversity of all kinds. EJ, a child who fearlessly sought out new friends, insisted we trek up and down our block, knocking on doors to ask if there were any children to play with.

In our search for new pals, we met warm and loving people who became our extended family. I felt blessed to be able to share EJ with them. And I thank them for enriching our lives by acting as members of *the village* it takes to raise an honorable citizen of the planet.

HOME IS WHERE THE HEART IS
Thank you, Peter, Paul and Mary, for sharing this with the world

On our corner, there's this nice man
His name is Mark, he's always smiling
He's got this mom who comes on Wednesdays

In the evening, with soup so steaming
He shares his house with his friend Martin
They're not brothers, they're not cousins
My little girl wonders all about these men
I take hold of her hand, I begin
CHORUS
Home is where the heart is
No matter how the heart lives
Inside your heart, where love is
That's where you've got to make yourself
At home

Through the yard live Deb and Tricia
With their drills and ladders and their room addition
My kid yells over "Are you having a baby?"
They wink and smile and say, "Someday, maybe"
Through their doors, go kids and mommies
Funny how you don't see the daddies go in
My little girl wonders 'bout the house with no men
I take hold of her hand, I begin
CHORUS

'Round the corner, here comes Martin
He's alone now, he tries smiling
He roams around his well-stocked kitchen
He knows that fate will soon be coming
My little girl wonders "Where will he live?"
I take hold of her hand and I begin
CHORUS

Martin sits and waits with his window open
His house is empty, his heart is broken
We bring him toys and watercolors
He loves to hear my little baby's stories
She's the gift I share, she's his companion

She's the string on the kite
She guides him up into the wind-up into the wind
My little girl wonders who will care for him
We take hold of his hand, we begin, let's begin now
CHORUS

MEET THE BABES

B ack when I toured on the college coffeehouse circuit, I often looked up friends—to crash on their couch, snag a free meal, or just hang out between gigs.

In 1976, after finishing a show at the state university in Stony Brook, New York, I called up a dear friend and music producer, Steve Burgh. I had met Burgh years before, when he produced John Prine and Steve Goodman in the Chicago recording studio where I worked.

Now a *macher** in the New York City music scene, Burgh was a great supporter of contemporary songwriters and artists. He loved to gather musicians in his funky Greenwich Village apartment filled with junky furniture and outrageously expensive instruments. The most talented itinerant folkies gathered at Burgh's place to hang out and jam, passing guitars (and joints) around his sun-filled living room, haphazardly learning from one another.

Steve invited me to one of those living room jam sessions. It was there I met Christine Lavin, another struggling folk singer. Thirteen years later, our paths would cross again.

By the fall of 1989, I had purchased a home with my husband, been in a car accident, stopped touring, given birth to a daughter (who was now three years old), and settled into writing and singing commercial music at our downtown Columbus recording studio. By that time, Christine Lavin was an accomplished and successful touring performer and a Rounder Records recording artist. She wrote brilliant, savvy, sophisticated satirical songs and had headlined at every major folk festival and folk club in the country. With her sparkly blue eyes, cropped blondish hair, and a mile-a-minute mouth, Chris had become a celebrated entertainer with a vivacious stage presence and sparkling charisma. Her career was in full swing.

Early in October 1989, Chris flew to Minneapolis to perform a concert. Her record company sent a member of their promotion/distribution team to fetch Chris from the airport and escort her to several radio interviews. By a stroke of good luck, this person was my sister-in-law, Ricki Gayle Fingerett.

Upon meeting Ricki and hearing her last name, Chris raised an eyebrow and said, "I once met a songwriter with the last name of Fingerett. Not a common name, so I have to ask, are you related?"

"Oh, for Pete's sake!" Ricki laughed. "She's my husband's sister. I have her new album—have you heard it?"

Ricki, a world-class marketing *maven*,* always had my back.

"Nope, but I'd love to," Chris said.

After the show that night, Ricki gave Chris a copy of *Enclosed*, my vinyl LP from 1983.

The next day on her way to the airport, Chris left the album in the cab.

A few days later, my phone in Columbus rang. EJ was cranky, and I'm pretty sure my garbage disposal was broken. I had been rushing to prepare dinner—never a pleasant time to call me on the phone.

"Hello!" I barked.

"Sally—this is Christine Lavin."

I nearly dropped the phone. *Christine Lavin?*

"I got your phone number from your sister-in-law, Ricki. I met her while touring and she gave me your album, but I left it in a cab. I'm wondering if you would send me another one?" Chris managed to expel this all in one breath.

Ricki had never mentioned meeting Chris, and I couldn't believe somebody had an interest in my work. Since having EJ, even *I* didn't have an interest in my work. But I decided to roll with it.

"It would be my pleasure to send you the album," I told Chris. "My sister-in-law is a hoot, isn't she?"

"I don't think you could have a bigger fan and supporter. By the way, I'm playing in Columbus in a few weeks. Wanna meet for lunch?"

"Yes to lunch—but you have to promise to let me treat." Now I was giddy.

"I promise, Sally! I'm looking forward to this." Chris gave me her New York address, along with her phone number and concert info. We shared cheerful good-byes and hung up.

I stood there in the middle of my kitchen, flummoxed by the entire conversation. Then I took a step, tripped over EJ's Fisher-Price Little People house, and sent minuscule furniture and plastic children skidding about the kitchen floor.

A few weeks later, Dan and I watched as Chris gave an amazing performance. Her songs, her stage presence—everything about her—was spectacularly entertaining. I was knocked out by her fabulous guitar playing, her comedic timing, and a voice that was simultaneously angelic and full of personality.

The next day, Chris and I met for our girls' lunch. I was not surprised to find that she was as warm and charming offstage as she had been onstage.

Chris had listened to my album and didn't understand why I wasn't "out there" touring. I told her that I loved performing, but after years of doing college shows and traveling the country, I had eventually burned out. My new life offered me great joy. Having a baby had truly changed my life, and someday I hoped to find my balance between performing and parenting.

"My mother dedicated her entire life to us kids," I told Chris, "and when we grew up, well, she just tipped right over and shattered. I don't want that to happen to me. So I still write all the time, and trust me, no one can take that away, but I can't travel like I used to right now."

"What about your husband? What if he watched your daughter so you can go back to performing again?"

Chris' sincere concern struck me. I certainly didn't have any mom-friends in EJ's playgroup who understood the lifestyle and creative passions of being a working musician.

"I'm sure Dan would love for me to get back to work," I said. "But I just haven't been able to put the pieces together." The logistics involved with performing overwhelmed me— where to gig, how to book the shows and then arrange the travel, who could watch EJ while Dan was in the studio—my heart raced just thinking about it. No way was I equipped to manage all of that while taking care of EJ.

SALLY FINGERETT

We finished our lunch and I drove her to the airport. We hugged good-bye, and I thanked her for her support and kindness. Chris was like a sun lamp. When her light shone on you, her warmth felt healing.

A few weeks later, Chris called.

"Sally, your song "Wild Berries" would be just perfect for this compilation of winter music I'm putting together for Rounder. I'd love to include your version from *Enclosed* on this project. Once people hear "Wild Berries," they'll want to hear more of you. What do you think?"

"I think . . . yes, please!"

And so, Christine included "Wild Berries" in her *On a Winter's Night* recording, and my life changed forever.

Three months later, in January of 1990, Chris called again.

"Sally, I wanna run something by you." She sounded rushed and excited. "My agent Kathy and I want to put together a group show—four women songwriters on stage together for just a handful of gigs, this summer. Do you want to join us?"

"Wait . . . what?" I couldn't believe what I was hearing.

"It would be you, me, Patty Larkin from Boston, and Megon McDonough from Chicago. We'd do eight or nine shows at clubs. Do you think you might be able to get sitters?"

"Chris, seriously? I'll have to talk to Dan and get back to you."

"You better!" Chris said. "Make it work, girlfriend!"

After EJ had been born, my every little mood brought about a song. When that mood had passed, I had a something to show for it. Now, Chris was offering me an opportunity to take these new songs out of the house and perform them in places I could never have dreamed of performing before. Here was the most gracious invitation from the most gracious performer—whose career was in the best place ever—to share a stage with her. It would only be eight or nine shows. I had to jump in with both feet.

As a professional musician *and* a husband, Dan was thrilled, and agreed that we would work it out, no matter what. And that's what we did.

In August 1990, Chris, Patty Larkin, Megon McDonough, and I met in Chicago for our first show. The next day we headed west and performed in Boulder, Salt Lake City, and Seattle. We ended that leg of the tour at the Great American Music Hall in San Francisco.

Together on stage, we performed round-robin-style—each woman took a turn in the spotlight, singing her own original songs. After our second or third night, we effortlessly began riffing and improvising harmonies together. Not since my Buffalo Gal bluegrass days had I felt this heady mix of musical, spiritual and social camaraderie. Patty, Meg, and Chris lovingly shared their talents, and through their friendship, I found the acceptance I didn't know I'd been searching for.

On the next leg of the tour, we played in Philadelphia, Club Passim in Boston, the Bottom Line in New York City, and finished off our adventure at the Birchmere in Alexandria, Virginia.

We were having the time of our lives, but we weren't making any real money. Our airline tickets and hotel room bills were paid with our own gig dough. Chris suggested that we record our last show at the Birchmere, in the hopes of making a little money by selling the recording at our (hopefully) future shows. That night, we asked the club's sound engineer if he would help us out. Without too much fanfare, he slid a tape into his fancy gear. At the end of the night, he gave us the recording.

Chris brought the tape to Amerisound and we spent a week together in Columbus, editing twenty live songs down to a fifteen-song collection. Later that year, Rounder Records would release the cassette (and then the CD).

But, before that could happened, we needed to name the recording. Chris remembered my song, "Do Me, Show Me, Buy Me, Love Me, Give Me" and suggested we go with something like that. We came up with *Buy Me, Bring Me, Take Me, Don't Mess My Hair,* but we wanted to add a tag line. We borrowed the California surfin' term from a scene in *American Graffiti*—where a teenage boy refers to a beautiful blond bombshell as a "bitchin' babe."

We were not four beautiful blond bombshells—but we could dream.

We settled on *Buy Me, Bring Me, Take Me, Don't Mess My Hair . . . Life According to Four Bitchin' Babes.*

And so the group was born.

It was delicious to arrive home from touring and smush my family. Throughout the tour, I had yearned for Dan and EJ. However, I didn't look forward to getting back to the kitchen.

To me, performing with the Babes had been a license to sleep in and eat out.

My kitchen missed me more than I missed it. Dan was not a housekeeper by any means. The remnants of his efforts were everywhere. My first morning home, I stubbed my toe on an enormous mound of rock-hard cereal. (To this day, I'm not sure if it was a pile of shredded wheat or Cream of Wheat—maybe both?) Whatever it was, the heap of mush had dried and cemented itself to the linoleum floor in the kitchen.

I simply retreated to my usual and customary coping mechanism. I grabbed my guitar and wrote this song.

SONG: BREAKFAST DISHES

Breakfast dishes, how I wishes
Someone would do all my dishes
All we had was cereal, Cream of Wheat, it's terminal
All those globs, combustible on breakfast dishes
He forgot to strain the juice
Now I'm chiseling the pulp loose
Sandpaper—that's what I'll use on breakfast dishes
Morning coffee clears the mind
But what to do with coffee grinds?
I'll use 'em twice, just saves time from breakfast dishes
Scrambled eggs in a frying pan
Little bit of cheese, mushrooms from a can
You ain't never, never, gonna see ham on breakfast dishes
Coffee cake, my favorite thing, Entenmann's, my heart sings
A sugar buzz—and I take wing from breakfast dishes
Breakfast dishes, how I wishes
Someone would do all my dishes
Private dinner for two, late last night

I served first-class victuals to Mr. Right
We left the table—we didn't touch a bite
VOILÀ, now they're breakfast dishes
Breakfast dishes, how I wishes
Someone would do all my dishes

After dining at wonderful restaurants while on the road with the Babes, I found reentry into my seven-by-twelve-foot galley kitchen difficult. However, touring with these crazy-funny women helped me make peace with my inner sarcastic biatch. I found it a very satisfying challenge to get out of my own head and reroute my naggy-rants and turn them into songs. I felt a surge of creativity and wrote songs that blended Old-Solo-Touring Me with New-Bitchin'-Babe Me.

This blending, however, could not be done in the kitchen. Just sayin'.

SONG: *TAKE ME OUT TO EAT*

I'm sitting in my kitchen, ooh, I'm wishin'
They'd love my cookin' or they'd quit their bitchin'
Gonna put my foot down, make him take me uptown
Dress like a debutante, go to a restaurant
Baby, take me out, baby, take me out to eat

I want a white cloth linen and a cool pressed napkin
A zinfandel from an organic vineyard
Where they've got Evian on-on-on every table
They let you sit and linger, long as your butt is able
Baby, take me out, baby, take me out to eat

Don't wanna hit the Hut—don't wanna slam no Mac
Don't wanna run for the border
Don't you give my no Kentucky Fried yech
I ain't no seafood lover
Don't want no chili dog, no pizza burger
Baby, your baby will not be drivin' though
Unless they've got a five-star review

I wanna leave my lipstick on fine bone china
Gimme decaf espresso, don't want no insomnia
Drink my water from a sparkling crystal
Get a monkey in a tux running to my signal
Baby, take me out, baby, take me out to eat

They got squid and leeks—I see those grouper cheeks
How about that garlic veal?
Can't we put aside our politics for just one meal?

They've got free-range potatoes, braised with a mango
Garnished with a twenty-dollar tomato
I don't care if it's tasty, don't care if it's good
I want you spending money—I think you should
Baby, take me out, baby, take me out to eat
You deserve a break today
So get up and get away—and take me out to eat!

Chapter Four

LITTLE GIRL

PLEASE WAIT...

FOR ME

LITTLE GIRL
PLEASE WAIT

Why is it that women love shoes? I don't understand why neuroscientists haven't gotten to this yet. We all call it "the shoe gene". . . so why isn't this on the hit list for geneticists?

I did not get the shoe gene. I couldn't care less what my feet look like, just as long as they hold the rest of me upright. For my money, it's about my personal surroundings.

This is why I know I am a card-carrying carrier of the housewares gene.

I do empathize with the emotional satisfaction my gal pals find in a new pair of pumps or stilettos, but I am irresistibly drawn to high-thread-count, Egyptian-cotton bed linens, goose down duvets, and sturdy ironstone dishware.

My addiction to these things is otherworldly. During the January White Sales, my spirit is eerily summoned to the mall. I levitate above the crowds of pushy shoppers, floating up and over the discounted stacks of Martex sheets and shams and past shelves heaving with Cannon and Fieldcrest bath towels. I am mesmerized by matching rugs and toilet seat covers. Overpowered by my own exquisite delirium, I meditate on shower curtains, toothbrush holders, and designer Kleenex box covers. I skippy-dance toward the kitchen section to fantasize over KitchenAid mixers.

But nothing does it to me like . . . dishes. I have a sick thing for dishes, for anything that rests on a table and sits under food. After years of whining and *hokking,* * I became the lucky repository for my family's unwanted china. I have everyone's, I have all of it, and I respect the legacy.

Aunt Lillian's "China with the Cherries" arrived first. She began her marriage with service for eighteen, but after forty years, it had been reduced to service for twelve if one person went without soup. Each elegant place setting contains eight pieces, making this a very formal collection. The plates come in three sizes: dinner, salad, and bread. The bowls come in two sizes: fruit cup and soup. The pièces de résistance are the beautiful juice and water glasses that are not made of glass, but of china.

After four decades, Aunt Lill had grown tired of her dining room's maroon and olive-green color scheme. The décor had been originally based on the "China with the Cherries." Buying new dishes meant she could repaint the walls and change the carpeting and finally replace every textile and accessory, from tablecloths to napkin rings.

So, after she realized that her sons weren't interested in the "China with the Cherries," she gave them all to me.

Next came my mother's "The Good Dishes" dishes. She heard about Aunt Lill's dining room do-over and had to copy her, of course. Shortly before my parents headed to Florida for the winter, Mom decided to leave the china in the Midwest—with me.

Her explanation went like this: "Sally, I might as well enjoy knowing you enjoy them, and G–d knows I don't need to *schlep** them down to Delray, and really, if I dragged them down with me, then I'd have to cook and serve on them. Then we'd have to invite people over and entertain, and I don't wanna feel guilty every time we go out to a restaurant that I'm not home cooking and serving fancy. And PS, how do people cook in that heat? I should leave them with you. Just try not to break any. Okay, Sally Girl?"

She spat this out in one breath. My mother required an audience when thinking and processing out loud. As her daughter, I was quite accomplished at following her train of thought, no matter how far off the rails she went.

My mother decided that my big sister would someday inherit "The Good Ring," and I would take early possession of "The Good Dishes." I was elated beyond measure. Adorned with tiny, flowing, pink-and-green flowers and gold-plated rims, this delicate ivory-colored set looks Victorian. With those painted flowers and shiny rims, these dishes are not allowed inside a microwave or a dishwasher, which means that "The Good Dishes" rarely come out of the breakfront—since they involve too much sink time. With matching serving platters, casserole bowls, and salt-and-pepper shakers, these dishes are magnificent and lovely and now . . . they belonged to me.

When I asked my mother where they came from, she said, "This set is hand-painted, and I couldn't tell you what it cost back in 1945—I got them from Sears, back when they were a really fancy department store, and you could buy fresh-made peanut brittle on your way out the door. Now, it's a place you go to buy kids' gym shoes, *drecky** clothes, and hardware for the garage."

Sears? Who knew?

Fifteen years before any of this china fell into my lap, pardon the visual, I had purchased my own "Plain White China" service for ten. My husband Dan and I had been radical hippie musicians when we married in 1979, and we jokingly told everyone that we were registered for gifts at the Honda dealer. After a few years of marriage, we had the resources to begin our own dining room legacy, and I bought the "Plain White." But I really had no emotional attachment to my boring china. So when Aunt Lill bequeathed her "China with the Cherries," and my mother did a drive-by on her way to Florida to drop off "The Good Dishes," I went nuts.

Dan also went nuts: "Why on earth do we need all that china? And, by the way, when was the last time you made dinner for company?!"

Ouch.

He was right, and I suggested hosting Thanksgiving. I would invite the relatives, knowing that all our womenfolk would quickly ask, "What can I bring?" Everyone would make her specialty, and I would roast a turkey. Voilà, a dinner party.

That Thursday morning unfolded beautifully. I meticulously followed my mother's instructions on how to cook the bird. The kitchen was bustling, and seven-year-old EJ was a wonderful helper. She peeled carrots, took out the trash, and *schlepped** stuff up from the basement. Then, rushing around the kitchen lost in my thoughts, I stepped on her. She didn't cry or whine but made a face I couldn't resist, so I set my daughter free to go play upstairs.

I moved into the dining room and shook out my mother's hand-me-down tablecloth. Next, I laid down the Kmart fake-lace cloth to camouflage the prior stains on my mom's old linen.

I put the candlesticks and a petite flower arrangement directly in the center.

Then I stood back and tripped on my own panic button.

Whose dishes should I use?

I was immobilized with terror. What was I thinking (or not thinking) to postpone this emotionally charged decision until the last minute? I must have been in ten kinds of denial to ignore the fact that—in my family—not using a beloved woman's dishes would cause her aging and blustery gray matter to boil over and spill onto her dinner plate.

If I used my mother's delicate pink-flowered set, Aunt Lill might understand, but Uncle Ralph would bark, "Where are those expensive dishes your aunt tossed away after forty years? I want to see them!" He was a boisterous guy who could turn thin air into a smoky cloud with an unlit cigar. But if I used Aunt Lill's "China with the Cherries," my mother would be off-the-charts offended. She had already asked me once if I had used the dishes. When I told her I was "saving them," her litany flew in on a broom.

"*Saving them?* For what? For who? Like they were in a passbook like money, you put the dishes in a bank? Or maybe you put them in the little safe deposit box where they make you sign your name and show your ID, and then they lead you into the little room and they set the bank table with your plates and saucers, and you look at them and think, oh, they're so pretty, I'm glad they're at the bank?"

When my mother's rants were seriously clever, this meant she was seriously pissed. She inhaled and continued.

"Listen, Sally Girl, my dishes aren't doing anybody any good just sitting in those padded china covers which, by the way, were handmade, and you should be careful with the zippers 'cause the lady who made them died, and you can't find this quality anymore, so go slow."

I *had* to use my mother's dishes. I *had* to use my Aunt Lill's dishes.

So I went for broke (enjoy the irony). I used *all three* sets. One place setting was Aunt Lill's, the next was my mother's, and the third was my Plain White, on and on around the table. I considered throwing in a place setting of my everyday Melmac plastic just for grins.

When I finished, the table looked awful.

I felt defeated and overwhelmed. But then my mood turned defiant. *So the table is* ongepotchket,* *so shoot me! Just don't shoot me while I'm holding these dishes!* I then turned hopeful. *Maybe everyone would think the table was cute and charming?*

I grabbed some aspirin and double-checked my wine supply.

Soon enough, the guests arrived with hugs and kisses. After a flurry of hellos and reports of traffic, coats were hung up and covered dishes beelined their way into my overcrowded oven.

"Mom," I said, "would'ja holler for EJ to come down?"

"Sure," she said. My mother loved to holler. "Elizabeth Julian! Grandpa and I are waiting for you to come and smush us and hug us, and I wanna see how you've grown, and what are you doing with your hair these days, and also, bring me a report card, and make sure you've got your shoes on?"

My mother had to sit down after this high-volume delivery at full throttle.

Down came my precious little girl to meet us in the dining room.

I smelled her before I saw her. I couldn't name the wafting fragrance, but it was reminiscent of the inside of my *Tante** Faigie's good purse. Clearly, EJ had been upstairs mixing perfumes and rummaging through my clothes, makeup, and jewelry. Hot-red lipstick, applied way beyond the lip line, lent her a scary circus clown vibe. She had given herself Cleopatra's eyes with my eyeliner or, possibly, her own black Crayola crayon. I couldn't be sure. Rouge was everywhere, from her cheeks on down to the knees of her jeans. She had taken off her everyday undershirt and replaced it with my black silk teddy. Shuffling and scuffling, she inched her way toward us, falling sideways out of my best high heels. She sounded like a wind chime, jingling in half a dozen of my better necklaces and bangle bracelets.

My daughter looked one part mischievous and adorable child, and one part streetwalker.

EJ stopped and studied the mishmashy table. With her little girl hands on her little girl hips, she said, with just enough bitchy, "Mom, do we *have* to eat off this scary-old-breakable stuff?"

I froze, horrified.

The women all turned their heads to stare at the table top, and then looked back at EJ. They couldn't figure out what to address first—the table or the kid.

They chose EJ.

They gathered around her to ooh and aah, clamoring for hugs and kisses.

"Look at the fancy lady!" said Aunt Lill, bending over for a kiss.

"Give Grandma a hug." My mother grabbed EJ. "Look how you've grown! But just maybe not enough for that top?"

Yah think?

Uncle Ralph, my favorite cynic, gave her a squeeze and said, "*Kutchkie,** you smell like a broad I used to know during the war."

I dropped down into a dining room chair. I was crestfallen, and the weight of this moment made gravity impossible to deal with. But I had to rally.

Time to divert, redirect, and turn this mess around.

"EJ," I said, "did you hear Grandma ask to see your report card?"

While her report card was upstairs in an envelope, *my* report card stood there half-naked in my private fancy underwear and jewelry, proving that I failed at both child rearing *and* table setting.

"Gramma, Gramma, don't move, I'm gonna get my school stuff to show you, I'll be right back." EJ turned and slipped one more time in my shoes.

"Hey, doll," I barked as she limped out of the dining room. "You wanna put on some regular-people clothes in case we decide to go out and play?"

"Okay!" She headed for the stairs.

I wanted to follow her up the stairs, get in my bed, and hide under my 600-thread-count cotton duvet cover. Being a negligent mother and a lousy daughter at the same time had wiped me out.

Maybe it's the wisdom of age and their years of experience raising children, but my maternal mentors recognized my embarrassment. They themselves had struggled in their youth to simultaneously be the perfect mother, daughter, and hostess, under the eyes of their own female elders.

I was immediately grabbed, hugged, and smushed by all, like I'd just been rushed by a sorority.

"She's so cute, Sally, what a personality!" said my lovely Aunt Lill.

"So you've got to find a better hiding place for the top, Sally Girl. It looks expensive," my mother warned.

Even Uncle Ralph laughed. "That kid came outta you?"

In the end, the meal was fabulous and the evening remained festive. My *ongepotchket** Thanksgiving table was easily over-shadowed by a seven-year-old covered in thirty-dollars-worth of Estée Lauder base and *shmeared** in matte lipstick that wouldn't fade away till mid-December.

However, hearing EJ verbalize her disdain for my precious heirlooms as "scary-old-breakable stuff" startled me. While her little-girl free spirit twirled and danced for company, I sat there stunned, realizing that my daughter would mature and pursue her own possibilities and passions, and disregard mine.

Then, for a fleeting moment, I was off the hook.

SONG: *LITTLE GIRL, PLEASE WAIT*

She was the one who kept you so young
Now she's growing
You're caught by surprise by the look in her eyes
You know what she's knowing
You sit back and stare into the space she leaves there
Your arms are so empty
She's borrowed your pearls
She wants to take on the world
You're the one not ready, you say
Little girl, please wait, little girl, please wait
Little girls will sigh, they might cry, but they must wait

There's so much to tell her
But you can no longer hold her
You pray in a whisper
You know it's only fair that she go through her share
Heartache will find her
Blindly you trust that she will grow up
In spite of what you tell her
What she must do is uncover the truth
There's no happily ever after—you say
Little girl, please wait, little girl, please wait
Little girls will sigh, they might cry, but they must wait

She's part of your history—her future's a mystery
She'll need to find levity as she takes her place
She helps set the table, antique lace and sterling silver
Her grandmother's china
You tell her the tales, women strong, women frail
Like hand-me-downs and heirlooms
A chip in the cup, a stain on the cloth, a useful existence
Whether she likes them or not
Someday, they'll be hers by default
They're a gift, they're a prison
They're for little girls who wait, little girl, please wait
Little girls, they sigh, they might cry, but they must wait

Will she seek loyalty inside family boundaries?
She might defy gravity, and just pull away
Little girl, please wait, little girls, we sigh, we might cry
But we must wait

POT OF GOLD

Since kindergarten, EJ had loved going to school and had always been a happy and successful student. However, one day in the third grade, I retrieved her from the bus stop afterschool and found her with a tear-stained face and a slump in her little-girl posture.

"EJ, honey, you look sad," I said softly. "Can you tell mommy what's up?"

She shook her head, with her lips pursed together and her eyes struggling to hold back tears. We walked the half block home in silence. When we reached our house, I opened the door and pushed the issue.

"Seriously, sweetheart," I continued, "kids are supposed to tell their mommies when something's not right, so we can fix it. Can you tell me?"

"Mommy . . ." The dam broke. EJ spoke and cried at the same time, releasing her words and pain together. "I was on the playground at recess, and Beth Kirk called me a dork, and she told me that I wasn't supposed to wear sneakers with a dress, *(sniff-sniff)* and that my socks were the wrong color for the dress, *(sleeve-to-the-nose wipe)* and that I was going to Hell 'cuz a man named Christ isn't my saver."

"Oh, I see." I picked her up with a squeezy hug, walked over to the couch, and placed her on my lap. In my own childhood, I had been checked for horns by an occasional racist—but that was back in the late 1950s.

"Listen, baby," I started, "I can promise you a few things. First, because your family is Jewish, and Beth's family is Christian, we will spend our lives on earth believing in different ideas and doing different things. She has her church and we have our synagogue. What her family believes in is very real and true for Beth. Just like what Mommy and Daddy and Grandma and Grandpa believe in is very real and true for us. There's plenty of room on this earth for all the people to have their own ideas and religions and prayers. Are you following me?"

I looked into her eyes, long and hard, to express my seriousness—and also, to see if she had glazed over yet.

"Yeah, Mommy, but she made me feel bad. I thought my socks were pretty."

Oh, I see we're done with the Christ thing, and now we're on to fashion.

"Sweetheart, your socks are fabulous and beautiful, and you have the right to make sock choices. This is America and don't you forget it."

I wanted to crawl into bed and weep. I found these kinds of confrontations exhausting. Of course, I expected EJ to occasionally find herself excluded from a birthday party or a playground game—but I had no tolerance for religious prejudices.

I held my tongue the rest of the day, but inside my head, I imagined the tirade I would have loved to present to my daughter:

Listen, my beautiful and 100% pure Grade-A Jewess, complete with baby-naming papers, trust me, you will never land in either Beth Kirk's heaven or Beth Kirk's hell, so don't you worry.

I dreaded having to write a note to report this event. But what if Beth Kirk was just the first child to throw these sentiments EJ's way? I had to find out if this issue would be ongoing.

Then next day, EJ took my note in a sealed envelope and gave it to her teacher—a lovely (and Jewish) Mrs. Greenberg—who in turn, handed it over to the school's principal—a very strict and determined (and African-American) Ms. Banks.

Ms. Banks called me straight away to assure me that, as principal, she would handle this directly. She suggested I wait, and someone would get back to me. *Oh boy, she sounds as serious as a heart attack.* I nervously wondered if I had done the right thing.

Or would I just become known as "that tightly wound Jewish lady"?

A few days later, Beth's mom called.

"Sally? This is Joan Kirk." She had a warm, polite voice.

"Hi, Joan," I replied cautiously. "Thank you for calling."

"I'm so sorry about what happened. I wanted you to know that Beth will be apologizing to EJ at school tomorrow. Also, I'm hoping that you'll accept my apology. We had some out-of-town guests last weekend, and I believe Beth picked this up from one of their little boys. My husband and I had a lengthy chat with her, and I'm sure the issue will be put to rest."

The knot in my *kishkes** loosened. This scenario was easy to forgive. "Thank you so much. I totally get how kids pick up stuff—and it's always a surprise what they remember."

"I thought of something that might help the girls move past Beth's verbal boo-boo," Joan continued. "Why not bring EJ to the next Girl Scout Brownie meeting and see if she'd like to join? She'll know a few of the girls from class, and maybe she'd like to cultivate more friends outside of school."

"That's a lovely idea," I said. "When EJ comes home tomorrow, I'll let her tell me how it worked out between her and Beth, and then I'll see if she'd like to go to the meeting."

After we hung up, I took deep breath and thanked everybody's' G–d for making this go well.

Joining the Brownies proved to be a tremendous success for EJ. The kerfuffle between her and Beth was quickly forgotten and they became fast friends.

Over the next few months, I watched as a group of second- and third-grade girls coalesced into a finely tuned Brownie-machine. They volunteered to collect toys and jackets to benefit the less fortunate and held a children's book drive for a pre-school, all the while earning badges as symbols of their effectiveness and success.

EJ remained the only Jewish girl in the group. As winter approached and everyone was buzzing about Christmas, EJ and I treated the troop to a Chanukah party. In place of the weekly Brownie meeting, everyone gathered at our house. We showed the girls how we light the menorah candles and sing our blessings. We told stories of our temple's destruction and the magic oil that burned for eight days when the tiny amount should have lasted only one night. We served potato pancake *latkes** and fried jelly rolls, a custom that represents the abundance of the oil. We taught the girls to play our dreidel-spinning game, and gave them pennies to use as the center pot prize. At the end of the party, EJ and I sent each child home with a gift bag full of miniature dreidels (complete with instructions for the parents) and Chanukah *gelt**—golden-foiled chocolate coins.

For several weeks following the party, appreciative parents called to thank us and tell us how their daughters had loved hearing the stories of our Jewish history and learning our Chanukah customs. Several parents also mentioned how thoughtful we had been to invite their children into our world during such a hectic holiday season.

EJ and I explained that this was called a *mitzvah**—a good deed—and we thanked *them* for allowing us to do this mitzvah of sharing our family's traditions.

By the following spring, EJ had become a passionate Brownie, with her uniform covered in accomplishment badges. All the girls were excited for the big annual pre-summer camping overnight in the woods. "Camping" for these girls meant sleeping in a lodge-style cabin with bunk beds, an attached bathroom with all the amenities, and a full kitchen with an eating area.

I had never been a Brownie, but I had spent a night or two in the woods, and this Brownie trip sounded like a hoot-and-a-half. I volunteered to be one of the chaperones.

With ten girls and four moms, we caravanned thirty-five miles to the Girl Scout campground. We drove down a bumpy gravel road and parked our four vehicles next to our assigned cabin. As soon as we stopped the cars' engines, the girls bolted toward the cabin and claimed their bunk beds, shouting and hurling sleeping bags and knapsacks everywhere.

Joan and I dragged in the groceries while the two Brownie-Troop-Leader-Moms lugged plastic milk crates full of art and nature supplies into the main room and hollered for the girls to gather and start their projects.

Within minutes, everyone was spread out on the floor with crayons, Elmer's Glue, and Popsicle sticks. The Brownie-Moms guided the girls in building a Popsicle-stick replica of the very cabin we were staying in.

Joan Kirk began putting away the groceries and organizing the kitchen. Since I was in charge of bedtime and had no chores at that moment, I joined Joan.

"What's for dinner?" I pried open a brown grocery bag and saw cans of Campbell's tomato soup.

"Pot-of-Gold—it's a Girl Scout tradition." Joan almost saluted as she said this.

"Pot-of-Gold, huh? Never heard of it." I loved kid recipes and looked forward to learning something new.

"It's a blast. The girls will pour the ten cans of tomato soup, along with equal amounts of milk, into a camp soup pot. While that's heating up, the girls take blocks of Velveeta cheese and . . ."

"Wait—Velveeta?"

"Yep, can you stand it? Velveeta!" Joan kept going. "Anyway, the girls place a cherry-sized hunk of Velveeta cheese inside one of those Pillsbury quick-bake biscuits from the tube-can over there, and squeeze the dough around the cheese. Then, they'll plop the biscuit-covered cheese balls into the boiling tomato soup. Everything simmers for about twenty minutes on a low flame . . . and you've got your Pot-of-Gold!"

"How, um, *interesting.*" I paused, unsure what to say next due to several important considerations. First, I doubted that EJ would eat the Pot-of-Gold. She suffered from lactose intolerance, and might take a taste out of curiosity, but wouldn't be able to tolerate more than a spoonful.

As for me, a raging germophobe, the thought of eating Pillsbury's version of Play-Doh, manhandled by ten little girls, and then dipped in a cream soup that had been sitting out for hours, sent me over the edge. This dish could not have sounded more disgusting, and I desperately needed to soft-pedal my way out of this alien-cheesy-tomato-apocalypse.

"Um, Joan? Unfortunately, EJ has issues with dairy, and well, hmmm, I've got to watch my cholesterol," I said, trying hard not to sound like the liar I was. "No one's gonna care if we don't eat from the Pot-of-Gold, will they?"

Joan looked over her shoulder to make sure no one would hear her as she leaned in and whispered to me.

"Puh-lease, are you kidding? No one in their right mind eats this stuff. We've got peanut butter and jelly as alternatives. This Pot-of-Gold is kid crap!"

Crisis averted.

For our dinner, the girls put together a lovely banquet-style table with paper plates and folded paper napkins. Once we all sat down, they ravenously plowed through the entire Pot-of-Gold. Slurping and splattering, they finished every drop of the tomato soup sauce.

As EJ made her way through her second peanut butter and jelly sandwich, the girls were curious why she hadn't even tasted the Pot-of-Gold.

"Cheese argues with me," she told them.

"Honey," I corrected, "don't you mean it disagrees with you?"

"Yeah, sometimes cheese disagrees, and sometimes it argues, depending on how mad the cheese gets in my stomach. But, for sure, my stomach and peanut butter love each other!"

From our chairs, we moms directed the after-dinner clean up. These ten little-girl-bossypants all wanted to sweep the floor with the brooms that were too big to handle. No one wanted to dry the dishes, so we had a system—if you wanted a turn at sweeping, you took a turn at drying. Everyone agreed, and after a flurry of kids tripping over one another, the place was, hmmm, put away—sort of.

With an hour left before sunset, we laced up our walking shoes and bundled up for a hike in woods. The late spring air, mild and windless, allowed the two experienced Brownie-Moms to take their time, sharing their brilliant leaf-knowledge and courageous worm-holding expertise.

As we trudged through greenery, the girls asked about the forests, the ozone layer, and the animals. The two Brownie-Moms had already taught the girls how to improve their ecological footprint by not wasting water during our kitchen cleanup and by drawing on both sides of the paper before discarding their artwork. Here in the forest, they learned just what it was they were protecting.

"G–d really did a nice job with this forest, didn't he?" Sarah said. At almost nine, she was the first of the group to have braces, poor thing.

"Yep, he did," said one of the Brownie-Moms. Her brilliant talent was seizing every opportunity to spiritually guide the girls, without using religion. "Just think of all the different creatures of the forest, and the different ways they eat and build their homes, and all the work that goes into getting along as they share the same forest."

I ran up to this Brownie-Mom, grabbed her by the elbow, and whispered, "I adore you!"

The sun began to dip behind the forest trees and we turned around to head indoors for bedtime. We stepped up the pace, marching and chanting, "*Left, left, left-right-left, I left my wife and forty-eight children alone in the kitchen in starving condition with nothing but gingerbread left, left, left-right-left.*" In a blink, we were back inside the warm cabin, where Joan had stayed behind to build a fire in the fireplace.

I proceeded to police the tooth brushing and face washing. I marveled at how quickly the girls put on their pj's and moved about their tasks. They brushed and washed and primped and tried not to giggle too much lest someone take their place at the sink. I stood there, impressed by their cooperation.

"Mom?" EJ cornered me by a toilet stall. "I told the girls that because you sing songs for your work, you'd sing for us if we were good. Isn't everyone good? Aren't we all really good?"

I couldn't resist her, ever.

"EJ, I'd love to. Let's get everyone in their sleeping bags, and I'll make you proud."

Ten little girls scurried to their chosen bunks and slid into their slippery sleeping bags. After a few tossed pillows and teddy bears, everyone settled down with just a few shushes.

I started singing "This Land Is Your Land," and though they were tuckered out from their full day of adventures, they began to sing along softly. After a few more choruses, the singing slowly quieted down, replaced by the rhythm of mouth breathing and little girly snores.

At that moment, I realized why I had picked "This Land is Your Land." I have always loved this Woody Guthrie song because it speaks of the basic human rights all people are entitled to. Everyone deserves to live full and happy lives, here in our country's wondrous and expansive geography. No matter our skin color, our religious beliefs, or even the socks we choose to wear on any given day, we are equal in our responsibilities to protect and take care of this land, AND each other.

In this room, ten little girls slept on the promise of doing just that.

WHEN I WAKE UP FROM THIS NIGHT

Raising children while trying to instill a sense of righteousness, fairness, and soulfulness, in addition to the basics of hygiene, has been an outrageous challenge.

After her first Girl Scout camping trip, EJ's awareness of the world around her and her role in this world quickly became tremendously important to her. She became a devotee of every children's book and PBS program that showed concern for the environment and its well-being.

One day, after picking her up from school, I rolled down my car window and spit my gum into a grassy field. EJ screamed and scared the crap out of me. When I pulled over to see what was wrong, I saw her crying in the backseat.

"Mom, I can't believe you did that!' she scolded me. "A bird is going to eat your gum and choke on it and die, and then little birds won't have a mommy and it will be your fault."

Stupid me, I had always assumed that gum was biodegradable, and I never once thought a critter might croak after swallowing a small piece of Dubble Bubble. I apologized up and down to EJ. I promised to put my gum in a tissue next time and to never do anything like that again, ever.

That night, after her bath and tooth brushing, EJ climbed into bed for our nighttime ritual. We read a storybook together, and after the last page was turned, we began our nightly game of "Tell Me What to Dream, Mommy (or Daddy or Grandma or Grandpa)."

In this game, the grown-up du jour starts telling EJ a story, and with her eyes closed, she imagines the story in her mind. After a few sentences, the grown-up du jour stops speaking, gives her a kiss, and says, "Take it away EJ!"

Alone in her bed, EJ silently runs the story in her head, knowing it's going to lead her to a great dream. She only needs to fall asleep to find it.

On this night, for "Tell Me What to Dream," I started a story about a bird-mommy and bird-daughter who made it their life's work to announce to all the other bird-families that any and all chewing gum found on the ground was poison. No flying bird should stop and peck at the gum, but should stay away and go look for yummy worms and berries instead.

This news was very important. The bird-mommy and the bird-daughter helped all the bird-families make posters and write stories for bird newspapers. TV bird-announcers interrupted bird-TV shows to spread the news and make sure everyone understood. It needed to be a very big bird-deal.

That night, I woke up to the fact that this was her world I was living in, and I better behave. Or else.

SONG:
WHEN I WAKE UP FROM THIS NIGHT

Every night at eight o'clock
We lay our heads for pillow talk
Mommy, won't you tell me true
Let me ask these things of you
When I wake up from this night, will there be a morning
Will the sun be shining bright, what will I find dawning
When I wake up from this night, will there be a forest
Will the selfish, greedy ones take the big trees from us
When I wake, will the rain stop coming
When I wake, will the sun stop shining
When I wake, will the gardens growing
Stop from loving me—tell me please

When I wake up from this night, will I be awakened
By sirens from a nuclear site, accidents can happen
When I wake up from this night, will there be tomorrow
Will the earth have had enough, enough of all this sorrow
When I wake, will there be oceans
When I wake, will I still be frightened
When I wake, will there be horizons
That I cannot see—tell me please
Who on earth is gonna make it right
When I wake up from this night

Here I lie, right beside my daughter
In my soul, I've journeyed to protect her
More than that, it's my job to teach her
How to love this land—I take her hand, I say

When you wake up from this night
Yes, there'll be a morning

The sun's gonna be shining bright
With new ideas dawning
And when you wake up from this night
We'll start a new beginning
We'll show the earth her due respect
Create new laws for living
When you wake, we're gonna work together
When you wake, we're gonna start all over
When you wake, we'll take back forever
We will rise up strong—we don't have long

When you wake up from this night, oh darlin'
YOU AND I are gonna make it right
When we wake up from this night

DISCLAIMER: Funny, I never doubted EJ's riff on the topic of birds and gum. In later years, I checked Snopes.com and learned that it's still up in the air, pardon the pun. Let's face it—between humans stepping on it, and animals possibly getting hurt by it, chewed-up and discarded gum really shouldn't hit the ground.

MOMMY'S SOUND IS GONE

"**M**y mommy can't come to the phone right now . . . her sound is gone."

My eight-year-old daughter had found a way to speak to people on the phone when I could not.

I could not speak, I could not sing. I would sneeze and I couldn't even give you an "achoo."

A few months earlier, in February 1994, the Four Bitchin' Babes had a gig in Maine. While waiting patiently at the gate at the Columbus airport, I suddenly became cold and sweaty. The air felt stale. I knew this feeling. *Really? The flu? On tour?*

This sickness fell on me like a veil. I felt a grip tighten around my neck, like thumbs pressing into my voice box. I tried to clear my throat, but there was a thickness in there that wouldn't budge. I went for a cup of tea, something hot to soothe and loosen up the disgusting yuk. Then my head fogged up, my sinuses shut down, and I knew I was in trouble.

And in my business, there is no sick pay and, as I would learn later, no workers' comp either.

When I met up with the Babes at the Portland airport, I was hesitant to share this irritating malady. We'd had a special agreement when touring, which stipulated:

No mommies (Do not expect your fellow Babes to mother you.)

No husbands (No husbands will serve as mouthpieces for any Babe.)

No babies (Please check all children at the departure gate of your originating airport.)

I didn't want to bother them or annoy anyone with my misery. For me, this was the sorority I was never asked to join at the college I never went to. We were best friends from childhood who didn't meet until our late thirties. All four of us had our own struggles, on top of the demands of travel.

But, minutes after retrieving our luggage, the Babes noticed I was suffering. They bombarded me with homeopathic herbs and spices, tripping over themselves to come to my aid. That night, I warbled and coughed my way through the show. I was so miserable that death would have been an upgrade.

That Sunday we all headed home. As soon as I walked through the door, I put together a chicken soup and left it to cook on the stove all night. When I awoke on Monday—my sound was gone.

I was diagnosed with paralyzed vocal cords, a mysterious illness that even the best ENT specialists couldn't figure out. The most brilliant and highly recommended doctor at The Ohio State University's hospital could only say, "Gee, so sorry. If your voice doesn't return in a year, we can do an implant of sorts, so that in the very least, you might possibly return to speaking."

The official term was idiopathic nerve paralysis. I had been taking care of myself. I could not make sense of this vocal cord tragedy. There was nothing anyone could do but wait and see if the condition reversed itself.

I was living every singer's worst nightmare.

I tried to be productive. I learned to communicate via computer. I became an email *maven*,* which allowed me to correspond with my family and conduct business with the Babes. Upon realizing I couldn't yell at my daughter, I printed out signs using huge bolded words, with directions like **"BRUSH YOUR TEETH"** in eighteen-point letters. Then, in italics, I added the softer, kinder afterthought: *"Don't forget to rinse."* Occasionally, I'd hand her hushed little secrets in barely readable six-point type saying, "I love you, don't worry about me, we'll get Mommy's sound back."

I tried a plethora of holistic modalities—psychotherapy, reflexology, Rolfing, shiatsu, and some kind of woo-woo light therapy where I sat in front of digitally manipulated light bulbs that finessed and altered my energy on a cellular level. I also tried a hypnotherapist who specialized in past-life regression. I did acupressure, acupuncture, liver cleanses, colon cleanses, and ionic footbaths, where I sat with my feet in water in order to remove heavy metals through the skin of my tootsies. I studied with an Alexander Technique guru from South Africa, and a Feldenkrais Method specialist from Israel.

Nothing helped. My sound did not return.

During the course of my alternative therapies, I visited a lovely and magical massage therapist from Sandusky, Ohio, who dangled crystals over my chakras and said, "Sally, your throat

193

chakra is fine. It's your heart chakra that's lousy. What is it you can't say? What's stuck in your heart's voice that needs to come out?"

After that, I carried those words with me. They stuck in my *craw*. I spent months and months trying to listen to my own gut. I then realized . . . since I couldn't speak, I was being asked to listen—to everybody.

My own self included.

For ten months, I laid low. My biggest challenge was dealing with the sadness in the eyes of the people I loved. I wasn't in pain, but my loved ones were—for me.

During this time, Christine Lavin, my dearest Babe pal, sent my song *Home Is Where the Heart Is* to the amazing Peter, Paul and Mary. As social activists, they felt this song of tolerance and compassion fit right into their repertoire, and they recorded it for their *LifeLines* CD for Warner Bros.

Having Peter, Paul and Mary document a composition of mine was a game changer. This one accomplishment gave me the strength to keep chugging. Even without my voice, I felt like a real songwriter, authentic and established, all thanks to my Christine.

"What's stuck in your heart's voice that needs to come out?"

I carried that question with me constantly during my year without a voice. Instead of speaking, I watched, listened, and paid very close attention to the world around me. I began to see this illness as a blessing.

One morning, a few months before my fortieth birthday, the words that had been stuck in my heart made themselves known.

They came quietly, with no thundering clouds or choirs of angels heralding the news.

Just a burst of the unknowable becoming known.

Suddenly, in our kitchen breakfast nook, alone with my morning coffee, I began to cry. I cried as if I were watching my own life come to an end. But my life did not end— it would only change. My marriage to Dan, however, would end two years later.

FYI: Two weeks after that moment in the breakfast nook when my inner voice freed itself, my voice returned to me. *Emess.**

During the next two years, Dan and I did everything possible to save our marriage. By the time we separated, we had been in couples counseling on and off for eight of our seventeen years together. We were no strangers to "marriage is hard work." But we had married young and quickly and . . . young.

Dan and I remain wonderful friends, and he is devoted to EJ. To this very day, we *still* work together— in fact, we spent hours and hours in the Amerisound studio working on the *Mental Yentl* CD that goes with this book. He will be in my life forever.

Our marriage was over in 1996.

In 1998, he produced the tracks for this song.

SONG: *PRIVATE PLENTY*
Co-written with folk legend, Tom Paxton

CHORUS
I lay me down, surrounded by the glory
I lay me down, surrounded by the glory
I lay me down, surrounded by the glory
Of my own private plenty

There's a rock and there's a hard place
Where everybody spends some time
Cold rain on a sad face
More worries on a troubled mind
I believe there's a secret place waiting deep within
You never know just what you'll find
You might discover peace of mind, when you lay down
CHORUS

We're all walking in the desert
Stumblin' underneath the sun
Suffering from the same hurts
Thinking we're the only one
Never knowing of that secret place waiting deep within
Never taking time to find just a little piece of mind
CHORUS

You know the world is bound to spin with or without you
Let it go, look deep within, what more can you do
But go lay down
CHORUS

Chapter Five

SWF W/KID
SEEKS SMOOTH

MY PORCH

Once the moving van left, my ten-year-old daughter, EJ, and I crossed the threshold of our new, but used, seventy-year-old house.

School had just ended for summer vacation, and we had a lot to accomplish before her day camp program began in two weeks. We had furniture to arrange, closets and drawers to fill, a kitchen to stock, and of course, some good, old-fashioned mother-and-daughter hissy fits to throw when we veered off task.

EJ and I worked hard each day, lugging and hauling, unpacking and organizing. Late in the afternoon, after hours and hours of good, productive work, we would stop and reward ourselves by going outside to enjoy our new neighborhood. EJ rode her bike up and down the block, while I collapsed in a lawn chair, overwhelmed with exhaustion and stunned by the realization that being the sole owner of this house was going to be a fairly significant gig.

Within a few short days, my happy-go-lucky daughter slid right in with the kids on our street. Meanwhile, I found myself sucked into a vortex of lawn envy and became obsessed with yard work. I did my best to look like I knew a thing or two about nature, but instead, I trimmed the bushes too low, killed the grass, and accidentally dug up the roots of lily bulbs.

In spite of all this, I adored being outside and soon made friends as well. These gracious new neighbors found my lawn-care mistakes charming and offered tremendous support. They generously lent me everything from hoses and sprinklers to WeedWackers and shovels.

Upon hearing that I had purchased my own home, my girlfriends surprised me with the best housewarming/divorce gift ever—a complete set of tools from the Sears Craftsman Club.

I loved my presents—not just because they were shiny and new, but because these possessions gave me independence, which, during that first summer, was also shiny and new.

My girlfriends' insistence that I could do anything gave me a raging case of *get-out-of-my-way-I-can-handle-that*, and I took my tremendous hubris to the library and researched in the stacks. I quickly discovered helpful strangers illustrating the secrets of unclogging a garbage disposal, putting a new bulb in a toilet tank, and filling nail holes with flour and water. Mesmerized by do-it-yourself tutorials, I soon believed, wholeheartedly, that I could do anything.

For my first decorating project, I wanted to re-cover the seat cushions on my four kitchen chairs. The cushions' fabric covers were old and cruddy with baby food splats, finger paint, and red-wine stains. From a library book, EJ and I learned how to unscrew a seat cushion and remove it from the chair frame. We grabbed one of our chairs and performed this task perfectly. With the seat cushion now free, we turned the cushion over, and with a flathead screwdriver, we dug under the gritty staples that anchored the fabric to the cushion's wooden platform. Wiggling the staples away from the platform, we yanked them up and out. This freed the nasty and yicky old cloth cover from the cushion.

We decided to replace the cushion covers using a vibrant mauve-and-pink floral Martex bedsheet, which I had originally purchased for a sleeper sofa bed we no longer possessed. We meticulously measured and cut the fabric, and then stretched the flowered material over each seat cushion, pulling it down around the sides. Next, we needed to secure the new cover to the bottom of the platform. EJ held the fabric in place, while I loaded the staple gun.

Ready for action, I placed the nose of the staple gun against the fabric and squeezed with all my might. *One–two–three—fire!*

BOOM! It was amazing! *BOOM!* It was thrilling! Thirty BOOMs later, the cushion was gorgeous. We reattached the cushion to the chair frame—Voilà!

And so began my love affair with the staple gun. From my solar plexus, down my arm, and out my hand, I felt a surge of power I'd never felt before. The staple gun offered both a hearty physical release and an immediate sense of completion.

I want more! I thought.

To thank my neighbors for their lawn support, I offered to re-cover kitchen chairs up and down the block. I went from being the wacky next-door neighbor to an upholstering Rambo with a staple gun. *And I was good.*

By midsummer, after tackling many minor do-it-yourself projects around the house, I began to get itchy. There was one project calling out to me, and it was the mother of all tasks—rescreening our back porch.

EJ and I both loved that back porch. In the evenings, we sat on our rusty antique glider and ate our after-dinner Fudgsicles. Rocking back and forth, we made up songs to the rhythm of the glider's squeaks. I eagerly listened to EJ's stories of who gave her the last Twizzler from their camp lunch bag, and which boy splashed her in the pool. But, soon, the annoying mosquitoes made their way through the grapefruit-sized holes in the screens and chased us back inside. I was sorry to miss that lovely transition when dusk turns to night. And EJ could have stayed out there forever.

So, I decided that, with my trusty staple gun in hand, I would redo that porch and I would redo it right. This house was my castle—and my castle needed new screens.

By now, after a few months of nonstop house projects, my buddies at the local hardware store adored me. I regularly brought them home-baked goodies in exchange for their time and knowledge. When I walked into the store, they'd scurry to put on a fresh pot of coffee and we'd settle in for a *schmooze*,* some treats, and a DIY lesson or two.

Rescreening an entire back porch was intimidating, so this particular store visit required something special. I baked a batch of mandel bread, a walnut-and-cinnamon Eastern European biscotti that was perfect for dunking. These über-macho guys went crazy for these cookies, and as they ate, they gave me a twenty-minute tutorial on shoe molding. I learned that I would need these long strips of wood to hide the raw edges of the newly stapled-down screens. The hardware guys suggested I reuse the existing shoe molding, because if I bought new shoe molding, I'd have to paint the new shoe molding, and miter the corners of the new shoe molding, so I thought, s*crew the new shoe molding, I just want to play with my staple gun and keep the bugs out. Message received.*

They also instructed me on the various types of screening and the nuances of ensuring a tight and lasting installation. I coughed up big dough and went for the high-quality screen mesh and bought more wood nails than I could ever use in a lifetime. I cherished their expertise, and with stern warnings to measure twice and cut once, my hardware boys sent me home, ready to fly solo. I knew I could do this, and like the mandel bread, *I'd be good.*

The next morning, I grabbed my daughter's boom box, plugged it into the garage outlet, and cranked up the oldies station, ready to work.

First, I gently guided the very important, much discussed, and overrated shoe molding off the porch frame posts with a flathead screwdriver and the forky side of a hammer. I needed to protect these tired old pieces of wood molding so they could be reused.

My hardware boys had suggested I lay the pieces of molding down on the ground in the order I removed them, making sure to re-create the shape of each panel as it had been on the porch. This would help me remount them properly when all was said and done.

With the shoe molding off and successfully restaged on my driveway, I now needed to remove the staples holding up the nasty old screens. Each five-foot-high by three-foot-wide screen panel had been mounted using at least one hundred staples. This meant that I had to pry loose and pull out *six hundred* rusty staples.

With my flathead screwdriver, I dug underneath the staples to pry them up, so I could pull them out with my needle-nose pliers. But these tiny bits of wiry metal wouldn't budge from the porch's exterior posts. I stormed into the kitchen, grabbed my best and pointiest knife, and mercilessly attacked the obstinate staples. Gouging some impressive holes and scratches in the wood, I wiggled and yanked, until finally—two hours later—the worst was over. The filthy, decrepit screens floated off the posts, and I hurled them into the trash.

After unrolling the new screen, I measured perfect rectangles with my all-purpose T square, and carefully cut six identical pieces. Using wood nails, I temporarily mounted the new screens right where the old screens had been. I saw the beginnings of progress, and *it was good.*

Loading my staple gun, I knew the day's big payoff was moments away. Pumped and ready, I went around and around the six large screen panels, concentrating on each gratifying aim, squeeze, and hit.

I was forceful, *BOOM!* And loud, *BOOM!* And fast, *BOOM!* And I was yelling . . . *BOOM!* . . . and unaware . . . *BOOM!* . . . of my words . . . *BOOM!*

"Take that, you ex-husband, you!" *BOOM!*

"Take that, you coffee shop owner, *BOOM*, who slipped me a mocha java, *BOOM,* when I wanted plain coffee with soy milk. *BOOM!* But nooooo, *BOOM,* you refused to taste it. *BOOM!* And you had to argue with me, *BOOM*, and I looked like a fool. *BOOM! BOOM! BOOM!* Take that, Clifford, *BOOM*, and remember, there's *never* a good reason, *BOOM*, to wipe your boogers on my daughter." *BOOM!*

And then it was over, with all six panels tightly stapled to the porch.

As I put down my staple gun, my right hand began shaking. I felt as if I had lead running through my veins, and my right arm dropped to my side. I had a sudden need to sit down, so I plunked my tush right onto the grass and stared into space. A few blinks later, my vision cleared . . .

I surveyed my fabulous handiwork and immediately copped a cerebral buzz. Or was it a blood sugar issue?

Suddenly, I was hungry. I felt emotionally, physically, spiritually, and *dangerously* hungry. I grabbed my car keys, locked up the house, and drove to the grossest burger joint I knew. I treated myself to a cheeseburger, fries, a Coke, and a Tums. It was heaven. *And it was good.*

As I drove back home, my eyelids drooped and I felt the food coma setting in. But I still had to complete the finish carpentry work and get the big-deal shoe molding reinstalled. I worried that the afternoon would pass as quickly as the morning had.

Back on the job, I stood before the porch with the molding in one hand and a nail in the other. For some reason, I couldn't figure out how to bring the hammer into play. I needed three hands—one to hold the molding in place, one to position the nail, and one to swing the hammer. How could I not have thought this through? Had my greasy lunch had rendered me stupid?

What would my hardware boys do? *Think, Sally Girl!*

TWO-SIDED TAPE! I'd been using it to hold my life together for years, and I had several rolls in my kitchen junk drawer. Within minutes, I had stuck a lengthy piece of two-sided tape to my first long strip of molding. I pressed the molding against the porch post, then set about hammering.

How smart is this, huh? I'm so good.

I put a slew of nails between my lips, and if not for the vanilla lip gloss with sunscreen, I could have been a real carpenter. Up, across, down, and across, with my double-sided adhesive system in place, I nailed each piece of molding onto the porch posts, and it looked great.

And then I was done.

I closed my toolbox and stored the extra screen for whatever one keeps extra screen for. I went inside and headed upstairs for a well-deserved shower.

EJ arrived home from camp and greeted me. "Mommy, look what you did! It's like a real person did the porch, I love it! You did so good, Mommy, what's for dinner?"

To celebrate, EJ and I ate our pasta dinners on the new and improved back porch. I lit candles and filled our plastic wine glasses with grape juice. We drank a toast to the bugs who would no longer bug us.

Marveling at the clean and fresh view of my backyard, I felt like a land baroness. I had created the perfect space for the two of us, and in doing so, I learned that with the help of great neighbors, terrific girlfriends, the library, and my friendly hardware boys, I would continue to kick some serious ass and get things done. It was thrilling to think that, rather than nag, beg, or hire, I could dream it, plan it, do it, and—ultimately—brag about it.

It was then I realized that my daughter and I would be more than just fine, *we'd be GOOD.*

RECIPE: Naomi Garfinkel Fingerett's Mandel Bread

So good you'll get invited to every party, they'll want you should bring it

This is the cookie I make for parties and for gifts and, of course, for my beloved hardware boys. Because of these very cookies, my porch rehab was a brilliant success and that helped me get good money when I sold my house, so I'm indebted to this recipe. My dedication to this cookie, which I'll admit is fairly labor-intensive, has upped my stock on many levels, and I'm invited to parties because people know it's what I'll bring.

DISCLAIMER: I have been told by scores of Christmas People that this cookie "tastes like Christmas!" You couldn't go by me, but you could go by them.

INGREDIENTS:

1 cup salted butter *This means 2 sticks, or Crisco if you want* pareve.
2 cups sugar
4 eggs
2 cups chopped walnuts *I do this in the Cuisinart.*
4 cups flour
3 teaspoons baking powder
½ teaspoon salt
1 teaspoon cinnamon
1 teaspoon vanilla extract
1 teaspoon almond extract
A shaker of cinnamon-and-sugar mixture**

**For the very end of baking, you'll need a sugar-and-cinnamon mixture for sprinkling. I mix 1 tablespoon cinnamon to 2 tablespoons sugar, but you do whatever you like. No judgments.

DIRECTIONS:

Preheat oven to 350 degrees.

I use a KitchenAid mixer with that huge, white triangle thingy, oh my goodness, it's such an easy event because of this. But if needed, just take off your jewelry and smush by hand.

Cream butter and sugar. Add eggs and mix. Add walnuts and mix.

In a separate bowl, sift together the flour, baking powder, salt, and cinnamon. (Or don't sift. I myself am way too lazy to sift, I'm just sayin'.) Take 3½ cups of this flour-and-seasoning mixture and add it to the batter in the KitchenAid bowl. Mix and blend well. Then add vanilla and almond extract and mix some more. Now, throw in that leftover ½ cup of flour-and-seasoning mixture. If the dough is too sticky, you can add a little more plain flour to make the dough somewhere between bread-dough-firm and raw-cookie-mushy.

Remove the dough from the bowl and put on a floured surface. Cut the dough into 3 pieces. Since I'm neurotic, I weigh the 3 pieces on a food scale so I know they're all equal.

Using two 17- x 13-inch cookie sheets, place **one** hunk of dough on one sheet, and **two** hunks of dough on the other sheet. Due to my oven specs, I have to use two oven racks, both in the center(ish) area of the oven.

Now comes the molding and shaping the hunks of dough to create the biscotti shape. But first this message . . .

DISCLAIMER: I've been making mandel bread for years, and I've found a few secrets along the way to minimize the *tzuris**

and frustration. Though this recipe might very well seem like way too much work, and you might feel like throwing your sticky, doughy hands in the air, cursing me as you pitch this book down your garbage disposal—I'm telling you that you'll be thrilled with the outcome. This recipe yields a ridiculously large batch that you can freeze for what seems like an eternity, should you not eat them all at once. And PS, good luck with not eating them all at once.

. . . And we're back with the dough-shaping instructions.

Pat and shape each hunk of dough into long, narrow logs measuring 3 inches wide, 1 to 2 inches high, and almost as long as your cookie sheet. Make sure you stop 2 inches from each end of the sheet. The dough will grow and spread as it bakes.

Put one cookie sheet on one rack, and the other cookie sheet on the other rack.

Bake for 22 to 23 minutes, THEN SWITCH THE COOKIE SHEETS TO THE OTHER RACK. Bake for another 22 minutes or so. The switching helps each log balance top and bottom baking. **Initial** baking time should total 40 to 45 minutes. With my oven, I find them perfectly golden, but not too dark, after 42 minutes. You just don't want them too dark, as you've still got more baking to do.

Don't make that face at me. Yes, there's still more baking to do. I said **initial** baking time.

After the initial 40 to 45 minutes, take both cookie sheets out of oven. KEEP THE OVEN ON.

Place cookie sheets on a towel so you don't hurt your countertop. Seriously, I'm doing you a favor here. You also don't want the cookie sheets sliding around when you go to cut the loaves. Read on.

Starting with the cookie sheet that has just the one loaf on it, take a sharp knife and cut the loaf into 1-inch slices. (Maybe you'll wear an oven mitt on the hand that's not holding the knife so you can hold onto the loaf with one hand and not get burned?) As you go, lay each slice down on its side, and line them up in rows. There will be room on this first cookie sheet for cookies from the other cookie sheet. Slice the other two loaves as well, filling up each cookie sheet with cookies on their sides, however it works.

Now you have two cookie sheets full of the biscotti-mandel-bread-things and they're ready to be "toasted." Sprinkle the cinnamon-and-sugar mixture** over the two trays of cookies. Put one tray back into the oven on the higher of the two shelves you've been using (but not broiler height). Leave in for 7 minutes. When done, remove and put the other tray in for 7 minutes.

When done, carefully turn all the cookies over on their other sides, sprinkle with the sugar-and-cinnamon mixture and repeat the 7-minutes-a-tray baking process. It's this toasting that gives the mandel bread its shelf life and hardness—and makes these cookies perfect for dipping into a hot beverage. You don't know what love is till you've dunked one into a shot of Jack Daniel's, which is what you deserve if you really take this recipe on.

THE QUEEN

Here, in my house tonight, I am the Queen-Single-Mum. It's Saturday night and I will not be wearing makeup. I will not stand in front of my closet frustrated that I own lovely things that no longer fit. I will not be going out to a bar to hold in my stomach while I hold an overpriced cocktail.

Tonight, I will stay home, watch movies, eat Twizzlers, and make brownies. I have allowed my eleven-year-old daughter to host a few polite and drama-free girlfriends. They have been banished to the basement where they will dance to music videos, dip Double Stuf Oreos into room temperature milk that had an iffy expiration date to begin with, and have a wonderful time and not bother me.

It is dire that these girls understand what is expected of them on this one very precious evening. To drive the point home, I gather all six excitable young women and ask them to stand in a circle. I shove a copy of *A Wrinkle in Time* into the center of their huddle.

"Girls, put your left hand on this book and your right hand in the air," I say.

A few of them play team sports, so this comes off as cool, and they do as they are told.

"Now, repeat after me, but add your own name where I tell you to, okay?" I take a deep breath and begin, "I, Angie–Marla–EJ–Katherine–Bailey–Colleen do solemnly swear . . . "

"I, (*all the names bungled over each other*), do solemnly swear," they repeat. Except for Colleen, who looks horrified.

"Colleen, honey, what's the matter?" I ask.

"I wanna make the promise, but I'm not allowed to swear." Colleen's red watery eyes are about to spill over.

"Oops, you're absolutely right, dolly," I assure her. "Okay, girls, I'm going to ask Colleen to forgive me and I want a do-over. Let's try it this way." I pause to take another big breath. "I, then say your name, do solemnly promise . . . to leave EJ's mom alone unless there's an emergency."

"Wait, what kind of emergency is okay?" Angie panics.

"Mom, really? You're being goofy weird!" says a very perturbed EJ.

"Okay, okay." I'm beginning to wish that I'd never started this whole hookey-doo. But now I've got to just barrel through. "You can come upstairs for bathroom breaks or to call home. Okay, let's try this again!" I am determined to have a little more fun with the girls before I ride off into my carbohydrate stupor.

They place their hands back on the book.

I begin the pledge one more time. "I, I know who you are by now . . . promise to leave EJ's mom alone, unless there's an emergency."

"I promise to leave EJ's mom be," one girl says.

"I promise to not pee or get hurt," another girl says.

"I promise to only come upstairs if I'm really thirsty," yet another one adds.

"I promise to leave EJ's mom alone in an emergency," says I don't know who.

"I promise to not tell my mom that I was asked to swear." Colleen is laughing, thank goodness.

"I promise to yell at my mom later over this whole thing!" EJ says, with significant vehemence.

I leave them and head upstairs. I know I have frustrated them and they will want nothing to do with me for hours. I gather my treats from the kitchen, and grab the TV remote and the latest *People* magazine. After locating my phone on the kitchen table behind the napkin holder, I am ready to settle in for the night. Prepared with everything and anything, I will not need to budge an inch from my couch. Finally, here in my kingdom-palace-living-room, where I reign over all things breakable, I am set to have a Queenly blast.

Monday through Friday, when being a real-life Mum is imperative, it is I who am subservient to my daughter EJ (DBA Princess Dirty-Room). All week long, I'm an amazing example of Earth Mother Fantastic. I'm kind and loving, patient and serene, and, of course, forgiving and thoughtful. But, occasionally, I require a Saturday night where I take to the couch armed with bowl of chips or a plate of pastries, along with a nice cup of whatever I feel like.

Then I "let it go."

On this Saturday night, I am Queen Bother-Me-Not-I-Don't-Give-a-Damn. I am the self-proclaimed ruler of Couldn't-Give-a-Shit Island. I give lazy a whole new meaning and take selfish to new heights. It's rare that I say no to driving giggly girls from mall to mall and basketball game to pep rally. However, every now and then, a woman's gotta let it rip and proclaim for just one evening, *"I'm the boss of me and subsequently you, so stand back!"*

I am a realist, and I do know that I'll hear from the kids during the course of the evening. I only hope that the scene I made earlier in the basement hasn't ruined my daughter's childhood completely, but served as a warning that it must be REEELY REEELY IMPORTANT before they come to the Queen with a request.

Sure enough, not twenty minutes into my decadent slug-fest, where I'm at risk for a sports injury from relay cookie eating, a young girl appears. Marla, who is adorable with amazing hair and surprisingly hip prescription glasses, nervously enters my space, too petrified to speak. My eyes are glazed from a sugar buzz, and I think I see that she's holding a little white flag. I try to focus and realize she's waving a toilet paper cardboard roll with just a few pathetic squares attached. This urchin politely asks for assistance, but she has interrupted my deep and satisfying high-fat and processed white flour coma. I struggle with my lethargy and the surfacing of some horrible inner Cruella de Vil. I search my soul for the will to not frighten this poor thing whose legs are crossed and could easily wet her pants at any moment.

I've got to have a conscience around here somewhere . . .

"Sweetie, go ask EJ," I command her. "She'll get it for you."

Marla curtsies and backs out of my regal living room.

As the evening proceeds, Princess Dirty-Room and my other loyal subjects appear to be doing their adolescent best to follow orders. On any other night, I'd allow my daughter to invite her BFFs to sleep over, but that event would be fraught with the possibility of an unexpected sick kid, a bad dream, or someone's mother requesting to retrieve her in the early morning hours for a soccer game or religious event. Tonight is not the night for such kindnesses.

Normally, I'm a nice mom, a hip mom. The girls love to include me in their girl talk as I make nachos or pizzas for them. But tonight, I have made it very clear that my royal behind requires a royal rest coupled with an unrestricted free fall into the abyss of junk food.

Tonight, Queen Bother-Me-Not-I-Don't-Give-a-Damn has appointed herself the star of the *QUEEN ME SHOW*. This show has been written and produced by ME, directed and edited by ME, arranged and scored by ME, and the front row seats are saved for ME . . . The Queen!

Should the *QUEEN ME SHOW* enjoy a successful Saturday night run (e.g., no girl-trauma, skinned knees, or puking), it will be good for one and all. Sundays are lovely after a good Queen-centric Saturday night and there's no telling what wonderful outcomes might be rendered after such a self-serving event.

The next day, as the early morning sun appears, though no one in their right mind is awake to greet it, sleeping spirits are magically lifted across the land. Mysteriously, the national flag of Saturday night's Couldn't-Give-a-Shit Island has been taken down and neatly folded for next time. A new squeezy-mushy-huggy-lovey flag unfurls on this wonderful Sunday morning. Miraculously, the island's name is now the Land of Here-Let-Me-Do-That-for-You.

In this new world order, no shrill early morning wake-up threats waft from the kitchen into Princess Dirty-Room's consciousness via the cold air return on her bedroom floor. The mini-royal is allowed to sleep in and rise naturally, and waffles appear for Sunday brunch. This unexpected kindness causes the Princess great confusion and skepticism as to why all of sudden her Queen Mother is gracious and generous and reasonable.

Huh, say whaah?

The Queen's sincerity is running high and there are emotional rainbows and virtual puppies and cotton candy feelings floating through the warm, fuzzy ambiance of the castle. Princess Dirty-Room finds this a good time to tell her mother that she has a track meet, a book report, and an oatmeal map of Australia due the next day.

In one deep breath, the Queen softly releases three basic instructions: "Throw your uniform into my hamper, you have the computer from now till dinner, and the Quaker Oats are on top of the fridge." All is calm. All is well.

Long live the Queen's Saturday night.

SONG: *DON'T MESS WITH ME— I'M SOMEBODY'S MOTHER*

She's sitting at a red light, waiting for a green light
When the Porsche Carrera comes on speeding through
She puts on her siren, she's heading out to chase him
Gonna hand him a citation with how do you do
She says, "I clocked you going eighty"
He says, "Little lady, girl, you must be crazy
Honey, are you sure?"

CHORUS
She says . . . "Don't mess with me, I'm somebody's mother

I've taken on much tougher than you
I've given birth to sons and daughters
I part the waters, then I walk through"

She's runnin' up the court steps
With her purse and briefcase
Grabs her robe and gavel, says—"Here comes the judge"
She'll hear the prosecution, defend the constitution
Gonna hand down her decision
You know she will not budge—Case Closed!
CHORUS

Don't mess with Mama, don't be a fool
The hand that rocks the cradle
That's the hand that makes the rules, baby
Don't mess with Mama, you know what I mean
Like when Mary said to Joseph
"Better get that stable clean"
Baby, don't you bug her, remember your own mother
If you're gonna go up against her
Just remember she's a sure and steady boulder
CHORUS

I'm gonna, walk on, walk on, walk on, walk on
I'm gonna part the waters I'm gonna walk on through
I'm gonna, walk on, walk on, walk on, walk on
I'm gonna part the waters—just like Mrs. Moses
I'm gonna walk on through!

GREETINGS FROM
THE LAND OF LIME JELL-O
AND REALLY BAD SANKA

At seventy-seven, my strapping and handsome father was proud of the fact that hadn't spent a night in a hospital since an appendectomy at the age of sixteen. But that streak was about to come to a screeching halt. He was scheduled for surgery to check out the mass on his colon.

And now, for the first time in their marriage, Dad realized that he and Mom needed help. Ever the caring husband, he was concerned for my mother's emotional well-being during what could be a miserable shift in their lives. He needed me to come down to Florida to help out with my mother, who had become immobilized with worry.

I am the youngest of three and had a special talent for dealing with all things Naomi, just like my father.

As soon as I arrived, my mother and I made a pact to work together to make him happy and comfortable. We hovered over my dad and organized this hospital stay as if he were going to sleep-a-way camp. The first items on our packing list were his cassette player, headphones, and tapes of classical recordings.

Whether it was a vacation hotel, a long trip in the car, or a night on the couch after a tiff with my mother, he had to have his music.

When surgery day arrived, Dad was all set with his razor, pj's, and a first-class collection of tunes. My mother grabbed her pocketbook, a pill bottle full of who knows what, some tissues, two candy bars, a roll of Tums, and four magazines.

"Okay, kids, get in the car," I barked, and we headed for the Cleveland Clinic in Fort Lauderdale.

We drove in silence. My parents were never silent, not ever. I was hoping I would come up with something to say as I parked the car, but even I couldn't put a sentence together. I grabbed my dad's bag from the trunk and led my folks inside the hospital to the reception area. After some paper work and anxious waiting, a nurse came to take my dad.

He grabbed my mother and launched into a heartfelt "I love you, Naomi." Dad turned to me for a hug and his customary "Take care, Sally Girl," and then shuffled off, with the nurse guiding him through the doors.

My mother sighed loudly, completely unaware of her personal volume. "If he comes out okay, I swear I'll stop yelling about the computer."

Mom and I made our way to the waiting room to begin our vigil.

We sit. We wait. We read. We eat. We chat. We fight. We sweat. I walk. I'm back.

Two hours later, the doctor appeared to report that the mass on Dad's colon was benign. They surgically took what was necessary, and Mr. Fingerett was indeed a very lucky fellow. They were closing him up, and we could visit him in a few hours.

Unbelievable! This was amazing news! My father had lost three much younger siblings to cancer, and this was not the expected outcome. With shared excitement, Mom and I decided to celebrate.

My mother looked at me. "I could eat . . . how 'bout you?"

I replied, "What, are you kidding? Let's!"

And together we agreed it didn't matter what or where, just as long as we had a change of scenery.

The nurses suggested a wonderful place right next door—and if we got there before five o'clock, we'd be able to catch the tail end of the early-bird special.

Gleeful over the prognosis, my mother had an effervescence I hadn't witnessed in years. She said, "Sally, don't 'cha just love Florida? If you're willing to pretend this is a late lunch, you can get a nice meal on sale."

The restaurant was noisy and festive at four thirty in the afternoon. We were seated in a booth, and as my mother was no stranger to the early-bird event, she flipped an open menu my way to hurry me along.

Suddenly, I saw an old man walking toward us from across the room. I couldn't take my eyes off him. He looked like an ancient human fossil. His skin was translucent. He was a linear collection of sharp angles and protruding bones, wobbling as he planted his walker with every step. A frail, white-haired woman accompanied him. Her rounded back hunched over in such a severe curve that she looked like a walking question mark. As they passed our table, the old man hacked a phlegmatic cough that chilled me to the bone.

Unaware of all this, my mother put down her menu. "Sally Girl, what looks good to you?"

I closed my eyes, trying to erase the vision of this couple. I was not successful.

"For some reason, Ma, I'm not that hungry."

She looked at me in horror. "What are you nuts? Your father is going to live and be well! Of course you're hungry!"

I turned my head back toward Florida's very own 2000 Year Old Man, and my mom's gaze followed. She gave him a long, hard stare, then brought her teary eyes back to me. My very own shrinking mother grabbed her water and took a huge gulp, followed by a *"Kinahora poo-poo-poo.*"*

This mantra is the old-world way of saying, "But for the grace of G–d . . ."

Returning to the hospital after dinner, we found my dad sleeping a merciful sleep in his private room. My mother settled in among her collection of diversions—outdated *Family Circle* Magazines, two Hadassah newsletters, and a *Rolling Stone* she had no use for.

At seventy-five years old, she had entered that blissful age where one can sleep in a chair. I told her I found this creepy because, when her mouth and face were totally relaxed, she appeared to be dead. I constantly reminded her that she could expect deep and powerful shoves so that I'd know she was alive. But during this hospital adventure, I thought it best to let her sleep. And sleep she did. She crossed her arms, tucking them on top of her huge and vast bust, which rested on top of her huge and vast purse, which rested on top of her huge and vast lap, which was parked on a small and tentative chair. For the next seven days, this was how my mother sat during our visits. Her purse served as physical and emotional support, never once resting on the huge and vast floor.

With her eyes closed and her mouth wide open, she began snoring harmless tiny baby snores. I reminded myself that she only *looked* a little bit dead and we *were* in a hospital, so I needn't worry. I took this as a cue to stroll about the hospital floor and check out the joint.

I grabbed the puny plastic ice bucket and went searching for ice chips. Out in the corridor, trying to look officious, I peeked into room after room. I was taken aback by what appeared to be sons and daughters watching over bedridden parents hooked up to a variety of scary machines. Though we all seemed to be adults, I empathically felt that they also had a screaming inner child, petulant and frightened, silently demanding to know, "Whose idea was this? I'm not a grown-up! *Why am I in charge?!*"

After reaching the end of the hallway and filling my bucket with ice chips, I turned around and headed back to my dad's room. The corridor seemed so long and winding. Was I lost? Suddenly, and with the nerve one feels when severely exhausted, I was driven to do some snooping. *Why not stop and chat and find out more about these people sitting at the foot of these beds?*

My first stop was Mrs. Kohlberg, the gallbladder in Room 411. Her handsome son sat in the turquoise lounger at the foot of her bed, calmly reading.

"Excuse me." I knocked softly on the half-open door.

I was unaware that the door was made of metal, and my *tap-tap-tap* came off much louder than I'd anticipated. He put down his *Wall Street Journal* with such a snap he scared me. At that point, we were even—I had shocked him and he had shocked me.

"I-I-I'm sorry to bother you, my name is Sally and my dad is the colon resection down the hall in 401, and I'm taking a poll. I'm wondering . . . are you Mrs. Kohlberg's son?"

"Yep, I'm Jonathan, the youngest," said Jonathan, the youngest. He told me he was a day trader from Chicago, and he had no idea how long he'd have to stay in Florida to take care of his mother. He looked drawn and sullen, the kind of dark and brooding handsome that made me nervous.

I shuffled the ice in my bucket to announce my forthcoming excuse to flee. I began to inch away from the doorway. "Well, I'm the baby of my family too, and this is the biggest gig I've ever had. I hope your mom gets better soon."

He smiled. "Thanks, stop in again."

Next up was Room 409 A & B, where Mr. Grakowski and Mr. Beidsman lay sleeping. The two women in attendance had to be daughters. They looked worn-out but cheerful. Were they sisters? But why would two daughters do the job it only took one daughter to do? The thought of sharing this task was lovely, but I wondered if that ever really happened.

"Pardon me," I interrupted, "I hope I'm not disturbing you. I'm taking care of my dad down the hall, and I'm just curious, are you the daughters? And, if so, where do you fall in your family's birth order?"

Miriam Cohen (née Grakowski) said, "I'm the baby of four."

Susan Hackman (née Beidsman) threw in, "I have an older brother—that's it."

It was like a party in their room. There were photos of their families everywhere. The girls were having a picnic of sorts, playing Scrabble while their fathers slept. Somehow, they had discovered the *really good* vending machine, and I saw snacks and junk food everywhere. Holding out a bag of M&M's, they motioned for me to come in, and we quickly fell into an easy banter. I enjoyed their warm and delightful company for a few more minutes, but my ice was melting and my mother would be jealous if she caught me out schmoozing. We decided to meet again later, and I left feeling lighter from the social connection I was unaware I had needed.

Before my third and final stop, I thought, "Why continue?" I had my answer; I knew the deal. But I couldn't resist this one last room.

There she was—clearly "the daughter"—dressed in high-stakes, professional attire. She had an air of bossy importance about her, as if she'd left her office in some big city and flown to her mother's bedside here in Florida. She wore a stunning power suit. Her heels were pushed away into a corner, and she was reading with her feet up.

I was a woman with a mission, looking at a woman with a mission. I thought she'd be a gal who might appreciate a really ballsy intrusion.

"Excuse me," I said, leaning on the doorframe, more in than out. "I'm just walking the halls so I don't lose my mind completely, and I was wondering if you might help me with something."

She got up and slipped her heels back on. She nervously ran her fingers through her hair for a touch-up. Her hair went from fantastic to amazing with one sweeping gesture.

"Hi, come in, please. I'm Sheila. What can I do for you?" She reached out to shake my hand.

I assumed this meant I should come in. I quietly entered her space and shook her hand like we were men at a conference.

"Nice to meet you, Sheila. I'm Sally," I said. "I'm here for my dad, and I noticed that many of the patients have their children caring for them. I'm looking to understand—why us? Do you have any brothers and sisters?"

Sheila folded her arms across her chest and nodded. "I've got an older sister and an older brother, and they're not coming. They told me they couldn't break away." Her voice rose, sharp with anger. "But, frankly, I think they just won't break away."

She quickly looked away, staring out the hospital window. "I'm sorry. I don't usually talk that way."

"No, no, I get that," I said. "How was it decided that WE drop everything to be here and our siblings don't?"

I thought about my own miserable morning. I had spoken with my teenage daughter who whined that nothing was going right in my absence, leaving me shrouded with guilt.

"Well, Sheila, here's the deal." I pointed toward the door. "I've been walking the halls on this floor, talking to people. There's a Jonathan, a Miriam, and a Susan, and I think we should all grab coffee together in the cafeteria. You interested? Coffee's on me!"

Sheila chuckled. "Oh, that would be lovely. I'm in!"

I turned to leave, then paused. "On second thought, the coffee is on *MY* older brother and sister. I'll collect from them later, believe me."

My vindication would be her vindication.

A little while later—with my mother still asleep in her chair—Jon, Miriam, Susan, and Sheila and I gathered in the cafeteria of the Cleveland Clinic in Fort Lauderdale, commiserating and laughing, unglued by the fact that we were each "the baby" of our families.

We all wanted answers to the same questions: How did we get here? Why were we chosen? And when did our brothers and sisters covertly get together and induct us into the office of "Kid in Charge?" We spoke of our siblings' weaknesses, busy schedules, and well-meaning intentions, knowing full well that we really were better at dealing with our ailing parents.

It just felt good to bitch and be heard.

We fell into a heated debate over what flavor of Jell-O causes the worst stains on bed linen. We laughed and cried and hugged each other, then grabbed more of the homemade oatmeal raisin cookies that Miriam had brought from Green Bay, Wisconsin. This brief encounter gave us all a much-needed outlet for our repressed bitterness. We realized that, as a group, we were quite special. Ultimately, it was our open hearts and tremendous sense of familial piety that drove us to be there when our parents needed us the most.

"You know what we are?" I suddenly said. "We're tender grapes."

Everyone looked at me quizzically.

"It's what my dad calls kids like us, the ones who are always there for their families." I paused for a second, then quoted my father, " 'Tender grapes will ripen on the vine still attached to the garden wall as it grows up and over. Sweet and earthy, these grapes stay lush under the heat of the sun, while clinging still in torrential rain.' "

My new friends smiled and nodded. They understood. We had all realized that, in the end, it truly didn't matter if the other grapes fell away or couldn't linger.

It only mattered that we did.

SONG: CLOVER
For my parents

I see the twilight, just over your shoulder
So many stars holding together
Just like these heavens
We're constant and brilliant
Silver-gray spinning together

We have the moon, we have the dawn
In between, we're dancing in clover—in clover

I see in your clear eyes, an unspoken question
How one simple wish hands you a lifetime
Why were we chosen to share all these moments?
My heart of hearts, I have not one notion

But we have the moon, we have the dawn
We have our dances in clover —in clover

Now there goes a young pair, held fast in their passion
Entwined in desire of the moment
Will they, or won't they, have wishes and lifetimes?
Some questions have not an answer

But they'll have moons, they'll have their dawns
They'll have their dances in clover
They'll have their moons, they'll have their dawns
They'll have their chances in clover, until it's over

JDATE AND
THE INTERNET DATING
POOL

Following my father's surgery, I spent several weeks in Florida caring for my parents. Upon returning to Columbus, I felt that I might like to find a *menschy** guy to grow old with. Someone who would have no problem sitting on a bench in the mall, patiently holding my purse on his lap, so I could run around inside a T.J. Maxx trying on everything my heart desired. This devoted man would want me to take my time and enjoy.

I had recently discovered the perfect place where one might find such a *menschy* guy.

JDate—the online dating service for Jews.

My Nashville friend, Kari Estrin, recommended JDate after I complained to her that I was going to be the only female at an all-gay Thanksgiving dinner. Kari looked at me sideways and suggested I might try hanging out with someone who might like to kiss me, you know, in a *romantical* way.

When I first signed up for JDate, it was relatively painless.

What was *not* painless were the various dates I went on. One man lied about his age by ten years; one man showed up in a toupee, even though his date-page photo had shown him as bald and actually very cute. One man asked if he could order my dinner for me, and I thought that was so very sexy. However, after the waiter placed my beautiful dish down on the table, my date made a fuss (over what I couldn't tell you) and demanded that my dinner be taken back to the kitchen. All before I could even lift my fork.

Outside of the actual *dating* part of online dating, I did enjoy the introductory writing aspect of it. At night, after EJ had gone to bed, I spent hours trolling the photos, being picky and choosy—and then I would take a flying leap and start an email communication. I was surprised to discover that getting to know someone slowly and deliberately, through precise and well-edited words, offered me a very satisfying escape.

Since EJ would be heading to college in a few years, I opened up my geographical availability. I made a conscious decision to audition potential cities where I had friends and family. I took a gander at the men in those cities.

I began a lovely email relationship with a comedy writer out in Los Angeles.

His emails were fast and furious, funny and razor sharp. With twenty-three hundred miles between us, and nothing to lose, I allowed myself to banter freely with him.

After three weeks of delightfully intriguing missives, we agreed to have a person-to-person chat.

For me, this is how I truly get a feel for someone's demeanor—by listening to that person's voice, cadence, and the natural flow of words and charm. Like his emails, Mr. L.A. Writer Guy was quick-witted and articulate, and had an air of confidence I found manly and attractive. Then, at the end of our very first live phone chat, he made a *glaring* gaffe—an offhand statement that felt kinda slick and yicky to me. After hanging up the phone, I immediately sent him an email to let him know that I caught it, and that it needed to be addressed.

> **ME TO HIM:** Listen, *Shmendrick*,* do you realize that you ended tonight's phone conversation with "I love you, good-bye"? I have a feeling that you're not aware that you said this. Advise?

> **HIM TO ME:** Darling . . . that may have sounded like "I love you," but "love" was spelled "luv" when I relayed the phrase. Ahem . . .

> **ME TO HIM:** Oh, yeah? Okay, I'm looking in the dictionary under the word "Luv." Give me a minute. Here it is: **Luv** (n.) "A disposable diaper sold at most 7-Eleven convenience marts, for families who find themselves caught with their pants down and out of nappies. These diapers are not cheap, and frankly not even disposable, but certainly beat the crap (pardon the pun) out of wrapping the baby in toilet paper." Thanks for the clarity. Just don't think that because you said this, you can ask me to powder your ass.

Mr. L.A. Writer Guy laughed at my off-the-cuff definition. We continued writing and chatting for a few more weeks, but I never got the feeling that there was anything substantial below his *shtick** and smarm. I soon realized that he'd been working his way through all the JDate women east of the Mississippi when he found me. Disappointed, I took a break from internet dating and disabled my JDate page.

With a free Saturday night in August, I drove EJ and a slew of her pals to the Ohio State Fair. I set them free on the midway to play games and ride the rides. I took off by myself and enjoyed the summer air while consuming unlimited amounts of junk food, as no one was there to judge. I had a terrific time.

Overstimulated by the midway's flashing neon lights and the barkers' high-octane hawking of their games and attractions, I accidently overdid it by eating cotton candy, fried Dumbo ears, and ice cream. I didn't get a tummyache—but I did fall into a coma-like state from the carbohydrate overload.

I shuffled over to a kiddie chair by the Ferris wheel and plopped myself down. I found myself mesmerized by the young teenagers holding hands, necking, petting, tongue mixing, and performing other displays of public affection. The boys wore tight blue jeans and muscle shirts, while their dates kept tugging at their insignificant tank tops, which constantly threatened to malfunction and go horribly wrong.

I closed my eyes and pretended that I, too, had a date for the fair. He would have won the toughest midway game, and I'd be holding a giant stuffed animal that wouldn't fit in the car.

At that moment, the wind picked up and I swore I heard a whisper in my ear.

I love you, dear. I love you, dear. I love you, dear.

Then someone shoved me.

I opened my eyes and stared at the little snot-nosed kid standing in front of me.

"You're in my chair, you're in my chair, you're in my chair!" he whined.

That was the last time I ever ate fried dough, cotton candy, and ice cream all in one evening.

However, these items, consumed individually, are perfectly safe.

SONG: *TRUE LOVE*

Just a little vision, just a little night walk
In the moonlight, by your side
Come a little closer, in the distance
There's a sadness in the tide
Walking up along the lake
Careful of the steps we take, lovers passing by
They're so quiet you can hear them sigh
CHORUS
I'm hearing—true love, true love, true love
Forever mine—be my true love—forever mine

On the boardwalk, under neon
And a crazy August sky
There's a chance of thunder
There's a chance that I might fall into your eyes
Something breezes through my hair
Or did you whisper something in my ear?
Sounds like I love you—tell me, tell me true
CHORUS

Don't you wonder why does summer
Hold such magic in the dark?
Strangers turn to lovers and
Gravity will not deny your heart
On the midway at the fair
You will see us everywhere
Like ducks all in a row
Love lines us up, love lets us go
And we shoot at true love.

WHAT MARRIED WOMEN
WANT TO HEAR

R *rrring.*
The phone jolted me awake.
Rrrring.

I looked at the clock. 9:30 a.m. *SUNDAY MORNING?* Really?!

Rrrring.

I groaned and picked up the phone.

"Okay! Okay! I'm up! Who wants me and why?" I said, though I knew full well who it was, and why.

It would be Lori, my best-friend-from-forever. Happily married for over twenty years, she had a sick and twisted need to live vicariously through my dark, stormy, tippy, and scary single gal social life.

"So how was it?" Lori asked, plowing right in. "Was he cute? Where did ya' go? What did ya' wear? What did ya' eat? What did ya' drink? Did ya' kiss?"

"Lorel, for goodness sake, we are grown women! I have'ta go make a sissy and then I'll call you right back." I was irritated, but she WAS my best-friend-from-forever.

"Wait, wait, are you gonna just pee, or am I waiting till you make coffee, too?"

"Let me go potty," I told her, "and I'll call you *while* I'm making coffee."

There was only so much talking I could manage until I had some caffeine. These Sunday morning recaps of Saturday night's post-divorce dating were always fun, but sleep is sleep. Everyone knows you don't wake a sleeping baby or a single mother whose kid is at a slumber party.

I hit the potty, washed my hands, and reached for my toothbrush. Then I stopped. Why bother? I'd been waking up single for a while and had discovered that coffee tastes so much better pre-toothpaste. *Look for the blessings where you can.*

Downstairs, I juggled the Mr. Coffee pot under the faucet with one hand and grabbed the phone with the other. I pressed the speed-dial key.

Lori picked up on the first ring. "Okay, we're back! Proceed!"

"Hey, whatever happened to 'Hello, how are you?' " I laughed.

"Screw you! You know I've been waiting."

"I apologize. You know I adore you and need you. Hey, I called you back *before* making my coffee, so shut up and listen as I pour water into the coffee machine thingy." I let the water trickle slowly from the carafe pot into the Mr. Coffee brewer for dramatic effect so she could hear the proof of my devotion. Then I flicked the "on" switch.

I'm such a smart ass.

"Sally, did you remember to put in the coffee? Sometimes you forget."

I shrieked. "Crap-on-a-crutch! Hold on." I pulled the coffee maker's plug out of the wall to halt the dripping process. "Damn it! Clearly, it's too early for me to be multitasking. I need a do-over."

"Okay, here's a thought," Lori said. "It appears now, with all this yelling and kitchen excitement, I have to go potty. How about I grab the Sunday paper and take the phone in with me? Get yourself comfortable, call me when you're ready, and we can start this catch-up session fresh."

"Sounds like a plan." I agreed. If she was taking the newspaper into the bathroom, I had time to make coffee *and* scrambled eggs, for Pete's sake.

Once I heard the hiss of the coffee maker, I was ready to tell Lori anything—whether it happened or not. I dialed her back and she picked up and continued without missing a beat.

"Hello, how are you . . . Bitch!" Lori said gleefully. "Proceed, take two, but hold on, let me flush. I want out of here."

"So did you have success in there?" I asked.

"Yes, I did, thank you. Now cut the crap—pun intended— and tell me about last night's date!"

"Well, let's see . . . he was nice, I guess." *Yawn.*

" 'Nice'? Are you bullshitting me? 'He was nice'? That's it? Seriously, why do you torment me like this? You said you adored me!"

She was right on this count. She *was* my best-friend-from-forever.

"I'm sorry Lor-*i-leh*. I'm just tired. Let me get a big sip in." I slurped my coffee for fuel and took a deep breath. Then I gave her my all.

"Okay, let's see. First, I liked that he was on time. Then he took me to that little place in Grandview where, if you sit by the window, people can see up your skirt, but we ate in the back and I was wearing pants, so it didn't matter. He was okay with drinking merlot, which was a blessing, but only drank half of his, which was a blessing, then he picked up the check, which, as you know, was a blessing. He spoke politely of his ex-wife, which is where I glazed over due to the fact that I drank his merlot. Frankly, because he was cute and I was nervous, I didn't dare eat in front of him. I think I might have been a little tanked, but I couldn't say for sure. Hey, because I couldn't say for sure, does that mean I was tanked?"

"No, you weren't tanked." She paused. "So do *we* like him?"

Lori was my self-appointed cheerleader on all things "men," and with our tremendous history together as friends, we were, in fact, a *we*.

"Do *we* like him?" I knocked back another huge gulp of coffee. "Hmmm, I don't know, let's summarize. He doesn't drink much, he's got some nice manners, and he had the class to spare me the icky divorce details, so, yeah, I might maybe kinda-sort-of like him."

"*Nu*,* so what did he wear?" asked Lori the *Yenta*.*

"Actually, he did good," I admitted. "He wore faded blue jeans, the ones made with the good kind of blue. He had a black V-neck sweater with . . ."

"Was it itchy?" Lori interrupted.

"Itchy? What difference does itchy make?"

"Are you kidding? If it was itchy, it's a cheap wool sweater, but if it wasn't itchy, it could have been merino wool, or even cashmere, which means he has a few bucks. I can't believe you don't know this. It's a good thing you have me."

Lori said this all the time, and it was true. It was a good thing I had her.

"I don't think it was itchy, but I only touched his arm once, and I don't remember feeling anything itchy or scratchy. Does that mean I was tanked?" I asked.

"No, you weren't tanked. You only get tanked on old-fashioneds with Maker's Mark, or Hershey's chocolate syrup. Forget about it. Go on—black V-neck sweater of undetermined quality . . ."

"Okay, yeah," I continued. "Under his sweater, he wore a starchy, white button-down shirt, and it was unbuttoned enough to see he had really terrific chest hair. And he had a goofy scarf his twelve-year-old daughter made for him, so he lost a few points for bad accessories, but he gained a few points for being a good daddy."

At this juncture, Lori switched into true interrogation mode:

LORI: Yeah, yeah, okay, he's a good daddy, with good chest hair. But is he a good kisser?

ME: Huh?

LORI: Did he kiss you, did you kiss him back?

ME: Pardon me?

LORI: Did he walk you to the door and plant one?

ME: He helped me out of the car if that's what you mean.

LORI: Come on, did you do the goodnight kiss thing?

ME: Seriously?

LORI: Did he lean in and grab a kiss, or offer a kiss?

ME: I'm sorry . . . what?

LORI: Were his lips open or closed? Did he try to French you or was it a peck?

ME: Can you hear yourself?

I felt like I was on a party line in *Bye Bye Birdie*, and we were just about to break into song about Hugo and Kim.

Lori reeled herself back in. "Was he romantical? Did he put his arms around you?"

"Well, actually, there might have been some sparks," I said. "We sat in my driveway and made out like teenagers. His daughter's handmade scarf got to me, in a good way, I mean. I don't know why, but it did. Maybe I was tanked."

"NO, you weren't tanked! You might have been buzzed, but I know how you roll. Sipping your glass of merlot plus sipping his glass of merlot over the course of an entire meal, does not equal tanked. Trust me. Now, if you had eaten two molten lava cakes for dessert, which I have seen you do, then I'd say you were most likely shit-face-tanked."

Lori really *did* know me well.

She paused and lowered her voice. "So Sal, *(dramatic pause)* did he cop a feel?"

"You're insane! Lorel, it was a first date!"

"I think you're holding out on me," Lori whimpered.

I sighed. "Sweetie, this guy was driving a car with Cheerios stuck in the gearshift column, and even with an empty box of graham crackers on the floor of the backseat and possibly a cheap, itchy wool sweater, the guy had some class. It was what it was, and PS, it was a first date! No man in his right mind would place his hand anywhere near a middle-aged woman's chestal area during their first encounter."

"You're right," Lori said. "But, promise me, Sal Pal, that if you see this guy again and he puts down some good moves, you will *immediately* make mental notes and file a detailed report?" She sounded a little sad. "You know how I love to hear about the sexy kisses of the single."

"Sexy kisses of the single? Don't married people kiss?" I asked. "I hear you guys can kiss whenever you feel like it."

"Yeah, but what if after twenty-two years, no one ever feels like it?" Lori said.

And there you have it. This is what my best-friend-from-forever, who had been married for forever, wanted—stories from the dating pool. Lori knew that, in these stories, I took the risky plunge, while she got to stand by with the emotional towel. She was a proud coach who misses the exhilaration of competitive swimming but will have nothing to do with a bathing suit.

I heard Lori's husband, Bill, interrupt her on the other end of the phone. He often sidled up while the phone was attached to Lori's ear and loved shouting at me about nothing.

"Hey, Sally, bring me bagels!" he yelled.

"Shhh," Lori admonished Bill. "Sally's telling me about last night's date and how they necked in the car."

"That's terrific. Ask her if he plays golf."

"Bill, we don't give a shit if he's Arnold frickin' Palmer," Lori said. "If he's a lousy kisser, we have no use for him."

Bill then mumbled something about the garage, and Lori lovingly told him to scram.

Hey, Lori," I said, "remember when you were all jazzed up and in Bill's face with kisses because he took out the trash without being asked?"

"Yeah." She sighed. "Who knew that watching a man take initiative with a garbage can would be such a turn-on? That went into my journal, three pages worth, and he was a very lucky man that night, winking-winking."

"Well," I said, in a lilting, singsongy voice, "It might not be Paris . . . but you'll always have trash day."

She burst out laughing, and then surprised us both with a shriek.

"Oy, I gotta pee, I gotta pee! No, no, don't laugh, your laugh makes me laugh, stop, I'll talk to you later, quit it, hang up on me NOW! I'm hanging up on you NOW, I don't care who hangs up first, I'm not gonna make it!" *CLICK.*

I'm fairly certain she wet her pants.

On those rare occasions when we had an afternoon to ourselves, Lori and I would curl up on her couch with herbal menopause tea. We'd pretend that PowerBars tasted like Tootsie Rolls while overthinking and overdiscussing the pros and cons of every guy I met. We'd nitpick a variety of victims down to their Gold-toed socks. Wrapped in our shared case of arrested development, Lori and I longed to be sixteen again: before kids, middle-age spread, failed marriages, complicated histories, and for sure, before anyone had ever heard of spilled Cheerios decaying in the cup holder of a late-model Toyota Camry.

Every now and then, when a new guy turned out to be a total *yutz,** Lori received validation that married life was the right choice for her: safe, secure, and wonderful. With me, she had visitation rights into a life she really didn't desire for herself, but enjoyed knowing still existed, for someone, somewhere. In exchange, I was given undying devotion, unconditional love, and permission to borrow her husband when my stuff broke. It was the win-win relationship of truly enlightened girlfriends.

All she really required were a few safe splashes from the shallow end of the dating pool in the form of an occasional tale of the sexy kisses of the single. I could do that for her.

There were many friends who took great care of me during those early years of being a divorced single mom.

I had a tag team of gal pals who called me on the telephone late at night and kept me company while I walked through the house and locked the doors and turned out the lights. At forty-two years old, I had become neurotically terrified of the dark—both inside and outside the house. Every night like clockwork, I'd get a call from some wonderful friend who would remind me that all was good, that I'd be fine, that EJ would grow up in spite of all the crazy chaos, and that I was not alone.

Years later, it has become my turn to make those late-night calls. I reach out to a newly divorced girlfriend as she ends her day, home alone with sleeping children. I'll chat with her as she closes down her house for the night. She might be sleepless from anxiety, so I remind her that these days will pass, she will be fine, her children will grow up in spite of all the crazy chaos, and that she is not alone.

SONG: *LONG LONESOME ROAD*

Some might say the world's a lonely place
With heartache all around you
Moon and stars hover high above—no love looks upon you
Close your eyes to catch your breath

Your spirits start to falter
You've done all that you can do to make love come true
You might as well try to walk on water
Inside your head, you think about
What's been said—you couldn't work it out
Why don't you let it go—all you really need to know
You are not alone
CHORUS
I see that long and lonesome road you'll be walking down
I will walk along—I will be right beside you

Each morning, you awake with the same heartache
Another day, another worry
Trouble won't let up on you
Your heart and soul are growing weary
You're tired of being strong, being on your own
Lost your courage—lost your backbone
There's no rush, straighten up
Take your time, I'm here to lean on
I've got your heart right here, that's what friends are for
Together we'll get there, better than before
Why don't you let it go—all you really need to know
You are not alone
CHORUS

You can count on me night and day
You must believe me, when I say
I won't let you down—together we can turn this around
You are not alone

Chapter Six

WHAT DOESN'T KILL YOU—MAKES YOU FASCINATING AT COCKTAIL PARTIES

THE PERFECT DEATH

In September of 2000, my folks made the drive up from Florida to spend Rosh Hashanah and Yom Kippur with us in Columbus. They missed the changing colors of fall and cherished having time with EJ as she started a new school year.

After spending a few weeks with us, my parents planned to drive to Chicago to visit Aunt Minnie, whose health had taken a precarious turn. We called Aunt Minnie "the Energizer Bunny" for surviving thirteen surgeries during her nine-year battle with breast, colon, and even appendix cancer. She had gone through amazing risks to be *cured* of cancer, but the doctors were running out of ideas.

Mom had become emotionally unglued by my Aunt Minnie's declining health. After struggling with being overweight her entire life, my mom had lost forty pounds in a just a few months. She told me that it physically hurt to eat.

"You know, Sally Girl, I think G–d is playing a cruel joke on me. Here I am at seventy-six and it's too late to wear the really adorable and fun clothes, and *now* he makes weight loss easy? Ah, *nisht gefehrlach.** I'm sure it's just a worry ulcer."

Immediately upon arriving in Columbus, my mother grabbed my kitchen phone and called Aunt Minnie to check in and confirm travel plans for the Chicago leg of their journey.

My mother began to pace back and forth in my narrow kitchen, her voice getting louder with each step. "What do you mean I can't come and see you?" she yelled into the phone. "We drove all this way, and Bill spent all kinds of money on getting the car fixed so we could visit. I'm at Sally's now, just seven hours from you. I don't understand."

Mom fell silent and closed her eyes as she listened to Minnie. Then her mouth twisted with anger.

"Goddammit, Min, what the hell is wrong with you? Who gives a shit how you look—I'm your sister. This is insane, you have to be kidding! Put Bernie on the phone."

She stopped speaking and listened again. Then she leaned over and put her elbows on the counter top for support.

I made my way to the stove, thinking I might make some tea. She would need it.

"Put Bernie on the phone, Min," Mom said in a scary, quiet voice and then paused. The next second, she stood up straight and screamed, "PUT BERNIE ON THE GODDAMNED PHONE!"

I heard a click as Minnie hung on up my mother. My mother slammed down the receiver.

"Can you believe this?" She looked up at me as I stood there holding the kettle. "My own sister doesn't want me to see her this way. What way I ask you? She says she's all puffy from her chemo and she can't handle having company. I'm her sister, what's to handle? What a load of shit this is. Can you believe?"

She turned to my dad, who sat at the kitchen table, and hollered, "Bill, you gotta call my sister and talk to her. What on earth is wrong with her, I ask you?

"Na, simmer down," my father pleaded. "She just can't handle company. Have a little *rachmones** and understand what she's dealing with."

My mother was not wired to comprehend this kind of rationale, and my dad knew better than to attempt reasoning with her. But he always, *always*, gave it a shot.

Over the next three days, there were numerous hysterical phone conversations between the two sisters.

In the end, Mom declared herself victorious.

"I'll show Minnie! We'll go back to Florida without seeing her, and it'll be on *her* head!"

And so my parents drove straight back to Florida, heartsick and confused.

My mother's health worsened. Over the next six weeks, she went from doctor to doctor and had three MRIs and two endoscopies. Surgery revealed stomach cancer. Due to the severity and widespread damage, the doctors' only option was to remove her entire stomach along with affected sections of her esophagus and colon.

While Mom was in the recovery room, the doctors sat down with Dad and informed him that they had installed a feeding tube under Mom's rib cage. She would no longer be able to eat normally or digest regular food. Instead, she would have to survive on a strict diet of Ensure, a liquid food substance, pumped directly into her small intestines through the feeding tube. I'd been waiting in Columbus for my father's call. When he gave me the news, I was stunned. My parents might have had an inkling that things were this serious, but I did not. I had genuinely believed that Mom had nothing more than a "worry ulcer."

"Sally, the doctors told me lots of people do just fine with these tubes." My father sounded very weary. "They said she'd be okay."

She'd be okay? The doctors had basically told him, "Oh dear, we're so sorry we had to remove your wife's *kishkes*,* but we've got them now, so she's good to go. Oh, but first, here's a list of what she can eat. Hah-hah, just kiddin', she can't ever eat again! Psych!"

But that wasn't what I said to my dad. Instead, I told him, "That's good."

I booked a flight to Florida and made arrangements for EJ to stay at her dad's house for as long as I needed to stay with my parents.

A week later, Mom came home from the hospital. She remained in bed, recovering from this surgery—to what end, no doctor would tell us. We were told to take care of her at home, and after she healed up a bit, there would be time to discuss a treatment plan.

My father and I diligently did as we were instructed by the doctors. In order to get her strength back, she needed regular meals. Four times a day, we measured the prescribed number of ounces of Ensure. We clumsily poured this miserable chocolate milk into a measuring cup and then emptied the cup into the funnel attachment of the feeding tube. The Ensure slowly drained through three feet of tubing before delivering the nutrients into her poor body.

This feeding procedure was more than Mom could stand. She began to meditate on a bleak future of never eating again. To her, not being able to enjoy hot dogs and pastrami made for a compelling argument that, at this point in time, life wasn't such a big *metziah*.*

At that point, my mother realized that she had been given a socially acceptable get-out-of-jail-free card.

"You know, the more I think about it," she said to me one evening, "cancer is like having a doctor's note to be excused from life, you know, should someone want that."

And *that* was what she wanted. She eventually told us—in no uncertain terms—that she was done. She wanted us to let her go.

My father was not ready to hear any such thing. He continued to measure her Ensure, using a calculator to estimate the number of calories needed to keep her going. He demanded that we keep feeding her, four times a day, while my mother steadily lost astounding amounts of weight.

She now complained of pain. Her insides hurt, her bones ached, and I could only imagine the unseeable things that the doctors couldn't tend to during that one surgery.

"Daddy," I said softly one evening, as I prepared some after-dinner coffee. "I'm calling her doctor to see what can be done about this pain. I think Mom is done fighting."

My father didn't answer. He just reached for the sugar bowl.

I handed him a mug of fresh coffee. "I think it would be okay if you, too, came out of the ring. She'll know you still love her."

"I know, Sally Girl, I know." My father put both of his hands around his warm mug and closed his eyes.

I took my seat at the table and we sat in silence, defeated together.

The next day, I contacted Mom's oncologist—and I was very clear with him. "I know you won't let her be in pain . . . but please, can we arrange it so that she's not in fear, either?"

And so began my mother's death.

We couldn't bring ourselves to stop the tube feedings, but we became more accepting of the course that nature would take. Mom made deliberate and good use of her time. She insisted my father take her to my Four Bitchin' Babes concert at the Kravis Center in West Palm Beach. She then made me promise not to tell him that she wasn't wearing underwear beneath her dress. After losing so much weight, she figured it was safer to wear nothing, rather than risk having her panties slide down to her feet right there in front of all the Florida *yentas*.*

Just a few days after the concert, she was confined to her bed.

One day, Mom's dearest friend, Rochelle, paid her a visit. Rochelle had been the owner of the famous pencil skirt that Mom borrowed the night she met Dad. She had been telling my mother what to do since they were fourteen.

"Naomi!" Rochelle said as she entered my mother's bedroom, "I've talked to an amazing stomach cancer doctor who said I should give you his name, and he could maybe have a look at you and get you fixed up and forget all about the tubes and the not eating. This is bullshit, Na."

"Rochelle, darling, that's really sweet," my mother said, her voice soft and calm. "But I'm exhausted, and I'm thinking maybe I'll just do this my way."

Rochelle's eyes widened in shock. "Naomi, you're only seventy-six years old! What are you thinking? Why aren't you fighting?"

"Dolly, come here." My mother patted the bed. "Come sit here and hold my hand, I wanna talk to you."

"Naomi, no! You're not going to die—I won't have it. We're going to get through this. Harold has a golf buddy who can get you into this specialist, and they can check this out, and maybe you can get a few more years." Rochelle's voice had slowly been getting louder, and now she was nearly shouting. "Why won't you try? I can't believe you'd give up like this . . ."

My father stepped into my mother's bedroom. "Hey, hey, girls, what's with the racket in here?"

"Bill," my mother whispered, "take Rochelle out and explain things to her, will you? Have Sally make her some tea."

Rochelle's face softened and she shook her head. She turned to my mother, leaned over, and kissed her. "I'm sorry, *cookie*, I just can't bear the thought of losing you." Rochelle's tears came hard and fast as she sat down on the bed. Together, the two women held hands and wept.

My father left the room and joined me in the hallway. We both stood there, witnessing the saddest and most beautiful moments two old friends could share.

My mother spent her days sleeping on and off, and when she had the strength, she'd call an old acquaintance on the phone. Her voice sounded weak and baby-like as she told each friend how much she treasured them and how grateful she was for their friendship.

She called my sister's husband and begged his forgiveness for all the meddling and all the fights they had gotten into over kosher markings on packages and silly things of tremendous unimportance. She admitted that he had been an exemplary husband and father and thanked him for being so good to her daughter Rozzy.

And then there were the phone calls to Minnie.

The two Garfinkel girls were both dying, in tandem, side by side in their own beds, thirteen hundred miles apart—Minnie, in Skokie, Illinois, and Naomi in Delray Beach, Florida.

My mother kept her door closed during these conversations, preferring to talk to Minnie in private. I sat in the kitchen with my father, desperately wishing that I could put my ear to the door and listen in. Instead, I asked my dad annoying questions, as if I was six years old again.

"Daddy, what on earth do they talk about?"

"What could they possibly be discussing?"

"Do you think they talk about death and forgiveness?"

"Do you think they wish they could go shopping and eat out?"

"Good lord, Daddy, don't you wanna know? This is so big!"

I hoped that, if I opened a verbal door, my dad would waltz right through. Instead, he quietly threw an old poetic *mind-your-own-business* in my face.

"Sally Girl," he said with a sigh, "what they have is a thing of beauty, and it's not for us to question."

One morning, while my mother slept, I thought I'd clean out the fridge.

My father walked in and picked up his keys. "Sally, I need to run some errands. What time is the hospice lady coming?"

"Soon, I think. Someone will probably show up in a few minutes."

"That's great," he said. "I had no idea these women would be so amazing. They're absolute angels."

From the bedroom, I heard my mother cry out, "Angels? Angels? Are the angels here? I want a David Berg hot dog with pickle-lilly!"

I slammed shut the refrigerator door and ran down the hallway. My mother hadn't been able to speak above a whisper for days, and now she was shouting.

I flew to her bedside. "Mom, are you okay?"

"Are the angels here? Are the angels here?" she asked, barely able to lift her head off her pillow.

"No—Daddy and I were talking about the hospice ladies being such lovely women."

"No angels?"

"No, Mommy, I'm sorry"

"Shit." And she laid her head back down.

My father's unending devotion to Mom's comfort couldn't have been greater or more loving. He massaged her limbs with her favorite scented creams while she rested in bed. He made sure her clothes and linens were fresh and warm. He insisted on doing certain tasks because he knew she felt more comfortable with him, rather than a hospice worker.

She was now as light as a feather, and together Dad and I would gently lay her in a tub of warm water with Epsom salts. I washed her hair while my father took care of her feet. We were quietly grateful for the time away from the sadness of the bedroom, and hoped the warm and soothing water gave her comfort.

During one of these baths, Mom perked up a little. With an eager smile and lucid gleam in her eyes, she slowly said, "You know . . . this is a *beautiful* and *perfect* death."

Right then and there, every broken sliver of my heart fell back into place like a finished puzzle. That moment remains a defining memory of my mother.

My father took care of my mother at home—until he tripped and fell down with her in his arms. I told him that he had done the angels' share of work, and it was time for Mom to move into the hospice facility.

Nine days later, she was gone.

SONG: *LET 'EM GO*

Let 'em go, let 'em be
They'd maybe like to have a look around
To see what they can see
Let 'em go, don't make them stay
There's an open door waiting for them
They'd like to go that way
You gotta let them go, you gotta let them go
You gotta let them go, when they want to go

Don't keep them here—nothing you can say
It's a selfish heart that longs to love for one more day
They need to go, they see the light
Shining on the silence—the grace, the peace of mind
You gotta let them go, you gotta let them go
You gotta let them go, when they want to go

Set them free, cut them loose
Give the gift of kindness a traveler can use
Let 'em go, let 'em be
Send them off with love, send them off with dignity

DAD AFTER MOM

The Brisket Brigade

After fifty-eight years of marriage, my dad was now a widower. He would be living alone in Florida and taking care of the entire house himself. My siblings and I worried about him.

Turns out, we needn't have been concerned.

Dad was an unusual guy for a man of his generation. He knew how to cook, clean, shop, do laundry, and pay bills. He had spent three decades monitoring my mother's lithium intake. The man had an abundance of skills and talents.

And, after many, many months of full-time caregiving for his dying wife, he had things to do.

Following a long career as an accountant and comptroller, my father took the next logical next step for a retired guy who loved computer technology—he began day-trading online. He loved to monkey around with money. He didn't enjoy big risks, but he had a great eye for business opportunities.

Dad also pursued his creative passions. He began playing his beloved violin once again. He reintroduced himself to his CD library of Gilbert and Sullivan operettas. He built furniture, repaired electronics, and baked and decorated cakes. He was an accomplished artist with buttercream frosting—no matter how many layers you challenged him with. If he had more frosting than cake, he'd decorate the kitchen countertop with colorful flowers and vines and leaves.

This was a man who could be alone and not be lonely.

Once word got around that Bill Fingerett was a widower, the aging single women in his gated Florida community were on him like sour cream on *borscht.**

At seventy-eight years old, he enjoyed perfect health. Tall and robust with a full head of silvery white hair, Dad had always been extremely charismatic and handsome, but here's what drove the ladies wild (*drum roll, please*)—he still drove at night.

As any self-respecting mature woman in Florida will tell you, the ability to drive at night was more attractive than a bottle of Viagra and a high-yield portfolio put together.

I called him several times a day, and often had to listen to him complain about "the brisket brigade."

"Sally Girl, I had no idea there were so many unattached women down here."

"Dad, you have to be kidding. What, did Mom hide you in a drawer all these years? There have always been more widows than widowers down there. For you, it's sellers' market."

"Sally, stop that! I was married for a long time, and I'm not interested!" he barked.

"I get that, Daddy! But you know, no court would convict you if you went to dinner with friends and there happened to be an extra *maidel** at the table."

"Nah," he said. "I'm just not up for a big gang of people. This is not so bad for now. I've got it all worked out. When I don't answer the door, they set their dishes on the ground and leave. I wait a few minutes, open the door, and see what they left me."

"That's pretty sneaky, Dad. What do they make for you?" I asked, seriously curious.

"It's all the same, and really, I like my own cooking just fine," he replied. "What bugs me are the notes taped to the tinfoil. I can't read the tiny handwriting. Maybe they all have arthritis, but I can't make out their names or phone numbers. These girls make it impossible."

Girls? My heart flipped a little to hear my father refer to these elderly women as girls. Good for him!

"Dad, do you call and thank them? How does this work?" I wanted to make sure that nobody thought my daddy wasn't a gentleman.

"Oh, please, of course I call them! I make sure to sound good and sad, and then they understand and offer condolences, and we hang up," he explained. "If the whole point of bringing me food is for me to eat, I do. If the point of bringing me food is to date, I don't."

I knew he was right. I also knew that he took a Brillo soap pad to each pot and pan and scoured it within an inch of its life. Of course, Dad didn't realize that when he returned their cookware in sparkling clean condition, each "girl" would be even more entranced.

I could easily imagine the conversations between Dad's neighbor ladies as they *kibbitzed** at the clubhouse bridge table. Over potato chips and Raisinets, Estelle Kravitz would share some gossip with her old friend Feygy Wurlizter: "Oy, can you believe that Bill Fingerett scrubbed thirty years of baked-on *schmutz** right off my old casserole pan? *Takke,** I could go for him!"

My father broke many hearts that first year, but never a 9- x 13-inch glass Pyrex baking dish.

ME AFTER MOM

Enter Michael

During my tenure helping Dad care for Mom, I often sat quietly in her room with my laptop. I worked on my little essays, emailed friends, and corresponded with EJ, who missed me as much as I missed her.

Out of nowhere, I received an email from JDate. *That's odd, I could have sworn that I had pulled down my page a month ago.* Apparently, I hadn't.

HIM: Hi, I'm Michael.

"Hi, I'm Michael"? That's it? What a yutz.* I went to the JDate website and discovered that my page was still there, right where I swore it shouldn't have been. I felt bad about my page confusion and wrote back to this Michael-person.

ME: Hi, Michael. Thank you for writing. Many things are going on right now . . . I'm in Florida, helping out my father because my mother is gravely ill. I'll be down here for an unknown length of time, while my ex-husband watches our fifteen-year-old daughter. I'm so sorry, but I will not be in the position to meet you for a long, long time.   —Sally

The Michael-person wrote back the most beautiful and caring note. We started exchanging light and easygoing letters. Sitting by my mother's bedside, I enjoyed the diversion of learning this man's backstory. We shared tidbits from our days' events and news about our kids. As our personalities unfolded, his letters became a life-affirming oasis during a horrific time.

I flew home to Columbus for a few days and agreed to meet Michael for lunch.

He was amazing. He was patient. He was a complete *mensch** ... and he was willing to wait until my life could return to normal.

Two-and-a-half weeks later, my mother passed away, and the rest, as they say, is mystery.

ME AFTER MOM

Forgive me, Mom, I get it now

I was forty-seven years old when menopause started nipping at my heels . . . and cranking up my inner furnace.

Late at night, I lay awake missing my mother while sweating profusely. I remembered when my own mother had been going through this miserable mess herself at exactly the same age. When she was forty-seven, I had been seventeen, and we were trying to survive those rough years in Calumet City. Back then, I was not clued into this hormonal lady stuff.

During my senior year of high school, I awoke one morning to find that the bitter cold winter had entered my bedroom. When I rolled over to rearrange my covers, I saw my own breath.

What the hell?

I grabbed my blankets and bedspread, wrapped myself up, and traipsed downstairs to find my mother. I assumed she'd neglected to pay the heating bill. While this was a simple mistake, I felt uncontrollably angry and was ready to ream her a new one.

I stalked into the kitchen and stopped short.

My mother was standing over the sink, smoking a cigarette and puffing her smoke out the open window, while dressed only in a half-slip and bra. She had been to the beauty shop the day before, and had slept with her coiffed hair wrapped in toilet paper. Years ago, someone had told her that this would keep her hair in place—a pointless exercise, if ever there was one.

She turned and greeted me. "Sally Girl, what's with the blankets? Aren't ya hot? Oy, it's so hot."

"No, Mom, it's not hot. It's winter outside the apartment, and now it seems to be winter inside the apartment!" Based on the cross breeze, I assumed she had opened every window in the place. "I can see my breath, CAN'T YOU?" I yelled like a banshee and blew some air her way to show her.

My mother seriously had no idea that the house had gotten so cold. And she didn't appreciate my frozen freak-out. So, in true Naomi fashion, she gave it right back to me. It was not pretty.

Many years later, it was my turn. I was a motherless woman in her late forties who suffered like nobody's business with these hot flashes. Like a good daughter, I accepted the fact that my personal situation was overwhelming proof that karmic penance is very real. I had been a raving-lunatic-bitch-of-death to my poor suffering mother, and this was what I got.

So, before I share the lyrics to this song I wrote with my Babe partner Debi Smith, I would like to take this moment to make a public apology:

"Mommy, I'm so sorry for being such a mean-spirited misery to you. Please forgive me for my terrible intolerance—I had no idea this aging thing would be such hell. And while I've got your attention, I'm wondering, in case you've been given any special mystical powers, if you might open one of your magical windows up there. I know you're thrilled that I'm experiencing this torment . . . but if you've got the time and inclination, might you accept my apology and make this nightmare stop?!"

SONG: *HOT FLASH*
Written by Sally and Debi, who suffered together—under stage lights, no less!

It's been a struggle—we've been fighting
For the permission to do our own thing
No one can knock us down
We're standing straight and proud
With our laughing lines and our furrowed brows
Some of us had babies—some of us had husbands
Some of us went solo—some loved and lived with women
We've worked in factories—we've got our PhDs
In big fat boardrooms—we're running companies
And now we celebrate each new direction
As we face the mirror each day
We accept our imperfections
We won't give our power away
We have come a long, long way, baby
When times get tough, and we have had enough
We have earned the right to say—we're having a
HOT FLASH!
Hot flash, for hundreds of years past
Your momma had them—and her momma had them
And her momma had them—and her momma had them
Hot flash, then it's a total memory crash
From sleep deprivation, hallucination—is that a mustache?
It's no big secret—we're getting older

No one gets out alive, we just get bolder
We struggle, we commit, we vow to never quit
Then we lose our grip from a HOT FLASH!
Hot flash, for hundreds of years past
Your momma had them—and her momma had them
And her momma had them—and her momma had them
Hot flash, then it's a gravity avalanche
A dressing room mirror brings you to tears—is that my ass?!
Get yourself a bowl of soybeans and cup of black cohosh
Book yourself a beauty treatment
When your brains have turned to mush
No more sleeping through the night, baby
You toss and turn while your body burns
You're a walking zombie till the morning light
First you are sweating—your body is baking
You crank up the AC—everyone's waking
Life is a mystery—life can be wonderful
You've got your history
You've got your inner girl
She's still inside your skin, just a little less estrogen
Let your next chapter begin with a . . .
Hot flash, for hundreds of years past
Your momma had them, and her momma had them
And her momma had them, and her momma had them
Hot flash, you're crumbling down like smoke and ash
You can be sure—there is no cure
We'd even pay cash, but here comes a news flash
We're so sorry, dear, it's not hot in here . . . it's you!

ME AFTER MOM

The Haunting

One night, about two months after my mother passed away, I settled in for a mindless slug-night of television. Without thinking, I grabbed a small package of chocolate-covered espresso beans from a condolence gift basket someone had sent me. In concept, eating coffee beans sounded disgusting, but they were delicious and I couldn't stop popping them in my mouth.

I foolishly forgot about the powers of caffeine and sugar.

A half hour later, I had to turn off the TV because I could no longer sit still. I felt like a rocket ship had been strapped to my ass. I decided to put this energy surge to good use and clean my kitchen. I detailed the fridge and sprayed the oven with oven cleaner. While I waited two hours for the stinky chemicals to work, I mopped floors and de-gunked the baseboards. Then I wiped down the oven. But I still wasn't tired. I grabbed a toothbrush and meticulously scrubbed the dish drainer mat and the rubber caulking around the sink faucet.

By now, the clock over the sink said 2:30 a.m.

Sitting down at the kitchen table, I began to organize and alphabetize my recipe box. I flipped through the torn bits of handwritten notes, newspaper clippings, and recipe cards from friends. Then I stumbled upon my mother's Sweet Dairy Kugel recipe, written in my own hand. I had taken down her instructions over the phone, desperate for something wonderful to make for a brunch party. Mom had dictated at lightning speed, as she knew the recipe by heart.

Now my own heart seemed heavy in my chest, and suddenly—miraculously—I felt like I could sleep. I re-filed the recipe, gently closed the lid, and put the box back on the shelf above the exhaust vent where my spices lived. I turned out the light and headed upstairs to bed.

Once I slid under my covers, I felt drained. I worried that I might sleep forever. Possibly the caffeine-and-sugar energy blast had run its course and I was crashing.

My warm bed felt wonderful, but the knowledge that I'd wake up to a sparkling kitchen felt even better. I stretched and rolled around, desperate to find a comfortable position. My mind wandered and my eyes stayed wide open. In this state of half sleep, I had a dream that felt like someone had turned on a TV behind my eyes.

My mother appeared to be floating above my bed, just like Fruma Sarah in that scene from *Fiddler on the Roof*. Fruma Sarah was the late wife of Lazar Wolf, the butcher, who was supposed to marry Tevye's daughter Tzeitel . . . oh, forget it, it doesn't matter here.

Anyway, my mother floated above me wearing her lime-green pedal pushers with a matching crop top from 1968. Her hair looked really good and I was surprised to see that, although it was after three a.m., she hadn't yet wrapped her perfect coif in its usual toilet paper cocoon.

Then my mother started to speak in a soft, lilting, unfamiliar voice.

NAOMI-GHOST: Oh Sally Girl, oh Sally Girl, it's Mommy.

ME: Huh? Mom?

NAOMI-GHOST: Hi, *kutchkie,** how are you? I have to tell you I'm so proud of that kitchen, it's magnificent. But really you should do your housework in the daytime and spend the nights in bed like the rest of the world. But I never could tell you what to do, that's for sure.

ME: Are my eyes open or shut, am I dreaming or not? I have no idea.

NAOMI-GHOST: Shh, Sally Girl, you're asleep and I'm driving this dream, so quit it and be quiet. Actually, I wanted to stop by for a little schmooze, that's all.

ME: You look really nice, Mom. That was always my favorite outfit. You got it at Korvette's, remember?

NAOMI-GHOST: Yeah, and do you remember I bought you the same one, only in your size, and we were mother-and-daughter matching. I loved doing that with you, remember?

ME: Yeah, Mommy, I do remember. Why are you here?

NAOMI-GHOST: Well, doll, I have to tell you that *I know.*

ME: What do you know?

NAOMI-GHOST: Don't dick around with me, Sally Girl. I know what you did with the Sweet Dairy Kugel recipe. And after I told you not to share!

ME: Mom, you told me not to share it for really crazy reasons.

NAOMI-GHOST: I told you not to share the recipe because it needed to be *your* signature dish so people would always invite *you* over. It was supposed to be the special thing that you—and only you—could bring. But noooooooo, you gave it to Audrey Hackman, Wendy Spira, and that Mindy from Detroit.

ME: Mom, people invite me over because of me, not because of a dish I make!

NAOMI-GHOST: Well, I know that now, but I didn't know that back then. That's why I'm here. I've watched you grow and become a terrific wife and mother. Jesus, you're even a terrific ex-wife— *kinahora,* * *ding-dong-dang!* Your daughter is magnificent, and you've worked hard, and you were so wonderful to me and Daddy at the end of my life. I can see how you are adored and treasured and admired and . . .

ME: Ma, that's nice to hear, really, but what is it I'm supposed to get from this dream? Can you get to it, already? I was almost asleep!

NAOMI-GHOST: Yes, Sally Girl, here's why I've come for this haunting . . .

ME: Haunting! Is this supposed to be scary? Honestly, Ma, the only thing that's scary here are those pedal pushers—other than that, not so much.

NAOMI-GHOST: *(shrugs)* Well, I told the committee up here that I needed to make a visitation down below, and they warned me to be menacing. But after a lifetime of scaring you, my *kutchkie*, I just didn't have it in me.

ME: That's the sweetest thing Ma. Really, I appreciate that. So what's on your mind?

NAOMI-GHOST: Well, it's been a while since I gave you that kugel recipe, and I feel it's time that I give you my blessing and that you should share it, out in the open with whomever you like. It should be enjoyed and celebrated for the fabulous kugel that it is, and so, I bequeath these words to you—RELEASE THE KUGEL!

ME: Wait, what? Do you mean "Release the Kraken"? Have you seen *Clash of the Titans* ?

NAOMI-GHOST: No, what's that? I'm just telling you that you can set the kugel recipe free—send it out into the world. I want you to remember that I love you, and I know that everything you cook is wonderful, and I'm sorry to have left you, but you've got my recipes—and in those dishes, I'll always be with you. You should pass them along wherever you choose.

ME: Thanks, Mommy. Whenever someone compliments my cooking, I always say, "I am my mother's daughter. I will always be my mother's daughter." I will always be *your* daughter.

NAOMI-GHOST: Sleep well, my Sally Girl, and do yourself a favor and lay off the chocolate-covered coffee beans. They're hard on your colon. And you don't even wanna know from the headache you're gonna have tomorrow.

When I woke the next morning, for a split second, I felt her presence as if she was still here. But in a fraction of the next second, reality sifted through my lids, and I had to accept that my mother was gone.

But her recipes remain. And I have been charged with an important task.

In memory of my mother, Naomi Garfinkel Fingerett, z"l, I will now—RELEASE THE KUGEL!

RECIPE:
NAOMI'S SWEET DAIRY KUGEL

So good you'll get invited to every party,

they'll want you should bring it

INGREDIENTS:

8 ounces broad egg noodles
5 eggs *They now know eggs won't kill ya, so stop worrying!*
2¼ cups whole milk, warmed *You can use skim, but don't blame me.*
1 8-ounce package of Philly Cream Cheese, softened
1 4-ounce stick of butter, softened
1 teaspoon vanilla
½ teaspoon salt
¼ cup sugar
Cinnamon to taste

DIRECTIONS:

Preheat oven to 350 degrees.

Cook noodles as directed. Drain.

In a blender, mix together the cream cheese, butter, milk, sugar, salt, and vanilla. Then add the eggs, one at a time. Pour the mixture into a greased 9- x 13-inch glass baking dish.

Add the noodles and swish around to distribute. Sprinkle a good dose of cinnamon on top to create a lovely brown coat. Optional: Sprinkle ½ cup raisins into the dish and push them down with your finger. My peeps don't do raisins, but I do!

Bake for 40 to50 minutes.

You're welcome.

DAD AFTER MOM
Enter the Dish

After a long while, the couples from my parents' social circle started *hokking** Dad to get out and take a crack at dating. Frankly, I think the men in his group were getting nervous, as their wives couldn't stop talking about what a catch Bill Fingerett was. Then there was a rumor of a certain Married-Mildred who attempted a pass at my dad, so the pressure intensified to get him off the market.

Rita and her second husband had lived nine doors down from my parents' house in the same gated community in Delray Beach, Florida. But the couples had never met each other. As I found out later, Rita buried her second husband at exactly the same time Dad lost Mom. Each of Rita's marriages had lasted twenty-five happy years and then ended sadly, with each man suffering from a lengthy and protracted battle with cancer. In each case, Rita cared for these husbands with devotion and dedication, and each man died in the comfort of his own bed in his own home.

Her two children and three stepchildren marveled at Rita's strength and ability to love. All five of them and their spouses invited her to every extended family milestone event and special occasion. She was delightful company, popular and busy, with boundless energy and a supportive social circle of friends.

Dad and Rita were introduced by mutual friends, and by the end of their first date, Dad and Rita fell madly in love. And that was that.

We called her "Rita the Dish." Not just because her zucchini *kugel** was like crack cocaine, but because she was a "total dish" in the Hollywood sense. Rita was a full tilt, knockout babe. At seventy-three, she was absolutely stunning, with red hair, a fabulous figure, and the smile of a happy, healthy, and centered woman who loved life and enjoyed everything. Like my dad, she had artistic passions. Rita sang in show groups

Daddy and the Dish—A shame you can't see her gorgeous red hair and coral nail polish.

and choirs, and my father was so impressed that she recalled all the English *and* Yiddish words to the songs of their mutual bygone era. She had a wicked mouth and a youthful liberal spirit. She was a prolific and talented potter and had filled her home with glistening ceramic wall hangings, whimsical fantasy creatures, and magnificent sculptures. She loved to prepare meals for friends and was knocked out by my father's interest in participating in the cooking.

I once watched them working in the kitchen together, singing as they made a fruit salad.

"Oy, you guys are so cute together with the singing and the chopping," I said.

"Don't forget the hugging and the kissing." Rita the Dish grabbed my father. "I know what a marvelous man I've got here. I show him my gratitude every night." She winked at me.

"Noooooooooooooooo," I screamed and covered my ears, laughing.

My father didn't know what hit him.

Within six months, Dad and the Dish made a commitment to each other. Dad agreed to downsize his life, sell his place, and move in with the Dish. They believed there was no need to marry. They would join forces, share expenses, and create a life together, maximizing what time they had left.

Though this sounded lovely, I went straight to mental. I was overwhelmed with spinning scenarios and questions. No doubt they were both extremely capable of caring for a sick loved one, but would this even be a reasonable expectation as they aged? What if the Dish predeceased Dad? How long would he be allowed to stay in her house until we found alternative housing? Dad was seven years older than the Dish. If he became ill and needed a nursing home, how would we separate him from the Dish in Delray?

During their six-month courtship, I had fallen in love with Rita the Dish too, and she with me. Admittedly, I was equally concerned about her as I was about my own father.

Was I the only one around here who was worried?

I gathered up my courage and talked to Rita.

"Dish, seriously? You've buried two husbands. Are you sure you want to sign on for a third guy who could get sick?" I had to ask. "What would happen then?"

"I love him, darling. That's that. I'm a big girl, and I own a pair of big girl panties. I know full well what this means. Today's answer is 'I can do this,' and if tomorrow's answer needs to be different, I'm confident that all you kids will understand. Any problems that arise, *kinahora poo-poo-poo*,* we can process as a team. There's time to lay out the worries and organize the details, but you must know that I am willing to tackle whatever comes our way. And by the way, your father is currently giving my kids this very same speech."

"Okay, then," I said, "I'm onboard if you'll have me."

Dad invited my sister, Rosalyn, and me down to Florida to start the task of disseminating the house. Roz, a rabbi's wife with five kids ranging in age from eleven to twenty-seven, would be sorely missed at home. We made a vow to haul *tuchas*,* and see if we couldn't get this move organized quickly.

However, there was no way out of those energy-wasting conversations that began every time we found something that moved us.

"Rozzy, look!" I was elbow-deep in my mother's bureau. "I found an entire drawer of girdles! Oooh, she had a black one! Go Naomi! You don't care if I take a bunch of them home with me, do ya?"

"Why would you want to do *that*?" My sister was busy in the linen closet, tussling with fitted sheets whose corners had gone awry.

I leaned over the drawer and was overcome by an olfactory memory. "Roz, you've got to come over here and smell this! It's a blend of shower curtain liners, brand-new dolls, and mom's perfume."

She groaned. "I'm not sticking my nose into Mom's business—it's bad enough to just *see* it. Don't you find this traumatizing? I swear I will not have my children going through my underwear drawers when I'm dead. Will you please remind me not to wear underwear toward the end of my life?"

"Sorry to say, Roz, but I'm fairly certain you'll be wearing diapers at the end of your life," I told her matter-of-factly. "But I *think* you're asking me to help keep your kids out of your personal things. My answer is no. I love you, but I think this must be a ritual that we adult children are supposed to go through. It gives us perspective."

"Sally, that's a load of crap."

"Rozzy, are you saying wearing diapers at the end of your life is 'a load of crap'? 'Cuz if so, that's a magnificent pun."

"Huh?" She looked at me with that big-sister stern face, which meant she had run out of patience for a conversation.

"I think I'm gonna take a few of the nicer girdles," I told her. "To me, they are a perfect reminder of how hard Mom tried to contain herself—through both medication *and* latex. Plus they smell like her and I like that."

Mom's bedroom was just the starting place. We had to tackle an entire houseful of stuff. My father refused to have a garage sale. He felt it was too personal and too much trouble, though he had no problem pressuring me to take everything back to my house, and keep it forever and ever. He believed that I should be the curator of the Fingerett Family Museum of Crap in Columbus, Ohio.

It became a running joke how each item around the house merited a "vibrant" discussion.

DAD: Sally, take this candy dish your Aunt Rose made.

ME: Dad, that's not a candy dish, it's an ashtray.

DAD: Your Aunt Rose made this, and it was your mother's favorite candy dish.

ME: Dad, look at the rim and see those scoops where the cigarettes go?

DAD: What's the difference? It's pretty and you put candy in there.

ME: Dad, it's an ashtray, it was made to be an ashtray, and it will always be an ashtray. Mom might have fooled you by throwing a few Hershey's Kisses in there, but that still doesn't make it a candy dish.

DAD: Why are you arguing? Take it and make me happy already!

ME: Okay, but give me the candy too.

After a few days of gutting Dad's place, Roz had to get back to Connecticut. Dad and I slowed down and focused on the boxes of family photos. We needed to minimize the volume and make order of these old cartons. I did not want this job, but like many responsibilities in my family, it became mine by default.

Dad and I sat for hours and hours. We dug though box after box, viewed album after album, and rescued important pictures stuck in frames with broken glass. There were loose photos from the 1940s backed with sticky tape that was no longer sticky. The entire living room floor was soon carpeted with a pictorial history of everyone we had ever known and loved, in addition to many relatives my parents couldn't stand.

We did our best to plow through and hold the reminiscing down to a minimum. Together, we successfully organized a few small boxes of extended-Fingerett-family photos to send to my sister and brother. We also compiled a special mini-version of a "This is Your Life, Bill Fingerett" photo album, full of his favorite people.

We were quite a team, my dad and I. After an entire five-hour shift—with a short break for graham crackers and coffee—we were down to two crappy, beat-up boxes. With an exhausted sigh, Dad sank down onto the couch and placed the one box next to him. I plopped down on the floor with the other box.

My box, a large forest-green dress box from the olden days of Marshall Field's, was as deep as a hatbox. I'm sure my mother had, at one time, carried home a coat or a dress in this box. I shook the lid to lift it away from the lower half of the box, revealing a collection of loose photos. I stared into this endless supply of faces. I didn't recognize any of them. How could this be?

My eye began to twitch.

"Daddy ?" I was incredulous. "Who are these people?"

He peered into the big green box. Frustrated, he leaned his head back against the couch. "Sally, I couldn't tell ya."

It was all too much. As he closed his eyes, he set a pile of photos down on the couch. They tipped over and a flowing cascade of snapshots fell to the floor.

I kept sorting photos and let him sit in peace. At the bottom of my box, I discovered two enormous black-and-white portrait photos. Both pictures, cracked and aging behind filthy glass, were mounted in splintering wooden oval frames.

I realized the photos were from my mother's side of the family. These antiques had survived her childhood in an orphanage and then spent the rest of the time buried at the bottom of this box, sequestered on a closet shelf. I had seen these two large portraits once—as a very small child—and then never again. I had forgotten that they existed.

One photo—a standard wedding still of my maternal grandparents—must have been taken sometime between 1918 and 1923. The other was a studio portrait of my mother at about four years old, with my grandmother, Rose Hertzberg Garfinkel, who would have been thirty at that time. Hefty and buxom, Rose stood next to an easy chair and faced the camera. My mother perched on the arm of the chair, with her back nestled against my grandmother. Rose had gently draped her arm around my mother's shoulder, and her hand rested protectively on little Naomi's forearm. It was a classic old-world mother-daughter photo except no one was smiling. Instead, I noticed that my mother was wearing my brother's face on her face.

I turned these old framed photos over. Stained and musty-smelling cardboard held them in place. Everything would have to be redone if these precious pictures were to be preserved. Gently, I started peeling the dried waxy backing off the frame.

"Dad, I'm opening these up. I promise that I'll have them reframed."

When he didn't respond, I looked over to find him asleep, sitting straight up on the couch.

I quietly retrieved a butter knife from the kitchen, and started prying off the rusty hardware. After loosening the frame, I removed the fragile, wilting cardboard sheet as carefully as if I was performing open heart surgery. When I popped off the backing, several small, stiff photos fell out from behind the aging portrait. They drifted to the ground.

"Holy shit!" I bent down to retrieve the photos that had spent G–d knows how many years hidden behind old frames. These small pictures had clearly been taken in Europe and had possibly been carried to America by my grandparents. Had my mother known these pictures were here? And, even if she knew about the photos, would she have known who these people were?

But there was no one to ask and no one to answer.

I knew my mother had contacted Yad Vashem—the World Center for Holocaust Research—in 1967. Through the Center, she discovered that her mother's two brothers had emigrated from Poland to Israel. This was stunning news to Mom, and three days later, she boarded a plane for Israel to introduce herself to her uncles and her many cousins. But that was in 1967 and this was now 2003. Generations had passed and contact had disintegrated.

My sadness was overshadowed by my shame. *How had I let important family members become strangers?* I dug through the big green box with renewed energy and purpose, trying to find some connecting features between these old-world cardstock black-and-whites and my mother's Kodak shots taken in Israel in 1967. I needed to find something that might link us all together.

It was decided that I should take these photos back to Ohio. I would display them on my grand piano and all around my house. I might not know who these people were, but I knew one thing—they were *my* people.

SONG: *FACES ON MY WALL*

To these faces on my wall, I long to know you
I long to learn about your life
About your husband, about your wife
And your children, what were they like?
Were they like me?

To these faces from the past, this glass will keep you
From the elements of time
That separate your years from mine
This family tree on down the line
Rows and rows of photographs

I hear your pidgin English whispers in my ear
I repeat those Yiddish phrases I hold dear
I struggle to remember—now it's my turn to remember
And when I come to visit, can you feel me near?
I touch the numbers on your arm as you stand there
So full of pride and wonder, how you made it out, I wonder
Yet you struggled to survive, you emigrated and you thrived
Here in America, you spared me from
The heartache of your life

Now you're framed in aging brass, your past is haunting
Oh, the stories you could tell
The war, the camps, the boat, the hell
Who here is left to tell your tale, if not for me?

Oh holidays, by candlelight, your story's told
Just like antique linen, history unfolds and we remember

Every family member
Recipes from memory generations old
Remind us how you celebrated, so very long ago
With tastes that we remember
In those kitchens full of wonder
And the aprons we hid under; *"Zies a maydeleh mine kind"* *
And now I take my turn
With these traditions that I've learned
Here in America, you spared me from
The sorrows you've endured

To these faces on my wall, I will protect you
I make a vow to hold you dear
I'll speak your name, year after year
Your voice will echo in my ear
You left your lessons here, inside my heart

I'm hoping that my children find some space for me
On the wall with all these souls
That's where I'd like to be remembered
I want to be remembered

In this gallery of life, I'll join these faces
As I look I realize—I have her smile, I have his eyes
And though my nose has been revised, I fit right in
With these faces on my wall.

fu·sion

Pronunciation: 'fyü-zh&n
a) The merging of diverse, distinct, or separate
elements into a unified whole.
b) The union of atomic nuclei that releases enormous
quantities of energy when certain light elements unite.

*Your presence is lovingly requested to witness and
celebrate the magical fusion of two families.*

*Max Stan, Aaron Stan, and Elizabeth J. Green
cordially invite you to attend the marriage
of their respective parents*

Michael Greg Stan

&

Sally Elaine Fingerett

Saturday, January 18, 2003

The *fu·sion* Room *at the Crowne Plaza Hotel*

33 East Nationwide Blvd. Columbus, Ohio

Cocktails 6:30 PM

Ceremony 7:30 PM

Dinner and kick-ass party to follow

HE BROUGHT BOYS TO
DIVA NATION

I'm a sucker for a freebie. My life is a constant quest for discounts and deals. I hate the thought of missing the semiannual Clinique makeup sale that offers free stuff with purchase. I'll spend the minimum, yet exorbitant requirement, and purchase the one large item, just so they'll throw in a petite zipper-pouch full of diminutive product samples that *I'm sure to fall in love with.*

The same thing happened when I married Michael. I took home the big guy, and he threw in the two little guys for free. And I indeed fell in love with them.

We set up house and pooled our three kids—my daughter, EJ (sixteen years old), and his sons, Max (fifteen) and Aaron (thirteen).

For the previous six years, I had been a single mother to just one complacent little girl and we had lived in a testosterone-free zone. In preparation for moving everyone into our blended family's new house, I figured all three *guys* might like a heads up on what to expect when living with a teenage girl and a menopausal woman.

So, I prepared a document entitled **The Tenets and Reasonable Rights of Diva Nation.** These rights include:

* **The right to relax** in various bathroom sanctuaries without someone entering—either by accident or on purpose.

* **The right to carry secret candy** in your purse and not share.

* **The right to bear elastic waistbands** around the house, including during dinner.

* **The right to stop talking mid-sentence**, glaze over, and forget whatever it was you were in the middle of saying—without outside criticism.

* **The right to carry an oversized purse** without harassment, even though it makes you slouch like an exhausted gorilla.

* **The right to turn one's own car** into a junk drawer on wheels.

* **The right to militantly feel above reproach** regarding certain character defects or humiliating behaviors such as: eating the entire last row of Oreos, refusing to speak until morning coffee has been ingested, not sharing your Jeni's ice cream 'cuz it was too friggin' expensive, plus any unfortunate events like over-sleeping, over-whining, over-sharing, over-interrupting, and any other overages incurred in general.

Leading up to our new life with "the guys," EJ dreamt that her *girl underpants* turned into *boy underpants* while going through the wash. Certainly, I would never pooh-pooh or minimize a sixteen-year-old girl's anxieties; however, I had bigger worries than thong-under-strings that mysteriously turned into tighty-whities. My overwhelming concern was . . . how could I become the LeBron James of stepmothers?

Friends with sons offered brilliant advice:

"Make sure to keep more food in your pantry than you could possibly need. Also, if the guys don't see it in the front row of the fridge, it doesn't exist."

"If you don't have to, don't go into the boys' bathroom. If they can't clean it themselves, hire someone—it's worth it. If money can clean it, it's not a problem."

And lastly: "For G–d's sake, if you hear the boys chuckle for no reason, don't ask, just open the window!"

After the wedding, when we were all settled into our new house, I cautiously ventured into my new role as the Stepmom. When the boys arrived home from school, I waited at the front door, at the ready and in-their-faces.

ME: "Hey guys, how ya' doin'?" **THEM:** *GRUNT.*
ME: "How was school today?" **THEM:** *GRUNT.*
ME: "Got any homework?" **THEM:** *GRUNT.*
ME: "Are ya' hungry?" **THEM:** "UH-HUH."

I couldn't believe it! I had just completed an entire conversation with two teenage boys.

It's a known fact that teenagers are moody, but I found the gender differences mystifying. Unlike the boys, my daughter was way more vocal. WAY.

ME: "Hey, lovey, how ya' doin'?"

HER (ALMOST-ALL-IN-ONE-BREATH SPITFIRE) RESPONSE: "Mom, you're not going to believe what happened to me today. Remember last night when I was up in my room and you yelled at me 'Clean your roo-oom' and I yelled, 'I caa-ann't—I have homework'? Well, you got me all riled up, and I forgot to pack my biology paper, and I got a bad grade. It's just not right! OOH-OOH-OOH, GUESS WHAT? Beth Kirk's mom took her to a hair salon for a fabulous haircut and highlights, and even waxing, can you believe it, up here (*points at eyebrows*) and even down there (*points to crotchal area*), I don't really know for sure. How come you never take me to the fancy lady hair salon? I'm too old for the Hair Cuttery, really, you never let me do anything fun and hip. Jeez! (*BREATH*) You're always running to *your girl* for *your* roots. Brown, Mom, your hair is brown, and they have aisles and aisles of brown at the grocery store, why can't you buy *that* stuff? It's just not right! OOH-OOH-OOH, GUESS WHAT? I bent over in the hallway today, and I think people saw my underpants, 'cuz when I stood up they all sang, 'I see London, I see France.' It's just not right, all my friends get their underwear at Victoria's Secret, and for goodness' sake, Mom, I'm wearing an Underoos bra! I'm sixteen! You never let me do what everyone else gets to do, I don't know why you can't be like the other moms, why me, why me, why can't you remember when you were my age, and how important it was to fit in, and be like the other kids, (*CRY-SNORT-CRY*)... HEY, HEY, HEY, (*BREATH*) did you go to the library and pick up that book we put on hold? You promised you'd get that book, did you get that book, I need that book, that book is for an important grade. Seriously, you didn't get the book did you? I can totally tell by that glazed look on your face. How did you become my mother, you're the worst mother ever, it's just not right, no, it isn't, and now we need to go to the library. But first I need to stop at the mall, will you take me?"

I loved her more than life itself. I also loved to yank her chain. I looked her square in the eye, and replied, "I'm sorry, honey, what was that?"

All my friends with sons were so excited for me to have my own "boy" experience. And though they were quick to give me advice, I felt as if they'd left out a few important details—just for sport. (Or possibly for spite?)

In those first few months, I learned, on my own, the rules of living with boys. And, so, I would like to share my lessons.

Here now are my **Top Tenets to Avoid Turbulence in Testosterone Town**:

* **Be advised that a household female** might awake on any given Sunday morning to discover an entire soccer team of twelve-year-old boys eating chips and salsa for breakfast in the kitchen. Therefore, wearing a brassiere is suggested. Also, maybe pants.

* **Be advised that a pack of unchaperoned boys** might randomly choose to buzz cut their beautiful, thick hair in the upstairs bathroom, using the good towels as capes. Be forewarned that those shorn curls and hair remnants of various lengths will continue to circulate through your laundry for at least six to eight wash cycles.

* **Be advised that a well-meaning and darling boy** will make an honest attempt to help in the kitchen and mistakenly use Joy dishwashing liquid in the dishwasher, rather than Cascade powder. Be prepared to forgive him instantly when he texts you a sad-sack picture of a flooded kitchen awash in clouds of foamy soap bubbles, with the words "I'M SORRY—WHAT WENT WRONG?" in the subject line.

* **Be advised to keep plenty of batteries** within reach for all boys who spend too much time on their PlayStations. Heaven forbid their handset batteries go dead at three a.m., and in a zombie-like daze, they drive their father's car to the twenty-four-hour quick-mart to purchase fresh batteries, only to be busted by the store's security cop for violating curfew.

* **Be advised that a seventeen-year-old boy** might come home from school and audaciously escort a blond and leggy sixteen-year-old *shiksa** goddess right past your office door and briskly lead her upstairs to his bedroom. As the only Adult Parental Figure at home, you'll need to quickly assess the situation before choosing whom to call first—the stepson's father, the stepson's mother, or maybe the girl's parents. After mentally playing out the uncomfortable scenarios that would follow any phone calls, the Adult Parental Figure should just fly up the stairs and boldly demand the kids cut the crap and come downstairs. You've got cookies.

* **Be advised that when you go grocery shopping**, you are not just shopping for two growing teenage boys and one fussy teenage girl. You will also need to feed anywhere from eight to ten of their closest friends, both male and female, who seem to prefer the comfort, care, and vibes of your home—rather than any number of other houses they could easily mooch from.

* **Be advised that when plans are made** for the Adult Parental Figures to book a hotel for a wedding anniversary overnighter just a mile from home, the boys in Testosterone Town will decide to throw a wild party of untold proportions. After the aforementioned party, they will clean up their mess in an effort to make it look like the festivities never took place; however, they will neglect to wash the floor, which will remain sticky and disgusting. In addition to not realizing that the dirty floor will be a dead giveaway,

they will also leave countless beer cans and bottles in the recycling bin. (So, while they might be extraordinarily brainless, the boys are, at least, committed to protecting the environment.)

In spite of all their *mishegas,** these kids have brought me abundant joy. They made me laugh and gave me purpose, along with great material. So don't mourn for me. I have developed a slew of stellar coping skills.

When under duress, my go-to first-choice coping technique is, admittedly, horribly fattening. However, this method *is* socially acceptable, easily accessible, and I've never been pulled over for driving under the influence of a Snickers. Even after having three too many.

SONG: *CHOCOLATE*

You made a beautiful dinner, fit for a king and queen
He said he'd be home early for a romantic evening
Seven thirty has come and gone, and now it's half past ten
You wonder why you're not surprised he shows up late again
Put away the Caesar salad
Put away the pasta and the garlic bread
Don't need no stinking entrée
You want something for your head
You know just where to find it, 'cuz you hide it from the kids
Underneath the Tupperware, behind the plastic lids
That's where you keep your chocolate, you gotta have it
You're chasing after chocolate, you need it now
But somebody ate your chocolate, they're gonna regret it
'Cuz Mama won't be nice till she's had a taste somehow

You'll sneak into the kids' room
You can't be heard you can't be seen
You're gonna raid their private stash
From last year's Halloween
You creep into their closet, and you hear a raging bell
They've booby-trapped the goody bag
Your kids know you way too well

That you would steal their chocolate, but you gotta have it
You're jonesin' for some chocolate, you need it now
You're ruthless for some chocolate, you can bet it
There's nothing you won't do for a little taste somehow

You'll rummage through the trail mix
Stealing all the chocolate chips
You'll suck it off a raisin or a pretzel that's been dipped
Grab a can of frosting, forget about the cake
You'll eat a roll of cookie dough you never planned to bake
You'll suffer through those
Chocolate-covered gourmet coffee beans
Up all night, but look at that!
You've got your whole house clean

All because of chocolate—gives you magic powers
Even your therapist agrees
The brain, it needs the chocolate
Got to—got to—give it some
Dark or white, milk, smooth and light, it's all right by me
You can pour it over coconut, cashews, caramel
Mold it into semisweet, ginormous nonpareils
Chocolate-covered cherries, chocolate-peanut-butter cups
There's even chocolate-covered ants, hmm, not so much
Junior Mints and Snickers, Milk Duds and Kit Kats
Did you know that Tootsie Rolls haven't any fat?
You've been through every nook and cranny

There's nothing to be found
Hershey's syrup in a can—pretty easy going down

Toast a glass of chocolate, hello, happy hour
Kahlúa, crème de cacao, smooth as silk
Why don't you throw some booze into your Bosco?
Who doesn't love what vodka does
To a glass of chocolate milk?

Back in the beginning, way, way back, with Adam and Eve
She was tired and weary, moody, grumpy, downright mean
A case of constant craving had her climbing up a tree
She picks a lousy piece of fruit, we've come to believe
She was looking for some chocolate
She was feeling punky, shoulda had a Chunky
Down and depressed, get a Hershey's Kiss
Before you swear off men get a bowl of M&M'S
Wanna feel the love—anything by Ghirardelli, Dove
You know you're alive, ah, when you eat Godiva
N –E–S–T–L–É'–S helps you feel your very best
Because it's chocolate

BONES AS CURRENCY

FOR LOVE

During that first round of Jewish holidays in the September following my mother's death, I would instinctively pick up the phone to ask her a cooking question. I would dial, stop short, clutch my heart, and put the phone down.

I did this twice over a three-day period as I struggled to prepare my Rosh Hashanah holiday meal. After I grabbed the phone for the third time, I slammed it down, feeling completely unhinged. I missed my mother, and I was now an orphan-in-the-kitchen, bereft of my go-to-cooking-*maven*.*

Finally, I called my boyfriend.

"Michael, I have a matzo ball question, and I need a mom and I don't have one, so can I use yours?" By this time, we'd been dating for only six months, and for a gesture such as this, protocol dictated asking permission. I tried to sound desperate, yet adorable, knowing that cozying up to a man's mother could easily be misconstrued as ass-kissing.

Thankfully, Michael chuckled. "She'd love it and frankly, you couldn't ask a better cook."

He gave me her number, and I put it on my fridge, a place of high honor. Then I took a few moments to gather my nerve. I had shared a meal or two in the company of Michael's parents, but I had never called them at home. I picked up the phone and dialed.

"Hello," said the warm voice on the other end.

"Hi, Maitzie, this is Sally, Michael's friend." I couldn't bring myself to say "girlfriend."

"Hi, Honeeey! How are you, love?"

I dove right in. "I'm stuck here with a matzo ball question, and Michael said it would be okay for me to borrow you, since I'm in need of a Jewish Mother."

"Goodness, yes, how lovely." I could hear the *plotz** and *kvell** in her voice. "I'm right here, Sally."

"Is it okay to freeze matzo balls? How would that work?" I asked.

Maitzie immediately began imparting the wisdom of the ages on all things *knaidlach*.* She gave me a master class on the scientific properties of Manischewitz matzo meal versus Streit's prepackaged mix. I listened to the nuances of choosing between plain boiling water and boiling water with a little Croydon House bouillon added for color and flavor. Then she shared every which way that one might freeze a matzo ball—how Essie Cohen likes to do it, how her friend Dolores screws it up each time, and what works best with limited freezer space. I learned that I could put tinfoil on a cookie sheet, spread out the matzo balls in one layer, and freeze. Once frozen, the balls could go into a Tupperware container, layer upon layer, but when I went to defrost them, I had to make sure to, once again, spread them out in a single layer.

This phone call was a total score. Maitzie had perfectly blended the Eastern European old-world ways of her own mother with the new-world ways of our modern conveniences.

We said good-bye, as I thanked her and thanked her and over-thanked her. I sighed with relief as my upside-down heart righted itself, and I floated into a safe place of belonging. I felt calmer than I'd felt in months, and as for the job of Jewish Mother—Maitzie was sooo hired!

After Michael and I married, cooking for my in-laws became one of my biggest pleasures. I made the culturally familiar *haymish** dishes that he and I were both raised with, embracing my place in this Jewish cooking continuum. I found familial comfort taking my turn at nurturing my newly inherited family. Maitzie found great joy in watching me work in the kitchen, because she knew I loved being there.

And, in return, I found great joy in watching Maitzie eat. Like my own mother, she had a peasant's passion for picking and sucking every last bit of meat, fat, and marrow that could be gleaned from a bone. Whether she ate chicken, beef, lamb, or even fish, there was due diligence to be done before a table could be cleared. Maitzie attended to the bones that an average bone chewer wouldn't bother with. No bone too small, no bone too bent or crooked or impossible to win over. She loved them all. She also loved me because I, too, was a bone chewer. This mutual passion allowed us a currency, if you will, with which we showed our love and respect for one another. Whenever Michael's parents came for dinner, I made sure that the bones of whatever we had prepared were left intact with the proper amount of meat on them. I served these meals with a side order of dental floss, placed right within her reach.

A few years into our marriage, Michael made a huge, traditional turkey with stuffing for my celebratory Christmas Day birthday dinner. With his parents on the guest list, Michael took great care in preparing the meal. He did this as a gift to me, but I also believed that—like me—he thrilled at seeing the pride in his mother's eyes. Just as I had been with *my* mom, my husband was *his* mother's favorite cooking protégé.

That night, before any guests arrived, I was setting the table when Michael lifted his magnificent, golden-brown turkey out of the oven. Cameras were called for and pictures were taken.

Then my eyes fell on the turkey neck . . .

I'd *never* seen such a wonder, with the beautifully seasoned meat pulled tight from vertebra to vertebra and roasted to perfection. As a rule, when entertaining my in-laws, I gave Maitzie preferential treatment. All available bones were sanctioned and gifted to our Beloved Matriarch. That luscious turkey neck had Maitzie's name all over it.

But on this night, I snapped, I short circuited, I fell apart, I lost my head, I had a psychotic break.

Why? I don't know why. But there, hovering over the pan, like a glazed-over zombie on autopilot, I grabbed the neck and started ravenously devouring it. I stood in front of the stove in a stupor of bliss and frenzy, picking and sucking. I chewed the bones to a pulp with adrenaline-infused, carnivorous determination. I was *possessed.*

The doorbell rang just as I was washing my greasy hands at the kitchen sink. Michael let his folks in, and I heard everyone oohing and ahhing over the amazing aroma. As I rinsed my soapy fingers, it hit me. I had just committed an irrevocable and terrible act of gluttony. I had been thoughtless and weak and selfish, and I had stolen the turkey's neckbone. I had ruined the night and cheated myself out of this high-powered and full-throttled opportunity to show my love and affection for this woman I adored.

I had just eaten the Holy Grail.

Not knowing how to shake off this nightmare, I joined everyone in the front hallway. I sheepishly offered guilt-ridden hugs and kisses, barely able to make eye contact.

Maitzie handed me her coat and said, "Happy birthday, Honeeey! Your house smells delicious."

"Thank you, Maitzie," I answered, quivering in my own private hell.

"I've been looking forward to this all day! Michael said this was going to be quite a celebratory meal." Maitzie was glowing, so happy to have been included. She paused to straighten her sweater and then continued, "Sally, I think you'll agree that, for your birthday, you should have the turkey neck, yes?"

I threw my arms around her in relief.

"Thank you so much!" I hugged her tight. "And thank goodness . . .'cuz, apparently, I agreed with you twenty minutes ago!"

In true Maitzie-style, she hugged me back with loud smoochie kisses and said with a laugh, "Oh, I know how that goes!"

Once again, I was reminded that when I was with my mother-in-law, I would always be in that safe place of belonging. And my upside-down heart would always right itself.

LOST DADDY—
KEPT THE DISH

My father and Rita the Dish lived together in Delray Beach, Florida, for seven years. Then, in the middle of their great love story, Dad was diagnosed with Stage 4 lung cancer. At eighty-seven years old, with the Dish by his side, my father bravely decided to fight cancer head on, undergoing thirty-five radiation sessions and three rounds of chemotherapy.

My siblings and I jumped in to help with Dad's care. Rita the Dish took him to doctor visits and radiation treatments. We wanted to allow Rita private time with Dad, but we didn't want her to struggle with the schlepping and the stress by herself. Roz, Steve, and I decided to take turns traveling to Florida to help them out. After that point, he was never without one of us.

My father had absolutely no intention of dying. He did everything the doctors suggested. He felt certain he could lick this miserable inconvenience. A brilliant and capable guy, he had conquered the quirks of the internet, mastered the art of substituting applesauce for butter in his homemade cakes, and most importantly, won the heart of the magnificent Dish.

But no go. Eight months later, it was over.

I was on tour with the Babes when Roz called, late on a Thursday night.

"Sally, Steve called from Florida," she said. "Daddy's gone."

"Oh, Rozzy, I'm so sorry," I said, my heart sinking. But I also knew his passing was a blessing; Dad had been in horrific pain for a long time. I sat down on the edge of the hotel bed. "Oy, what about the Dish? How do we proceed?"

It was well-known that Dad would be buried next to Mom in New Milford, Connecticut, where Roz lived. But, at that moment, I felt overwhelmed by the logistics of the next few days.

"The funeral people are flying Dad up from Florida, so they suggested holding the funeral on Monday," Roz said. "Can you get Rita's airline ticket for her?"

"No problem." I paused. "It's over, Rozzy. Poor Daddy."

"Yeah, can you believe?" She sighed. "I love you, Sally."

"I love you too."

We hung up.

The next morning, the Babes—Nancy Moran, Deirdre Flint, Debi Smith, and I—loaded the rental van for our next show. I shared the news of my dad. The girls were sweet and concerned: "What can we do for you?" "Are you gonna be okay?" "Do you need to leave the tour?"

"Let's eat." I said. And we headed out for breakfast.

I told them that the funeral would be Monday morning. My father had requested a simple graveside service. Rozzy's husband, Norman, was the rabbi at New Milford's Temple Sholom and would lead the burial ceremony in the Jewish section of their local cemetery. Ironically, the Babes were driving to a gig in New London, Connecticut, today. But our Saturday shows would be in Pennsylvania.

"Today's only Friday," I said, "and to tell you the truth, now that Dad's out of pain, I'll be okay. The hard part is over. I'd rather be working than waiting around Connecticut till Monday for a funeral."

Over breakfast, the four of us pieced together a workable plan. Today, we'd head to New London for our evening show. On Saturday morning, we would drive two hundred and twenty miles south to Sellersville, Pennsylvania, for matinee and evening performances. The girls suggested that Michael drive from Columbus to Sellersville on Saturday and join me at the hotel. Then, on Sunday, he and I could drive back up to my sister's house.

With this plan in place, the other Babes and I got in the van, and we headed out.

During our show that night, I couldn't focus. *What am I doing up here on stage? My father just died. Who's the travel agent getting him to New Milford? I hope Rita received the airline ticket! I wish I had time to bake some my mandel bread for the shiva—people love it. Yikes, did I remember to tell Michael to bring me some funeral clothes? Oh shit, I'm supposed to be singing the chorus in unison. Why do I always hop on the harmony instinctively?*

Oh, my father just died—the Babes will understand.

My fathered had loved that I had been able to make a *real living* in music. He had dreamed of becoming a professional musician, but admitted that he didn't have the fire under his ass like I did. When he told me he was proud of me, I reminded him that it was *his* passion for music, *his* work ethic and *his* determination that flowed through my veins and helped me make my life happen.

My dad's affection and generous spirit had been boundless, and I was confident that he would guide me through the weekend.

On Saturday morning at six a.m., the four of us hauled our tired bodies into the van for the journey from New London to Sellersville, fifty miles north of Philly. During the trip, I heard each girl call home, trying to make arrangements to attend my father's funeral on Monday.

Nancy called her husband, Fett, in Nashville, Debi called "her Michael" in DC, and Deirdre yelled into the phone because her dog sitter couldn't hear her over all the barking dogs.

I tried to let them off the hook. "I know you want to be there for me, but seriously, I don't want you to go through all this *mishegas.**"

As true friends will do, they ignored me altogether and continued to make their plans.

I couldn't have loved them more.

Bleary-eyed and exhausted, we pulled up to the curb of the Sellersville Theatre. We unloaded the van, threw our costumes into the dressing room, and started carrying our guitars and gear onto the stage. As I put my guitar case down next to a microphone stand, I heard a scream.

Followed by, "Shit, shit, shit, I can't believe I did that, shit, oh no, shit!"

I ran over to the edge of the stage and looked down. There, at the bottom of the stairs, our very own Nancy Moran lay in a crumpled heap. She was conscious and swearing and moaning in pain. She pointed at her feet.

Debi Smith and I yelled at her in unison, "Don't move!" Then we called 9–1–1.

The paramedics arrived and took Nancy to the hospital.

Thankfully, Deirdre Flint's parents lived in the area. They met Nancy in the emergency room and remained by her side until she was treated and released. Nancy had broken one ankle and sprained the other. The Flints, bless their hearts, brought Nancy back to the hotel and helped her settle into her room.

Meanwhile, we had to do our matinee and evening shows as *Three* Bitchin' Babes. However, with my broken heart, we were really down to just two and a half.

Upon returning to the hotel at eleven thirty p.m., we ran into Michael, who had just arrived. We *(lovingly)* ignored him and rushed to Nancy's room to find her sufficiently drugged up on some fabulous pain medication. In true Nancy fashion, she was reclining on the bed, laughing at the day's events.

"Hopefully," I said, "this will be the last time the Four Bitchin' Babes do a Two Point Five Bitchin' Babes show."

I was so tired that the part in my hair hurt. I gave Nancy a kiss and left to decompress with Michael. Debi and Deirdre stayed behind to assist our injured Babe in her room.

The next morning, Debi and Deirdre swiped a luggage cart, arranged Nancy atop the wheeled conveyance, and ferried her to our van. Then Debi drove the van to the Philadelphia airport and deposited Nancy into the loving arms of the nicest Southwest Airlines curbside guys, who provided her with a really snazzy wheelchair. Then Debi dropped Deirdre off in Philly, and drove the van home to DC.

Meanwhile, Michael and I got into his car and headed for Connecticut.

Late Sunday night, we picked up the Dish from the airport in Hartford. We all hugged and kissed and cried, then checked into our hotel and went straight to bed.

The following morning, the three of us arrived at the cemetery before anyone else. We got out of Michael's car, and when I put my arm around the Dish's waist, she gently placed her arm around my shoulders. We silently made our way up the slight hill to the graveside tent. As I walked with the Dish, I gazed at the beautiful New England landscape. The sun was shining and the leaves were bursting with color, creating a perfect autumn day. But when we came upon my parents' shared headstone, I stopped and forgot about everything else.

In the nine years since her death, a soft carpet of lush grass had grown over my mother's side of the plot. Dad's grave—at that moment—was a cavernous rectangular hole. The apparatus used to lower the casket had been put in place the day before. Soon, the pallbearers would carry Dad up the hill and place him on the bars. I peered down into the empty grave, and then looked over at my mother's side of the headstone.

Oy, my mother! I wondered if Naomi Fingerett had any idea what Dad had been up to these past few years. I wearily closed my eyes and tried to cosmically mind-meld with my mother. I hadn't planned to speak at that moment, but somehow, I found myself talking out loud.

"Well, Ma," I said with a sigh, "Daddy sorta-kinda-maybe strayed, just the tiniest bit. He waited a really long time before going out on a date. And really, Ma, if you look at the big picture, he didn't get too far and it wasn't for too long."

I suddenly remembered that I was standing next to the Dish. I slapped my hand over my mouth so hard and fast that the sting of my own slap made me gasp.

"Oh, shit, I can't believe I just said that." A tiny laugh bubbled up.

"Are you kidding me?" The Dish stared at me and began to giggle.

I fell into a full-steam laughing fit. If you've ever been to a graveside funeral, you probably know that any laughing is a precursor to wetting your pants, because in a cemetery, there are no options. Laugh or cry, you won't find a bathroom.

I crossed my legs, trying not to have an accident, and glanced back at my mother's headstone. "And trust me, Ma . . ." I hiccupped and tried to catch my breath. ". . . he was in really good hands."

The Dish rammed an elbow into my ribs. "Seriously? That's it? *Really good hands?*'"

I nodded.

Rita raised an eyebrow. "Screw that—he was in GREAT hands!"

Shrieking with laughter, we stumbled backward as the spikes of our dress heels dug deep into the earth. We held each other firmly and pulled our muddy shoes out of the ground.

"Okay." I took a deep breath. "That was a good one! But now we have to straighten up and fly right."

"Yes, darling, I agree."

Cars began to pull up, and the rest of my family climbed the little hill where Mom and Dad would spend their days. The Dish and I wiped away our smeared mascara and prepared for the burial service.

Back at my sister's house after the funeral, we settled in for our meal of condolence. The grandchildren went outside with their sandwiches to enjoy the last warm day of fall. My sister chatted with various close friends and congregants who had stopped by to pay their respects.

I sat with the Dish and ate off her plate. Understandably, she was too tired to eat. She began to talk about Dad.

"You know, darling, your father never cheated on your mother. Did you know that?" she said.

"Uh, no, I did not know that," I said matter-of-factly. "I would have assumed that however. But you have proof?"

"Well, he definitely had opportunities, you know. He once fired a girl who made eyes at him. He was a true blue guy." She paused. "Oy, I miss him."

"I know you do, Dish. Tell me more."

"I can tell you this, darling—there were a lot of things he didn't know how to do, until me, if you know what I'm meaning?"

"Hey, hey, hey!" I waved my hands. "We'll have none of that—I'm not supposed to know those things!"

"Too much, too soon?" she asked.

I thought for minute. "Nah, I'm okay. I'm glad that he had these experiences with you. I knew from the start that you were going to be a wild ride for Dad. But he always looked so happy, and he *was* so happy, and he adored you with all his heart and soul."

The Dish turned to me and cupped my face in her hands.

"I'll tell you what your father said about *you*, Sally, my darling," she said softly.

"What, Dish? Tell me."

"He said, 'If I ever have a chance to come back to this life, I want to come back as a child of Sally's.' "

Losing my last surviving parent was outrageously difficult. But my sorrow has been eased by the knowledge that I was gonna get to keep the Dish, and she was gonna keep me.

RECIPE: "RITA THE DISH" SHAIN'S ZUCCHINI KUGEL
My new favorite

INGREDIENTS

3 cups of grated zucchini slivers
½ cup of grated parmesan cheese
½ cup of diced onion
4 beaten eggs
½ cup Mazola oil
1 cup Bisquick
Garlic powder, oregano and season salt *This is where the really good cooks just throw it in by feel. All seasonings are too your taste, use more or less as you prefer.*

DIRECTIONS

Preheat oven to 350 degrees.

Beat eggs, add oil, add Bisquick, and everything else.

Pour into greased casserole and bake for 45 minutes or until nice and brown all over.

Enjoy!

THE TABLE

When I returned home to Columbus after my father's funeral, I spent an evening with a group of friends who had also lost both parents and now considered themselves to be *orphans*.

My mother had been an orphan as a child, and I had grown up with parents, so I wasn't buying the orphan thing.

I did, however, land on the fact that I had somehow become the new guard on the front line when it came to the children. *Oh, man, this was gonna be ugly. I don't wanna be the grown-up—I wanna be the baby.*

Then I heard a familiar, sarcastic voice in my head.

This voice—which sounded just like Alan Alda as Hawkeye Pierce from *M*A*S*H*—said, "Hey, Sal, guess what? Your folks are dead, and you're it. There are no more 'elders' to turn to for advice or cash. Those days are over, so you better buck the hell up."

Still, I wouldn't have minded a little more guidance and training for that head-of-the-table gig.

SONG: *THE TABLE*

For my parents

Year after year, the family gathers here—the table's set
Kids running around, the noisy sound of life
Holidays come and go, we're watching children grow
Candles are all aglow, blessings everywhere
You never knew that time could move so fast
Before your eyes
Somehow you blinked and thirty years flew by
Seasons bring new life in, those kids are having kids
A new generation lives, the old one's gone, it passes on
Take your seat at the head of the table
You've become the next in line
It's your time, to give of your heart as best you're able
You help the next one learn, so they can take their turn
When you are gone

You look behind you toward the kitchen, see the table where
You and your cousins sat not long ago
As children we're unaware of our parents' hopes and fears
They were shielding us those years till we were grown
And now we're grown
Now we sit at the head of the table
We've become the next in line
It's our time to guide with our hearts as best we're able
We help the next one learn so they can take their turn
When we are gone

Year after year the family gathers here, the tables set
Kids running around, the noisy sound of life
Honor the young, the old, treasure each story told
Those are the secrets we need to know
That history holds us to this table.

Chapter Seven

IT'S TIME TO CELEBRATE THE CRAZY

ONE EASY DAY

I refuse to watch violent or scary TV shows. I just can't seem to carve out precious free time to sit down in front of an oversized screen and watch a nightmare in living color. I can't look at zombies with their faces missing as they drag their half-chewed-off limbs and other dripping parts through some dark and creepy parking lot, on their way to have a beer with their wacky next-door neighbors who run the local meth lab.

Those heinous and bloody scenes are not for me. I've discovered that one quick accidental glance at any yucky visual will subliminally plant those horrifying messages inside my brain, where they will sit dormant and quiet until some future date, when the subsequent free-floating anxiety will randomly surface and convince me that the tall and handsome dryer repairman is, in fact, an alien who's wielding a nuclear power pack disguised as a Pringles can. He'll offer me a Pringle, knowing full well that I can't refuse a potato chip, and after one bite, I'll morph into an alien girl and become his drippy love slave, as he blows up my house and kills my husband and children.

Nope, I'll stick to watching cartoons, sitcoms, and my beloved late-night talk shows.

When it comes to my psyche, I need things easy and smooth, polite and lovely, charming and confrontation-free. I do not spend money on violent films, roller coasters, or the stock market. I'm all out of nerve. I used up my lifetime supply of bravery while raising children. I am now a lazy weenie.

I start each day hoping that the following twelve to sixteen hours will be worry- and chaos-free. But then I always seem to encounter random and silly aggravations that throw me into an antagonizing downward spiral, from which only red Twizzlers, M&M's, or pharmaceuticals can save me.

For instance, I'm entirely unable to tolerate any clothing that feels—even slightly—scratchy. I must wear my socks and underpants inside out, as I suffer from extreme tactile sensitivity. In recent years, I have found that many people have this same problem.

As a shopper and consumer, my nutty physical comfort issues are a challenge. Thankfully, I've discovered the perfect bra for me. I've worn the same style for years. I love it, know it, need it, want it, and I'm willing to pay the sixty-three dollars, plus tax, for it.

One day, it was time to refresh my supply, and I planned a nice outing to the mall to visit the one store that carries my brand. After an hour of frustration and inefficient foraging in the lingerie section, I panicked. I couldn't find my bra anywhere on the racks. (Oooh, *snap!* Oooh, *pardon the double pun!*)

I cornered the buxom saleslady. "What happened to Wacoal #3205? I've been wearing the same model for nine years. I can't find it anywhere!"

She shook her head. "I don't know what they were thinking, but they've discontinued some of their best sellers. Everyone is in a snit over this, me included." The saleslady pointed to her own significant chestal area to show solidarity.

She motioned me over to another rack, loaded with a different brand, and pointed to several bras. "Here try these. They might work for you like the old Wacoals. Let me know what you think."

I searched for my size among these foreign-looking bras. After grabbing three possibilities, I headed for the dressing room.

I angrily tossed my purse on the floor, took off my coat, and began the tortuous trying-on process. One bra's straps weren't stretchy enough for a comfortable wear. Another bra's underwire gouged me so high in the armpit that I couldn't put my arms down at my sides. The last bra I had chosen had a four-inch band around the back and with a row of five hook fasteners. *What the hell—this was my mother's bra!*

"How you doin', honey?" the saleswoman shouted over the fitting room door.

"Not good."

"Oh dear, let me see what I can come up with." She sounded pathetic.

For the next thirty minutes, I stood in front of the mirror, slowly sinking into a despair I hadn't felt since the last time I went through this—nine years ago. Bra after bra after bra, the saleslady proceeded to bring me everything in her department that had potential, but nothing fit—nothing worked. Finally, I could take no more. I put on my clothes, thanked the frazzled woman, and left the lingerie department.

I headed down the escalator to the first-floor makeup department to pick up a lipstick, hoping to salvage this shopping trip. I'd been wearing MAC's SeaSheer for an eternity. It was the perfect lip cover for me, with just the right pigment and level of glossy sheen, without being too oily or heavy. MAC products are pricey, so I had finished up every last drop by scooping out the remnants of lipstick with my fingernail and schmearing it on my lips.

When I say there was nothing left in the tube, believe me, even a bobby pin couldn't glean a thing.

"Hi, can I get a new SeaSheer, please?" I handed my empty tube of lipstick to the twentysomething beauty by the shelves of beautiful MAC products. Dressed in a short black skirt, black sweater, black tights, black shoes, and black hair, the only color she was sporting was on her face. *Nice touch.*

She took the tube and immediately frowned. "They stopped making this a while back. Let's find you a new color!"

"I'm sorry, what was that?" I stared at her.

"Follow me." She motioned at a display case. "We have tons of wonderful new shades and textures!"

Her perky attitude was gonna kill me.

"Seriously?" It was sinking in. "I have to start all over?"

"You'll be fine! Come on, it'll be fun!"

FUN?

This is what I *wanted* to say: "No, it will not be fun. I don't give a lab rat's ass about beautiful new shades. I want what I want, I want what I had, and I don't want to hear about anything new or anything discontinued. I have just spent an unsuccessful hour in a dressing room hoisting my girls every which way, and now you want me to be flexible and open to change—to go with the cosmetic flow? What happened to retail therapy? There is no therapy here, only issues. There is only hell now. It appears that I have discovered that there is, indeed, a hell right here in Nordstrom—which, by the way, I have always considered to be the Mecca of Retail Heaven. Until now. Peace out, bitches."

Thank goodness, this rant was only a silent thought bubble floating above my head. Otherwise, mall security might have gotten involved. I plucked my empty SeaSheer lipstick tube out of her hands and did my best nice-lady impression:

"Thanks, darling, but today's not a good day. I'm in a rush, but I'll be back."

Never.

And then there's my tea.

I have a tea that I love. It's called Lipton's Gentle Orange, and it's delightful. It's herbal, caffeine-free, and not expensive. I've been drinking it for years.

Lately, Lipton's Gentle Orange has been very hard to find. Certain stores won't stock it, while other stores had only one box, abandoned behind the more current flavors.

Of course, everyone suggested that I go online and just order the damn tea already, instead of chasing around town and complaining loudly. They were right. I found my tea on Lipton's official website and ordered a case that contained twelve boxes of tea with twenty teabags per box. Score one for the pushy geeks who shop online.

Eight months later, I went back to my favorite tea's website to order more, but there was no more. Lipton had discontinued Gentle Orange. They make something called raspberry-mango-butterfly-chamomile-lemon-flavored tea. They offer a tangerine-mango-rosehip-beeswax-zinger-flavored tea. They boast about their *most popular* orange-mango-passionfruit-jasmine-free-range-green-hay-flavored tea, but they have discontinued my Gentle Orange. I have vowed to forsake Lipton brand tea altogether. I have reached the end of my teabag ~~string~~ rope.

Thankfully, not every day threatens to be a shit-outta-luck day. Once in a very great while, I consciously notice the absence of heartache and crap. These are the moments in time where I stop and recognize that life has sent me an easy day.

EASY DAY PINK CLOUD #1

I was scheduled to fly from New York City, back home to Columbus, Ohio. Travel days carry a high risk of mayhem, but instead, this day contained a magical crazy-free journey.

On this day, my plane did NOT carry any children. Not a one. No one whimpered, screamed, or whined. No stinky overdue diapers wafted down the aisles. Also missing were adolescents with their annoying cell phones, yackety-yakking at offensive volumes and listening to headphones cranked so high you could play Name That Tune from across the aisle.

On *this* flight home, every passenger enjoyed the lovely quiet. We were just a bunch of exhausted, weary, hungover weekend travelers who all fell asleep at the same time and woke up just as we were preparing to land. The stewardess marveled at how no one had asked her for a beverage. For her, this was a career first. She called our plane "The Flying Nap."

It is on days like this that I'm totally enamored with life.

EASY DAY PINK CLOUD #6

One day in late winter, I ran inside a department store to wait out a pelting icy rain storm. Wet and aggravated, I turned to see a sale table full of winter sweaters. There, on top of a messy pile of cardigans and pullovers, I noticed the most magnificent taupe wool tunic, marked down to the equivalent of *almost free*. I bolted to the dressing room to try it on, whispering tiny prayers that the sweater would look halfway decent on me since it would be a bargain at twice the marked-down price. Designed with a deep V neck, the sweater had sleeves that easily rolled up and stayed up, and the length in the back was perfect. From behind, it hid a myriad of sins. I looked smashing in it. But more importantly, I had stumbled upon the rarest of fashion items—a discounted, itch-free wool sweater.

When I got home, I discovered that my last-minute, discounted top looked both sporty with pants and elegant with skirts. This new purchase soon became my first choice, go-to garment, one that I continued to wear and adore for at least a decade. Life again, had sent me a nice day, complete with a nice bonus.

EASY DAY PINK CLOUD #36DD

While on tour, I noticed that a large-busted musician friend was wearing a sports bra, and she looked very . . . well, let's just say, "put together" under her T-shirt. She had issues with large-sized synthetic and delicate foundations, and had decided to stick with sports bras. She went on and on about this sports bra's comfort and durability, and I was sold.

Returning home after the tour, I immediately shifted my focus from the expensive department-store lingerie racks to

Title Nine—my favorite catalog of women's athletic clothing. There, among the pages of skinny, active women in running shoes and yoga pants, I found a plethora of bras. I ordered a few different styles and tried them on in the privacy of my bedroom. I easily chose the best one for me, and then ordered a ridiculous number of them. Some for now and, of course, many for later.

The catalog rated each bra by how well your "girls" stayed put, and my favorite had received the top award—five dumbbells, the best of the best. This bra guarantees that if I were shot out of a cannon, my breasts and I would painlessly arrive at our destination in precisely the proper order.

And now, I'm good to go. I'm also good to run, dance, bounce, and hopefully, shut up about my boobs already.

As a citizen of the planet, I am aware of how life throws real sorrow and serious heartbreak at frightening speeds. It's during those moments you will find me, as a devoted family member, on the front lines with the best of them, ready to serve and shield my loved ones, body and soul, from all things dreadful. When I am needed, I am there in full frontal preparedness. And I will not be whining, pulling, or yanking at my clothing, because I will be dressed in seam- and tag-free underwear. Every day must start out as an easy day.

The rest of that day is not up to me.

SONG: ONE EASY DAY

I wake up in the morning with a sleepy face
I gotta drag my butt to join the human race
First I'm gonna meditate—set my pace
Right into one easy day
I throw back the covers, my feet hit the floor
I sit for awhile until I'm sure
I'm ready for the craziness outside my door
I search for one easy day
CHORUS
One easy day, one easy day
How lovely it would be to live trouble-free
For one easy day

In my easy day, we're all kind and patient
I keep my big mouth shut, no misbehaving
Everyone I meet, they're also navigatin'
Toward one easy day
Then I make a phone call, and it goes right through
A human says "Hello, what can I do for you?"
I get to say my peace, that's all I wanted to do
Oh, that's one easy day
CHORUS

What if you had a day—no one got in your face
No one ticked you off to put you in your place
I think I'll step aside and let the rats all race
And give them an easy day

What if we all woke up and there was no war
No more hungry children, suffering, poor
We can't be the only ones asking for—
ONE EASY DAY!

MY BROKER

Soon after marrying Michael, I realized that my husband saw me as a grown-up. Even though I felt like an adolescent on the inside, the truth was that my outsides were approaching fifty. Michael, in his good-natured and gentle fashion, suggested I start taking on some adult proactive tasks.

"Like what?" I whined. "Do I have'ta?"

In response, he fanned out my bank statements on the kitchen table. Somehow, after all my single-mother years of scrimping and saving, watching over every penny, squeezing every buffalo off of every nickel, and, frankly, being a neurotic pain in the ass during financial negotiations, I had finally clucked out a significant little nest egg. Therefore, Michael proudly pointed out, I had become a mature and established working-mother-artist, and the time had come to get rid of the *PASSBOOK* and get *A BROKER!*

Michael had a broker, and he thought I should have a broker.

I said, "Okay, take me to your broker!" But no, he thought I should have a broker to call my own. I didn't understand why we couldn't share a broker, but he lovingly explained how I should be autonomous and might prefer a female broker, so I could be myself and learn from the broker. Then I could share the teachings of the broker with my/our daughter, who would learn to recognize the value of outside advice, and maybe, eventually, she'd get a broker.

In essence, it became clear that everyone should have their own damn broker.

Of course, he was right, so I agreed to get my own damn broker. However, I had no idea how to *get* a broker—let alone what to *do* with a broker. Thankfully, Michael's broker had a female associate in the same office and she agreed to be *MY BROKER*. So I made an appointment with WENDY, heretofore known as *MY BROKER*. I was impressed with my follow-through and felt mature, but still a little hesitant and intimidated.

It had been a while since I last met with a financial professional.

During my divorce, I spent a harrowing twenty minutes glazing over and emotionally shutting down with *MY BANKER,* who helped me refinance the house after my ex-husband did the "quitclaim deed" thingy during our settlement agreement. *MY BANKER,* in our one and only meeting, gave me forty pieces of paper I didn't understand, along with some cookies and coffee. In return, I gave *MY BANKER* a promise of fifteen-years-worth of large monthly checks containing those wacky interest fees.

When I married Michael six years later, I sold that house, which added vitamins and iron to my nest egg, making it large and healthy enough to be worth protecting. As a result, I was now considering a long-term relationship with someone who would be my financial guidance counselor.

So, of course, I obsessed about what to wear.

Before the big day, a lawyer gal pal with a size-12 passion for Nordstrom allowed me to skim her closet for something gray and navy, straight and conservative. She told me my wardrobe concerns over one little meeting were complete crap, but I was hell-bent on looking like that person who needed a broker—i.e. her. First, she yanked my chain by making me try on stiff and itchy dry-clean-only outfits with darts and zippers. Then she generously lent me clothes, heels, and hose, along with tips on applying daytime makeup. In her heart of hearts, she clearly couldn't wait to see her wacky-free-spirited-musician-friend spend a day in her shoes, literally.

MY BROKER's office was in a brand-new building on the outskirts of our newly gentrified downtown. I pulled into the concrete, multilevel parking structure that had once been a meat-packing plant and drove up the narrow, winding spiral to the top floor. As I stepped out of the car, the sparkling blacktop looked as if diamonds had been paved into the surface. This gave me the poetic feeling that I was walking toward the potential wealth I would amass due to having a broker. Also, since *MY BROKER* was a woman, I had some kind of cosmic idea that these pavement sparkles were shards from the glass ceiling that *MY BROKER* had burst through on her way up to the top.

The view from my fifth-story parking space revealed an amazing dichotomy of urban construction. Down below, I spotted a lone undeveloped grassy field, full of cars and pickup trucks. Long-haired guys in ratty, old jeans hauled coolers past porta-potties and a stage being set up for some event. Maybe the construction workers were having a union meeting . . . or just a picnic?

But I had no time to gawk. I had a meeting of my own to get to—with *MY BROKER!*

I found the stairs down to the street, grabbed the railing, and paused to concentrate on my descent. I had no business taking hollow metal stairs in borrowed high heels, but I scoffed at the elevator because I had committed to "10,000 Steps" in my desire to be a youthful-looking old person. I slowly and deliberately wobbled down all five floors to the street. I crossed at the light, which I thought was very grown-up of me, and made my way to the glass-and-chrome world of high finance.

I breezed into the marble lobby with its sprawling wall of elevators. Just then, an elevator opened and a group of well-dressed, high-powered people flowed out like a school of minnows. After they passed, I entered the elevator, only to be caught in an overwhelming cloud of aftershave and perfume. As I pushed the button for the eleventh floor, I began a sneezing fit that lasted the entire ride up. With my nose running and my hand stuck in my purse digging out a tissue, I heard the ding announcing my arrival. The elevator doors opened. I looked up and saw a mammoth desk. The receptionist was right there, front and center, not twenty feet away from me.

Shit, no lobby? I'm here, right now? This is it?

I quickly turned my face to the back wall of the elevator and blew my nose with all the quiet force I could muster. In a panic, I swirled my tissue for one big deep dig up into my nostrils, lest I spend the meeting with *MY BROKER* with a huge shnork in my nose.

I stepped toward the receptionist and quickly scanned the space. Beyond her desk, glass partitions created a maze of transparent cubicles.

If I could see all these people, surely they could see me . . . and my drippy schnozz.

"I'm here to see *MY BROKER.*" I knew I sounded inane, but I was still completely preoccupied with my nose.

"Does your broker have a name?" said the twentysomething behind the desk.

Her eyes were aimed right at my nose. I was sure of it.

Within seconds, *Wendy-MY-BROKER* was walking towards me with a warm smile. Petite and naturally attractive with barely any makeup, she wore a royal-blue skirt suit, a hip and funky silver necklace, and low-heeled pumps. Her beautifully coiffed hair had that messy-on-purpose look which I coveted. We introduced ourselves with a handshake, and my easily irritated nose was relieved to note the absence of perfume.

I immediately liked her and felt a little more at ease, save for this nose issue.

She took me back to her office. "Would you like a cup of coffee? Or some water?"

"Water would be great," I said.

"I'll be right back."

As soon as Wendy left, I whipped out my compact mirror and studied my nose. All good in the shnork department—I was in the clear.

Wendy returned, handed me a water bottle, and took a seat behind her desk. She pointed toward the available client chair in front of me.

"Seriously, this is some office building." I hung my purse strap across the back of the chair. "All this glass, and everyone in suits. It makes me think about the Windex and dry cleaning bills." I laughed and, thank goodness, so did she.

As soon as my butt hit the chair, I slipped off the high heels that hurt like a mother. With the shoes off and my nose secured, I could now think straight.

Unfortunately, I had no idea what I was supposed to say or do next.

Wendy must have been warned that I would be an immigrant in the world of investing, because she started slow and easy. She asked about the kids, did I still enjoy all the travel and performing, and did I see myself retiring at any point? She made it seem like she had all the time in the world for me. I asked about her personal life as well, and I learned we both had daughters and loving husbands on whom we doted. More importantly, we shared the fears of not wanting our kids burdened with our own physical care down the line. She got IT, and she got ME.

"Ready to start?" Wendy asked.

I sat up straight. "I don't know much, but I'm excited to learn. Just think of yourself as my personal Mary Poppins."

Without a word, Wendy reached into her desk drawer and pulled out a root-beer barrel wrapped in cellophane. She dropped it into my palm.

"Spoonful of sugar?" she asked.

We had a great laugh, and she took off running. Wendy explained this fund and that fund, this percentage and that pie chart, and finally, how much money I should invest in conservative places, and how much she thought I'd be safe to risk.

IT ALL MAKES SENSE because she is wonderful, and I'm a grown-up, and we get each other! I wanted her to know that I was ready to commit to her ideas, so I took out a pen and drew a pie chart just for her.

"Wendy, I'm 100% in, so let me break it down for you." I pointed to my drawing. "In my pie chart, there's 30% faith, 30% trust, and 30% comfort zone."

She studied my pie chart. "Sally, that's lovely, but based on your math, we should all be happy you've come here today!"

It took my brain a few embarrassing seconds to add my percentages together, but then we both doubled over with laughter, and I couldn't have been more pleased. I wrote the check, and she said she would immediately get started on the various investment funds—with the goal that, in my old age, I could remain independent. I also opened a little fund for my daughter, so I could assist her down the line, should she need it. Whether her fund grew to be enough money for graduate school, or just an extra pair of flip-flops from DSW, I wanted her to know her mother cared.

I felt fabulous and independent, accomplished and in control. *Anyone* would agree that I had made some very grown-up choices.

I had been an adult for some time, but as a divorced single mother, I had spent years living hand-to-mouth and gig-to-gig. I knew my parents worried, yet I never asked for help. I had only recently moved into a wonderful second marriage, and with my daughter's plans to attend the college that had offered her a scholarship, I had been able to put my foot on the gas (literally). I had hit the road, touring all over the country, and squirreled away every dime. I knew that these were the years to work hard, and more importantly, save hard—just like a grown-up.

And now *Wendy-MY-BROKER* had painlessly offered clear and concise assistance that wasn't patronizing or sleep-inducing—but rather, exciting and empowering. Together, we would accomplish great things for my financial well-being. On top of everything she taught me, she even validated my parking. Could'ja bust?

I took the elevator down to the street level, ready to begin my new life. I am woman, hear me roar . . . about my accounts compounding annually, with no minimum balance necessary, and how everything could be liquid in just twenty-four hours if need be. All I had to do was call *MY BROKER*.

As I walked out into the Columbus summer sunshine, I realized that, in the euphoria of my financial hubris, I had exited the building through the wrong door. I stopped short and found myself in the tent-city circus and grassy field full of cars and porta-potties. I saw tie-dye T-shirts hanging from vintage VW buses. This festival was set up right at the busy intersection of "Broker's Office" and "Overpriced Restaurants." (*The very restaurants I'll be visiting once MY BROKER has done her job.*)

I started to giggle. *What's up with this grassroots 1960s-style festival set among these brand-new structures made of glass and chrome, buildings teeming with people wearing expensive suits and overwhelming personal fragrances? All this on a school day no less!*

I crossed the street and spotted a middle-aged guy with graying temples. His long dreadlocks were gathered into a swinging ponytail. With a lit joint hanging from his lips, he staked a Grateful Dead flag into the dirt. We made eye contact, and he shot me an approachable smile.

"Hey, what's with the tents and all these people?" I asked.

He passed the *doobie** to a slender, deeply tanned young woman with hair down to her *tuchas* and a bikini top that was primarily pointless. Music blared from his camper, and I struggled to hear him.

"Yeah, man," he said, "like tonight, the Grateful Dead's bass player is playing over at the Pavilion, and this is our version of a tailgate party!"

"You're kidding! Phil Lesh is here?" I jumped with excitement and landed off-kilter, my right foot falling out of its shoe. I felt too gleeful to care about what that must have looked like. "Do you know if I can still get tickets?"

"I couldn't tell'ya." He grabbed his girl around the waist, and she leaned in, physically marking her territory. They started kissing, and when I saw their tongues in battle, and the pot smoke wafting from their conjoined lips, I turned to leave.

"Thanks, man," I said, waving him off as I turned to walk toward the parking garage.

I paused and began laughing. I had said, "Thanks, man," as if I'd been transported back to 1972. I knew I looked like an aging PTA member on the outside, especially after having just met with *MY BROKER* and all, but on the inside, I was just like him—an aging hippie.

I quickly wondered if this gray-haired hippie guy had a broker, but then again, this gray-haired hippie guy might have *been* a broker! If my outsides didn't match my insides, possibly his insides didn't match his outsides either.

And, right then and there, I recognized my lesson. I had walked into a brokerage house with the purest intentions of behaving responsibly in this new economy. I didn't whine or cry, I didn't glaze over and space out. Instead, I listened, and learned, and made some educated decisions that felt right and made sense. And, as the universe witnessed my personal paradigm shift, it gave me a little perk by slapping me in the face with the smell of pot and a guy who was getting high one half block away from the box office where I could buy tickets to hear Phil Lesh.

Believing that my insides and my outsides might enjoy a little time together, I went home, threw on my jeans, put a picnic dinner together, and grabbed my "old man." It was going to be a magical evening and celebration of this new era.

This would be the "Night of the Living Deadhead Girl Who Finally Has a *BROKER.*"

PRAYERS FOR A BLOUSE

When I wore "the blouse," I felt like a fashion superhero. I'd be all flowy and confident with my sophisticated manner and graceful posturing, convinced that everyone saw only my fabulous taste in wearable art, rather than the personal and physical neglect that was now my ass. I called this blouse my win-win, slam-dunk, fashion-high-five. Finally, I felt like I was wearing and doing something right.

This blouse was my go-to blouse. My A-list piece of clothing that caused perfect strangers to say, "I love your top!" Thrilled, I would reply, "Thank you, I've had this blouse for eleven years, and it's never once seen the inside of a dryer." Of course, they would immediately give me the polite smile that one saves for the crazy, but that's understandable, 'cuz I was crazy in love with this blouse.

I purchased the blouse back in the summer of 2001. Though Mom had passed away just ten weeks prior, my sister and her husband had agreed that their daughter's wedding, which had been on the books for a year, should go on. Our family was emotionally upside down and inside out, and to make crazy crazier, my sister wanted me to bring my serious boyfriend Michael with me to this *simcha*.* She told me the wedding would be the perfect opportunity for our entire family to check him out.

Still, I was concerned with how things would go. When a family has a large life-cycle event, like a wedding, that follows a large life-cycle event, like a funeral, all rules and bets are off. How does anyone know where to stand, what to do, what to say, or how to behave, given the complexity and conflicts of the current joys and obvious sorrows?

But I surrendered, let my big sister tell me what to do, and invited Michael to join me.

Once we arrived in New Milford, Connecticut, we stopped by my sister's house to hug and kiss and connect. A few immediate family members were gathered together, and the collective laughter and excitement of introducing Michael helped me relax every muscle from my hairline on down. I knew the tone for the weekend was now set. Everyone felt easy and happy and knew just the right thing to say.

They also knew what to wear. I quickly saw that my family and guests were coiffed and sharply dressed and ready for everything. Having just spent months and months at my mother's side, I had completely spaced out and neglected to organize a wardrobe appropriate for a classic

The Blouse at the Grand Canyon

Jewish family wedding with a potential husband in tow. I mentioned to my sister that I felt horribly underdressed and unprepared. She lovingly suggested that, at some point during the weekend, Michael and I might slip away and do a little clothes shopping for me.

The Blouse in Pittsburgh

The next day, when there was a break in the action (i.e. eating), we excused ourselves to "run a few errands" before we were needed at the rehearsal dinner. Michael and I drove a few miles to the center of my sister's sleepy New England town. We decompressed as we strolled through the village square, looking into the windows of an ancient Ace Hardware store, a family-owned bakery with a fabulous neon sign from the 1940s, and an old café. Not a cute café like on TV, owned by some plucky, terrific cook, but one that the health department should maybe look into. We walked and laughed, joking and debating what food we might order with the least amount of risk in a place like that, when *BOOM*, we stumbled upon a little boutique. As soon as we spotted the hippie-style "alternative folk music" coffeehouse poster taped to the storefront window, we both knew that this would be the shop for me.

And, there in the window, hung the blouse.

It was cut long, like a short kimono, and made from several different versions of black-and-white mishmashy prints—one black-and-white print for the sleeves, a second black-and-white print for the collar and front pocket, and a third variation of black-and-white for the bodice.

I flung open the boutique door. An adorable little bell announced my arrival. I might have heard a saleswoman say hello, but I can't be sure, due to my focused beeline for the blouse.

I grabbed the hanger and turned the blouse around to discover a magnificent, vibrantly colored scene of Japanese geishas on the flip side. The outrageous pairing of fabrics made this a hip bowling shirt in the front with a walking piece of art on the back.

Whose lucky day was I having? It couldn't possibly have been more perfect for me.

The Blouse on the North Carolina Shore

But then I peeked at the price tag and gasped.

Oh, crap, was that out loud? I thought. I glanced from side to side to see if anyone was within earshot. Thankfully, no one seemed to have heard me. I grabbed the blouse and flew to the dressing room. I was in drastic need of something new, and drastic needs called for drastic measures, even if drastic prices garnered drastic responses.

I love these types of boutiques—the ones with quaint little dressing rooms and antique full-length mirrors. There was even a chair for Michael, where he could patiently pretend to be patient. I stood before the dressing room mirror and peeled off my ratty, wrinkled linen jacket, not caring the least where it landed. Then I slowly and gently slipped this new blouse over my customary black sleeveless tank.

The instant connection between me and this blouse was spiritual and otherworldly. I stood there glowing and giddy in front of the mirror, convinced that the blouse would be mine. Of course, this thought was immediately

The Blouse in Colorado

followed by my ritual mental and emotional headbanging.

> **ME:** How could I spend such a ridiculous amount of money in such haste—shouldn't I think about this for a minute?
>
> **ME SQUARED:** Well, you're thinking about it now, so check your watch, and after sixty seconds, shut up and go immediately to the cash register—or you'll miss tonight's dinner party.

> **ME:** Do I really need this blouse? Why is this blouse different from all other blouses?
>
> **ME SQUARED:** Because it's perfect in every way—it's artistic, it fits, it's machine washable, you look great in it. The only thing that sucks is the price, so shut up and go immediately to the cash register—or you'll miss tonight's dinner party.

> **ME:** Should I ask Michael what he thinks?
>
> **ME SQUARED:** No. You're a grown woman, and this blouse works perfectly with everything you own, and you don't have to ask permission or validate anything—so again, I repeat, shut up and go immediately to the cash register—or you'll miss tonight's dinner party.

ME: Hmmmmmmmmmmmmmmmmmmm . . .

ME SQUARED ADDENDUM: Let's face it. We know you really love this blouse, and if you wear it all the time, the Cost Per Wear (CPW) will be amortized down to a reasonable price. You'll just have to take good care of it, and extract the best CPWs you can. Now, seriously, press stop on this endless loop of doubt, get your act in gear, accept the fact that you're paying retail, and don't stress or worry, 'cuz your late mother would be very proud that you've decided to step up the jams on your appearance. She's nagging from the spirit world, and she's thrilled that you found something so lovely, and you should wear it in the best of health, but she, too, wants you to shut up and go immediately to the cash register—or YOU'LL MISS TONIGHT'S DINNER PARTY.

"I'm taking the blouse!" I hollered from the dressing room, exhausted from the struggle.

For the last twelve years, the blouse has been my truest companion.

I did marry Michael, and when we took our three blended kids on our honeymoon, the blouse was there. At my fiftieth birthday celebration, the blouse was there. When I moved my daughter into her college dorm and my dad into Rita's house, the blouse was there. We took vacations, hosted countless Jewish holiday dinners, moved the boys into post-college apartments, and if I was there, the blouse was there.

And now, it's been lovingly suggested by a few very brave and nameless souls that I let the *shmatte** go. It hasn't bothered me that the fabric is so faded and worn that you could almost read a book through it. But the horrifying truth is that when friends see photos of me taken over the past decade, they glance at me with furrowed brows and say incredulously:

"Seriously, that blouse again? Give it a rest, Sal!"

And so, finally, I'm giving it a rest—a permanent rest. While I've braced myself for this transition, I'm still a little weepy and completely weirded out that I'll no longer have the security of my glorious and colorful uniform.

I've decided that before I release this blouse from its life

The Blouse & the Dish, a year post-Dad

with me, I will write a few words, a blessing if you will. I'm going to light a candle and mourn the loss of the best shirt ever. Then, when this moment of gratitude is over, I'm going to sew myself another one. I've always considered myself an amateur seamstress, and though this challenge is as overwhelming as this loss, I'm committing to the creation of a new one. I can't think of life without it, and so I plan to take the karma and the reincarnation of the blouse into my own hands.

After years of making clothes and toys for my daughter, I know enough about sewing to know what I don't know. Based on much research, I've purchased a DVD from the public television show, *Sewing With Nancy*, to serve as my tutorial on how to make a pattern for a blouse from this blouse so I can make a new blouse. I hope the video is easier to understand than that last sentence.

So far, I have meticulously prepared everything. I'm all set up

The Blouse in Las Vegas

with my foam core board and pushpins and tracing paper and special disappearing-ink pens, just as Nancy has instructed. But my heart is beating erratically and I'm beginning to feel immobilized from impending separation anxiety, as the unsuspecting blouse hangs in wait for the Kevorkian moment. I've yet to take a scissors and cut the blouse along its seams. I'm dripping with sweat.

But I've horsed around long enough writing this piece. I must move forward and finish the prayer to honor and bless this one special thing that has been there for me for so very long.

In closing, I will ask the congregation to please rise for the reading of the dedication.

Dear G—d:
We thank you today for the gift that was this blouse.
We ask that you keep the memory of this blouse alive through all future generations of blouses to come. Allow them to swiftly and effortlessly flow through mine own hand. Lord, bless and guide these hands that I might design a skeletal pattern from these worn and weary itty-bitty pieces of cloth that sadly remain from this mighty soldier. Promise and vow unto me that you've seen to it that Nancy from *Sewing With Nancy* on PBS knows what she's talking about, 'cuz once I cut this thing up, it's curtains. Not, oh Lord, that I covet or think for one minute that I could make

window treatments, but as I rip unto this blouse and taketh apart, only your generous spirit and love can direct me to recreate a new blouse that could be termed both dressy-casual and truly fabulous while camouflaging my rear end. I beseech unto you to forward this message along to any other Deities of Textiles, or possibly Crafting, in case I'm praying up the wrong tree.

G–d, give me strength and purpose, and keep thy thirty-three-year-old Singer sewing machine from stupid and random acts of haste. Remove from me this short attention span that might render unseemly frustrations and wrongdoings that lead me to waste money I don't have on fabric I don't need. I pray that you will watch over me through my days and make of me a joyful success. In return, I will create a house of heavenly blouses and keep them holy, hmmm—not ripped holey—but, you know, spiritually holy. And in the name of Vogue, Simplicity, Butterick, and McCall's, I will commit to using only fragrance-free detergents and a light iron. Help me to replicate the joy and comfort I have received from this one true blouse.

In closing, I say to you, oh Lord, should you doubt my pure intentions and dismiss this prayer, I beg of you, and forgive me if you've heard this already, but I am quoting from your sacred bible story, *Fiddler on the Roof,* wherein it states, "Even a poor tailor is entitled to some happiness." **To this end, I say, Amen.**

Doesn't this make you nervous for me?
I had to eat three whole candy bars while doing this.
But don't judge.

WHAT'S UP WITH JEWISH COMPOSERS AND CHRISTMAS HITS?

When the Four Bitchin' Babes decided to put together a winter holiday musical revue for the 2012 touring season, I suggested we call it "An Evening of Shared Musical Traditions." I knew full well that any Christmas show that this gefilte-fish-and-bagel-loving Jewish Girl performed in would have to have a whole lot of Chanukah going on.

We agreed to write some new comedic holiday songs that represented our personal, yet twisted, views on what the "Season of Giving" meant to us. My bandmates hoped to showcase a few classic Christmas hits, and I took it upon myself to go searching for a few classic Hannukah hits as well. Unfortunately, I discovered that the selection was dismal—or rather, that there was no selection.

During my research, I also discovered that the majority of classic Christmas hits were written by Jews. Beginning in the Tin Pan Alley era of the 1930s and continuing into the '40s and '50s, Jewish lyricists and composers had produced wildly successful

Christmas tunes. Song after song after song, the astounding hit list goes on and on:

"Rudolph, the Red-Nosed Reindeer" and "Rockin' Around the Christmas Tree," both by Johnny Marks

"White Christmas," by Irving Berlin (a *cantor's** son)

"Silver Bells," music by Jay Livingston, lyrics by Ray Evans

"Sleigh Ride," lyrics by Mitchell Parish (born Michael Hyman Pashelinsky!)

"Santa Baby," by Joan Ellen Javits and Philip Springer

"Winter Wonderland," by Felix Bernard & Richard B. Smith

"Let It Snow!," music by Jule Styne, lyrics by Sammy Cahn

"The Christmas Song" (aka "Chestnuts Roasting on an Open Fire"), music by Mel Tormé, lyrics by Robert Wells. (My mother went out on a few dates with Mel Tormé in high school. She liked him, but he was "too fast.")

Not only had Jewish musicians composed many of the greatest winter holiday tunes of all time, but many famous Jewish pop artists have recorded Christmas-related albums as well. Barbra Streisand, Neil Diamond, Harry Connick, Jr., Carole King, Barry Manilow, Bette Midler, Kenny G, and BOB DYLAN have all released Christmas projects.

Once I learned that all these fancy-schmancy, famous Jewish performing artists had opened their hearts and hopped on the Christmas train, I eagerly set about preparing my music and *shtick** for the Babes' holiday stage show.

Meanwhile, I wondered why these magnificent composers and lyricists couldn't have taken a few minutes to give the Jewish people a little ditty to carry them through December's onslaught of joy to the world while walking through a winter wonderland. Would it have been such a terrible *shonda** to throw together a series of musical notes, shape them into a couple of verses, create a sing-along chorus with a good hook, and make sure it's got a nice bridge for musical relief and lyrical point making? I'm sure there were plenty of Jewish mothers who would have loved for their children to quit chasing after someone else's holiday traditions already and bring home a song that their family could sit down to Chanucha dinner with.

From my own childhood, I remembered the beloved "Dreidel Song," which was brought to America by Sam Grossman and Sam Goldfarb z"l.

I have a little dreidel, I made it out of clay
And when it's dry and ready, oh dreidel, I shall play

How was I going to put a theatrical sparkle and shine on the age-old "Dreidel Song"?

Update it, that's how. I preserved the melody, threw in some pertinent information regarding our Channuka history, included some quirky social commentary, and of course, wrapped it up with a nice little universal-lovefest-kind-of-sentiment at the end.

In keeping with the 'folk process'—which means choosing to contribute to the cultural and contemporary evolution of "The Dreidel Song"—I just went in there and put my spin on it, you should pardon my meaning.

SONG: THE DREIDEL DO-OVER
And now, a spin-off of "The Dreidel Song"

When I was a little girl, I loved the dreidel song
Every year at Hannukah, we'd all sing along
We'd sing, "Dreidel, Draydal, Dreydle, I made it out of clay"
I thought I'd take an old song for a brand-new spin today

CHORUS
We celebrate with spirit
We celebrate with lights
We celebrate the miracle with candles on eight nights

Long ago, the bad guys tore our temple down
There beneath the rubble, our sacred oil was found
It was just a thimbleful, not enough to last one night
But it burned for eight long days
Gave us this Festival of Lights
CHORUS

You see, because we're Jewish, got no holly—got no tree
Don't wear Christmas sweaters
Don't sit down on Santa's knee
Nothing can compete with how Christmas rolls on through
So we have Hanukah for folks like me and folks like . . . me
CHORUS

What's up with that fruitcake, what's up with eggnog?
Just fry potato pancakes, feh, an artery gets clogged
We love your Christmas cookies
Jack Frost nipping at our noses
Was Jack Frost a plastic surgeon
Did he do the nose of Moses?
CHORUS

With our family traditions, many customs, many ways
We celebrate this season, finding joy in every day
I have my menorah, you might decorate a tree
Together we all say a prayer for love, good health
Prosperity and peace!

* **Channuka, Chanucha, Hannukah, Chanukah** Eight days,
  four spellings, one wonderful holiday!

BOY ON WHEELS

My girlfriend Claudia had three rambunctious boys, aged twelve, ten, and eight. Her kids were known at school for their athletic abilities and terrific study habits, but what we neighborhood moms envied the most was her husband Rick's tremendous gratitude for how hard she worked as a wife and mother.

One day, after a Jazzercise class, Claudia was all abuzz over her husband's decision to take her away for a romantic weekend. They would be attending his boss's daughter's destination wedding at some fancy-schmancy Myrtle Beach Resort in South Carolina. Rick had taken care of all the plans. He had booked the grandparents to babysit for the entire weekend and instructed her to purchase a beautiful gown. For grins, he had reminded her to get a manicure *and* a pedicure.

Upon returning home from South Carolina, Claudia had a glow about her. It had been a fabulous weekend of sunshine, parties, and fun. Also, there had been private time to reconnect with Rick.

A little over a month later, Claudia started feeling unusually tired and faintly queasy. She immediately suspected that she was pregnant. A quick trip to her doctor revealed that a fourth baby was on its way.

To say that Claudia experienced emotional conflict (i.e. went nuclear) would be an understatement. She was so pissed she could barely speak to Rick, and if she did have something to say, she focused only on the topic of vasectomies. She was as serious as a heart attack.

Of course, as soon as Claudia gave birth and held her fourth baby boy in her exhausted arms, she ran out of anger. She knew the drill of raising boys, and once she was settled at home, she turned a blind eye to all the boy-crap that had taken over the house and the yard. Finally, she accepted defeat and ignored the garage, which had turned into a parking lot for Big Wheels, tricycles, Huffy BMXs, skateboards, Rollerblades, scooters, skinny-tire ten-speeds, fat-tire road bikes, a prototype Soap Box Derby-style go-kart, and of course, the little red wagon permanently dressed up for its annual stroll in the neighborhood's Fourth of July parade.

She could only sigh, one more boy, one more bike.

As a family, they enjoyed long Saturday afternoon bike rides through the neighborhood. Rick turned out to be natural Father Goose-type whose boys would pedal along in the wake of their dad's speed and power. He also laid down the rules and bylaws, decreeing that helmet wearing was a deal breaker, and bike maintenance was regularly required or the bike would be impounded.

Occasionally, Rick signed on for multi-kilometer charity rides with boys his own age—a posse of professional men over forty. Rick and his pals conducted intricate planning sessions over drinks and chicken wings. The guys spent hours dissecting details like the mileage between pit stops and the length of time it *should* take to get from the early-morning starting line to their first night's destination hotel. They placed bets on each other's performance and endurance, and who could go the furthest without a restroom break. And, most importantly, they would discuss at length which restaurant would be the best place to celebrate their big finish and monumental physical achievements with gourmet, grass-fed steaks and local craft beers.

Claudia marveled at how these big boys with big incomes bought big toys that required big performance outfits—just so they could look like big shots. These grown men blew outrageous amounts of money on must-have gear—tight spandex shorts with pads for their butts, water bottles that strapped to their waists, and prescription, multi-vision, progressive goggles with some kind of dental tool that perched on the sides of their heads to serve as rearview mirrors.

Still, Claudia was charmed by the fact that her forty-five-year-old husband had a pack of friends who would play outside with him. These buddies all shared an unsettling need for speed. This made Claudia ever watchful about keeping their insurance premiums up-to-date.

She also came to the stunning realization that she'd never met a boy or man who didn't share a fascination for all things that rolled on wheels.

Once, there was talk of the family taking a long and scenic bicycling vacation, but Claudia said no and stood her ground. Literally. Her *boys*, who had inherited their father's competitive spirit, were more than welcome to spend eight to ten hours a day on their bikes . . . without her. She had no intention of chasing them up hills, lagging behind, sweating profusely, and feeling humiliated while her entire family flew forward with boundless energy.

Nope, when it came time to negotiate a family vacation, Claudia believed that giving birth to four strapping sons allowed her the right to nix all bike seats and tight-stretchy-pants.

Okay, boys, go play outside.

SONG: *BOY ON WHEELS*
For the Eastmoor boys

Little tyke riding on his little trike
Roaring through the neighborhood
Sunny little towhead, tornado all in bright red
He's looking good
He's just a boy on wheels—he's just a boy on wheels
Mom's a little nervous—the kid's a little reckless
He up and goes
Papa says it's all right, Mom's a little uptight
Inside he knows—that's just a boy on wheels
He's just a boy on wheels
Wind up the wind, and away we go
There's no point in going, if you gotta go slow

Later when he's sixteen, racing on a ten-speed
Why walk when you can ride?
Up the streets everywhere, he no longer cuts his hair
It's his disguise, his Mama cries
Oh my, he's just a girl on wheels!
There's a motorbike in college
He smokes a little foliage out in L.A.
He tanks her up and shifts her, hangs out like a drifter
In Monterey, he loves the way it feels to be a boy on wheels
Here comes a girl, on skates she flies
She steals his heart—their life goes rolling by

Their kids are off and running, he thinks about retiring
He can't sit still
He needs to find the answers, to move a little faster
Up over the hill
She buys him brand new wheels, two-seater studmobile
Youth cannot escape him, when he's set in motion
It comes from underneath the hood
Got a sunburn on his bald head, tornado in a Corvette
He's looking good—he's just a boy on wheels
Wind up the wind, and away we go
There's no point in going, if you gotta go slow
If you're going on wheels!

I THINK WE'RE ALONE NOW

We are now empty nesters—all three kids have moved out. Of course, we still worry about them and remain devoted to their well-being, but for now, these kids are off the dole, and they have left the building.

In this empty house, I can now rock out and misbehave. I'm gonna live by my whims, use poor judgment, and do any number of dreadful and stupid things that would annoy a saint. I will do all the things I yelled at the children for—just because I CAN.

I will walk into the house, take off my shoes, and leave them directly in the center of the foyer.

I will sit in front of the TV with my index finger inside a peanut butter jar, and then monkey with the TV remote using my scuzzy peanut-butter finger. I will return the peanut butter to the kitchen, and leave the peanut butter jar lid on the coffee table under the newspapers in the family room. Where it will remain undiscovered for a week.

I will play with knives and matches without supervision.

I will stand in front of the open refrigerator for as long as I want, in case anything has changed since I peeked in there twenty minutes ago.

I will eat a donut before dinner, drink milk from the carton, and make scrambled eggs and leave the frying pan hidden behind the cookie jar for a minimum of two days, or three if I can stand it. And believe me, I can really stand it now.

I will no longer cut my bangs, but allow them to obscure my beautiful eyes and lovely face. Then, for no reason, I will cut my bangs with a cuticle scissors that I ran with before using.

I will use up the last of the cream cheese, put the lid back on the empty container, and return it to the shelf in the fridge. I will do the same with the butter, the cottage cheese, and every product that comes in a container you can't see through.

I will take the Sunday newspaper to the upstairs bathroom and leave it there all day, while someone else assumes that the paper was never delivered, becomes unhinged and bitchy, and calls the poor delivery boy to ream him a new one for absolutely no reason.

And in conclusion, now that I'm free to let it fly, I plan to greet each day as I damn well please. I will come out of my bedroom in only my nightgown. I will enter the kitchen and there will be quiet and calm. I will prepare an easy breakfast of coffee and toast with a side of serenity set to a background of nothing. My day will slowly begin, as it waits for me to decide what it is I might need to do, and possibly I might need to do nothing. But that will be my choice.

I might choose to step outside and retrieve the newspaper, and I can do that in my nightgown, because there is no one in the house who might yell at me for embarrassing them. I will then bend over to pick up the paper, and my nightgown will creep into my butt crack, and I will leave it there in solidarity that even my nightgown can do what it wants.

All three kids are launched and happy now. Our pride is something we have to temper on occasion, lest people hate us for our joy and *naches*.*

At this juncture, Aaron, our youngest, lives across town and works as a registered nurse on the oncology floor of a highly respected hospital. Max, recruited straight out of The Ohio State University's Fisher College of Business, spends his days at the Starbucks corporate office in Seattle, dealing with logistics and the supply chain. And EJ, who graduated Phi Beta Kappa with a double major in psychology and creative writing, has just moved to San Francisco for a big-time job as a project manager and producer at a software company.

See, I told you.

A few months ago, we decided to dismantle the kids' bedrooms and box up their chosen memorabilia of trophies, snow globes, and bar mitzvah centerpieces. Michael, in charge of the boys' rooms, had no trouble plowing through. He sold their furniture on Craigslist, packed up their childhood remnants in labeled boxes, and voilà—we now have two lovely guest rooms.

As the mother of the daughter, I'm in charge of EJ's room. Unfortunately, I take one step inside, and I have to lie down on her bed. I'm immobilized by the thought of parting with the *tchatzkes** I bought her out of guilt during those divorced-single-mother years. I fall to pieces when I think of the plastic storage containers in the basement, already full of stuff that means nothing to her and everything to me—her baby bath toys, her plush Bert and Ernie dolls, and even the musical mobile from her crib. And I've already bought more containers, because I know I'll be adding prom dresses, her retainer case, and summer camp pictures to my basement stash.

But I'm just not ready for this moment. So I've put EJ's bedroom cleanout on hold and decided to tackle something easier—my office.

My office is a finely tuned machine, with my files neatly organized and an abundant supply of pens that I steal from hotel rooms.

It's the *schmutz** and dust that I ignore, so I figured, *would it kill me to run the vacuum?*

While on my hands and knees, wiping down the baseboards and the power strip under my desk, I spotted a shoebox. This box, labeled "Songs I Meant to Write," contained a hundred scraggly pieces of loose-leaf paper with lyrics scribbled in a rushed hand. Underneath the paper scraps, I found a slew of the microcassettes I once used to record the musical ideas that would hit me at inopportune times—when my attention was needed elsewhere.

The earliest scrap dates back to 1986, when EJ was born. I guess I knew someday I'd have the time . . . and now the time has come.

SONG: *THESE ARE THE THINGS*

This is the song I meant to write when you were very small
This is the tune I had in mind, but you took off to crawl
I stopped short to catch you
Had to pull you down from ledges
I followed close, I hovered there
Just to save you from sharp edges
These are the things that mothers do
And I guess they always will

This is the song I meant to write when you turned seventeen
There were some words I had for you
But you were nowhere to be seen
You'd be dancing out on ledges
I was told to keep my distance
Then you grew up in spite of me
Finding beauty, grace, and brilliance
These are the things that young girls do
And I guess they always will

I knew this day would have to come, I'd have to let you go
I held you in my open hand, so you'd have room to grow
Someday you will do it too—it's just what women do

Here I sit—I'm finally with the song I meant to write
Nothing standing in my way, no one needing me tonight
You've left home, I'm on my own
Heart-to-heart, we're bound together
I know I did my best, you did the rest
It appears we raised each other
These are the things that women do
And I guess they always will . . . and I guess *we* always will

I AM NOW THAT WOMAN

If necessity is the mother of invention, then not knowing who you are and what you need is the mother of depression

I am now that woman whose eyebrows are no longer made of eyebrow.

I am now that woman who digs through her purse for candy, only to pull out a coffee Nip whose original wrapping has fallen off and been replaced by a Kleenex. As that woman, I'm happy to eat it.

I am now that woman, who thinks that, after forty-plus years of wearing lipstick, she should be able to apply it without a mirror. I would be wrong.

I am now that woman who stands in judgment over current trends in contemporary slang. I just don't get the whole "JUNK" and "PACKAGE" thing when referring to a man's down-below parts. Who came up with this? Who's in charge of these decisions?

JUNK is an old car you can't get rid of. JUNK is the stuff in your vanity top drawer that's never used, but never, ever, thrown away. JUNK is the tiny collection of broken pieces of hardware you live in fear of needing and not having. JUNK is the crappy food that comes with a gazillion emotional attachments. JUNK is what we eat to feel better, even though we know we'd feel better if we exercised and took our neurological pharmaceuticals at the proper time each day. JUNK can also apply to boogers, messes, and ickies of great grossness. More specifically, that stuff in your eye first thing in the morning, that if it is still there by noon, people will know you haven't washed your face. If you have a bad cold and that eye junk gets out of control, you have "conjunkyitas."

PACKAGE is a birthday present with wrapping, and hopefully, a gift receipt. PACKAGE is something that UPS or Amazon drops off at your front porch. Also, a PACKAGE would contain the JUNK you bought online, 'cuz it wasn't anything you could buy in public.

I am now that woman who travels with her own Coffee-mate in a plastic baggie. I refuse to drink a cup of coffee that's not specifically to my liking. Also, the Coffee-mate in the baggie makes me look like a cocaine dealer, and I think that gives me cachet.

I am now that woman who believes that even if you're not Jewish, but you were born and raised anywhere near New York City, you will "get" certain Yiddish words, like *mishigas,** *ongepotchket,** and *bagel.**

357

I am now that woman who, late in life, discovered beets. They are amazing and delicious when roasted with olive oil and garlic, or steamed and chilled with goat cheese in a salad. However, on the subject of *borscht*,* I stand firm. *Nyet.*

I am now that woman who attends a gourmet, chichi-très-très-boom-boom dinner party, raves about the nuances and the alchemy and the colors and the textures and the "plating" of the food, and then on her way home, heads straight to Burger King to talk smack about the snobs.

I am now that woman who sits in the lobby of a restaurant while waiting for a table, with a purse on her lap, arms folded across her chest, already complaining . . . it's too crowded and kids are running, and where are their parents, and oy, this is a lousy table—too noisy, *ach*, this is a lousy table—faces the bathroom, *nu-uh*, this is a lousy table—the people next to us are practically "doing it" right here in the dining room, we need to get reseated. Hey, anyone else having trouble reading the menu in this darkness? Can we get more bread, and what's with the butter? It tastes like cinnamon and sugar, or is that garlic? AND, for Pete's sake, those children are dreadful, and what's with heat in here—how can it be this dark AND this hot?

I am also that woman who will lie and say it's her birthday for a free dessert.

I am now that woman who, when she sneezes and laughs, will pee a little. And possibly fart.

I am now that woman who is in need of a nose-hair trimmer, but can't find the makeup counter that sells this tragic and embarrassing item.

I am now that empowered woman who finally conquers the internet and buys a nose-hair trimmer online. When it arrives and her husband asks, "What's in the PACKAGE?," she says, "Nothing, honey, just JUNK!"

And finally, I am now that woman who no longer bothers with New Year's resolutions. It's pointless.

SONG: WOULDA, COULDA, SHOULDA

I've got a problem with my ass, thought I'd like to lose it fast
I heard about a diet plan that's gonna help me do this
Cayenne pepper, lemon juice, then you make a cabbage soup
There's nothing here for me to chew, they must be kidding
I bought the stuff, and I got to work
In the kitchen, I'm a jerk
Surely, I can make a soup in a ten-quart pot
It was pretty healthy, I agree, looky here, calorie-free
Did I make it past Day Three? No, no, no, no I think not!
CHORUS
I woulda, I coulda, I shoulda, but I didn't
I didn't, no, I didn't, hmmm

I found a twenty-four-hour gym, up all night—come on in
Insomniacs can now get thin, oh baby, sign me up
I commit to get all buff and strong as
Soon as I'm done writing this song
I'm gonna hit the gym at the crack of dawn
And I'm not kidding

I'm up early, moving slow, I bitch and moan, still I go
Maniacs with gym bags in tow, filling up the parking lot
I see pretty women and pretty guys
Pairs and pairs of perfect thighs
In my ratty sweats, do I go inside?
No, no, no, no, I think not!
CHORUS

I knew that I shoulda, almost I coulda
Really I woulda, except for because
I was gonna, and I meant to, I wanted when I went to
But when I realized I was supposed to
Somehow, I no longer chose to!

I'm the boss of me, I'm oppositional
Telling me what to do is bull
I've got twenty voices inside my skull, negotiating
I'm a baby in a high chair banging my spoon
Doing only what I want to do
They're telling me to grow up, I keep meaning to
I'm gonna get right on it—*Nah!*
I woulda, I coulda, I shoulda, but I didn't
I didn't, no, I didn't, hmmm

Quintessential Naomi and her Sally Girl, 1973
I grew up, but I'll always be Naomi's Sally Girl

Sally, EJ, and Naomi, 1987
Celebrating EJ's first birthday and three generations of tremendous love

YIDDISH GLOSSARY

Bagel Really? You had to look this up?
Borscht A misuse of beets in the form of soup
Bubbe Grandma
Bubeleh Honey, baby, dear

Cantor The officiant of a synagogue who sings or chants the
prayers
Chuppah Wedding canopy to represent the openness of the
Jewish home that the couple will build together
Chutzpah The nerve, presumption, arrogance

Diaspora The dispersion of people originally localized
Ditzed No, this isn't Yiddish. It's a childhood term we all used
for cutting in line, giving a shove, or not getting invited to a
birthday party. Getting ditzed is really awful, and sucks like
you wouldn't believe.
Doobie Nope, you'll have to ask around
Dreidel A top used in playing a game of chance during the
festival of Chanukah
Drek Substandard merchandise, worthless, poopy

Emess The truth, the real deal
Ess, mine kinder "Eat, my child!"

Gelt Money
Gezundheit In good health, bless you after a sneeze

Halvah Means "sweet meat" in Turkish; a sesame seed
confection. My father told us this candy was made by special
Middle Eastern elephants who crushed the seeds under their
feet. He hoped to gross us out so we'd stop begging for
more. Not possible!
Haymish/Heymish/Haimish Informal, homey, comfy
Hokk/Hakk/Hock To bug, annoy, urge, be a pill. From *"Ner*
hoch nish du chinik" or "Don't bang on my teakettle"

Kibbitzing Schmoozing, gossiping . . . something you do with
your hairdresser—or your accountant, but only after she's
finished your books and the clock's not running
Kiddush The blessing over the wine
Kinahora Superstitious knock on wood
Kishkes Literally, guts or intestines—but can be used
figuratively as well; can also refer to a thick sausage made
with matzoh meal and spices
Knaidlach Dumplings, matzoh balls
Kugel A noodle dish made of anything you like, plus noodles
Kutchkeleh Term of endearment meaning "little duck" or
"duckling"
Kutchkie Shortened version of "kutchkeleh"
Kvell To gush with pride, swoon with joy
Kvetch/Kvetchy Fussy, prone to complaining

L'dor v'dor Hebrew for "From generation to generation"
Lantzman/Landslayt A Jewish immigrant's term for someone
who comes from your hometown back in Europe
Latkes A pancake, as in potato pancake

Macher Big shot, mogul, boss
Maidel A young lady
Maven An expert, a smarty-pants, but in a good way
Mechayeh Joy, delight; literally refers to something that has
brought you back from death to life.
Mensch One who does good deeds
Metziah A bargain, lucky find, often used sarcastically

Mishegas Crazy-making nuttiness
Mitzvah Commandment, good deed

Naches Proud pleasure, special joy
Nisht Geferhlacht "Not so terrible." "I've seen worse."
Nu? Well...? What's up by you?

Ongepatshket/Ongepotchket Overdone, messed up, garish

Plotz An act of losing your mind with joy or craziness

Rachmones Pity, compassion, empathy

Sabra A native Israeli
Schmo A person easily taken advantage of
Schmutz Dirt, grime, gross, yicky
Shiksa A Gentile girl or woman
Shlep To drag, lug, or carry
Shmatte A rag or dress you should have thrown away
Shmear/Shmeer To thinly spread something
Shmendrick A nincompoop
Shmooze To chat, flatter, network, kibbitz
Shonda A tragedy, a shame
Shrayer A person who cries and screams—a lot
Shtetl A small town or village
Shtick A comedy bit, an act, a piece of acting
Simcha A happy life-cycle event party

Takke/Tokke Can you imagine? Hard to believe!
Tante Aunt
Tchatzkes/Tchotchkes Trinket, knickknack
Tuchas Rear end, derriere, tush
Tzuris/Tsuris Trouble, woes, grief

Yenta Busybody, gossip, or specialist
Yutz An incompetent person with a cloud over his head

Zaftig Plump, round, fleshy, a sorta-sexy way to say
overweight, but be careful, we're not there yet
Zies a maydeleh mine kind Sweet little girl, my child

Addendum:

Mental Yentl A student of crazy

ACKNOWLEDGMENTS

For Pete's sake, how on earth did I ever think that I could finish a book, with all the crippling self doubt and mind wandering? But I did it, and here it is!

In reading other authors' acknowledgements, I see them thank a laundry list of writers' groups, workshops, and friends who critiqued their pages over shots of Jack Daniel's while chewing the literary bone. Though that does sound like a blast, my own unorthodox method and personal process was delicious on every level. I didn't want to stop. But at some point, I had to leave my desk to physically get my moving parts moving, and emotionally keep everyone's loving parts loving.

First, I'd like to thank my beloved editor, Katherine Matthews, a calm and cerebral presence, who made house calls in lousy weather. With her brilliance and experience, loving concern and attention, Kathy is a shining example of "If you want something done well—hire a working woman with three kids." She sees it, she feels it, she fixes it, and she's done. She says it's because she does yoga; I say it's just who she is.

Thank you to my family and friends: Ed and Maitzie Stan and the entire extended Stan Clan, Bill & Randi Cohen, Danny & Cindy Becker, Cheryl & Jackie Jacobs, Dan Green & family, Sharon Saia & Peter Zafirides, Larry Harris, Audrey Hackman, and of course, Rita *the Dish* Shain. Kisses to Janis Ian, Flash Rosenberg, Sarah Allgire, Allyson Casey, Xenia Palus, Judy Carter, Valerie Nemeth, and Bitchin' Babes past and present: Christine Lavin, Megon McDonough, Patty Larkin, Julie Gold, Suzzy Roche, the late Mary Travers, Camille West, Deirdre Flint, Nancy Moran, Marcy Marxer, and my Babe Soul Sister—the Hem to my Haw—Debi Smith Jaworek.

Thank you to my family of origin, Steve Fingerett and Rosalyn Koch, for the love and protection—and to their children, Allison, Shira, Jason, Yonatan, Erin, Matan, Adina, and Aytan, for your tremendously sharp senses of humor, while wearing your DNA with pride.

Thank you, Michael, for your love and guidance and amazing care and concern (and dinners!). Your selflessness and generous spirit have enabled my dreams to come true while you kept our world on its axis. To our children Elizabeth Julian, Max and Aaron, I treasure you, I adore you, and I am your student.

ABOUT THE AUTHOR

Singer-songwriter Sally Fingerett is a founding member of the highly acclaimed musical comedy group, The Four Bitchin' Babes. She collaborated on all nine of the Babes' cast recordings, starting with their first release in 1990.

Sally's multifaceted career as an award-winning composer spans more than three decades, with appearances on over seven hundred stages and the production of five solo CDs. Sally's song "Home Is Where the Heart Is" was recorded by legends Peter, Paul and Mary for their *LifeLines* CD and PBS special. Sally currently performs across the United States, touring with the 4BBabes, as well as appearing solo in her brand-new musical revue, *The Mental Yentl.*

Sally's guest appearances include Putamayo's Songwriter Festival at Carnegie Hall, Michael Feldman's *Whad'Ya Know*, and NPR's *Mountain Stage* and *World Cafe.* Her written comedy can be found in Random House's *Life's a Stitch*, a collection of contemporary women's humor.

Sally lives in Columbus, Ohio, with her husband Michael Stan. They have three wonderful children, Elizabeth (EJ), Max, and Aaron.

**For more information on
Sally's career, recordings, tour schedule, and writing,
visit her web site www.sallyfingerett.com**

FIND SALLY'S HITS ON THIS SPECIAL TWO-DISC SET

THE MENTAL YENTL CD .

SONGS from a Lifelong Student of Crazy

Award-winning composer Sally Fingerett celebrates her career highlights by releasing the thirty-three songs featured here in *The Mental Yentl* book!

PRAISE FOR SALLY'S MUSIC

"A wrenchingly vivid knack for contemporary ballads."
THE BOSTON GLOBE

"Sally Fingerett gives ample proof why she won the Kerrville Award for songwriting...one of the best lyricists on the singer/songwriter circuit."
THE CHICAGO TRIBUNE

"All the things you want in a lunch companion, Sally has managed to capture on this CD."
JANIS IAN

"Informed by both folk and pop sensibilities, *My Good Company* is brimming with good songs well sung. Remarkably consistent is the quality of the songwriting, an unwavering level of craft."
THE WASHINGTON POST

"A meditation on life with all its sorrows, contradictions, small joys, and moments of wonderment. Her voice and her compelling lyrics are rightly the focus of ten tunes."
THE CLEVELAND PLAIN DEALER

"Thank you, dear heart, your songs are beautiful. As for (the song) *The Red Man*, I have received many awards in my lifetime, but I cannot remember anything that has ever touched my emotions with such heartfelt warmth."
RED SKELTON

www.sallyfingerett.com